CREATIVE RESEARCH

CREATIVE RESEARCH

THE THEORY AND PRACTICE OF RESEARCH FOR THE CREATIVE INDUSTRIES

SECOND EDITION

HILARY COLLINS

BLOOMSBURY VISUAL ARTS
LONDON · NEW YORK · OXFORD · NEW DELHI · SYDNEY

iq8016

BLOOMSBURY VISUAL ARTS
Bloomsbury Publishing Plc
50 Bedford Square, London, WC1B 3DP, UK

BLOOMSBURY, BLOOMSBURY VISUAL ARTS and the Diana logo are trademarks
of Bloomsbury Publishing Plc

First published by AVA Publishing SA, 2010
This 2nd edition is published by Bloomsbury Visual Arts, an imprint of Bloomsbury Publishing, 2019

Cover design: Louise Dugdale

A catalogue record for this book is available from the British Library.

A catalog record for this book is available from the Library of Congress.

ISBN: PB: 978-1-4742-4708-5
ePDF: 978-1-4742-4709-2
eBook: 978-1-4742-4710-8

Typeset by Deanta Global Publishing Services, Chennai, India
Printed and bound in India

To find out more about our authors and books visit www.bloomsbury.com
and sign up for our newsletters.

CONTENTS

FOREWORD TO THE SECOND EDITION

The last few decades have seen the emergence of new trends in practice-based research in and through the arts. This has been due to a number of things, most noticeably the increased attention to the creative industries as a legitimate area of interest for governments and academic institutions. The arts are no longer seen as an exclusive activity, but have a changing relationship with a wider society. The means of production and of consumption are also rapidly changing. Artists, in their broader sense, are also the researchers.

Arts, like the sciences, are a form of human creativity that has found an institutional space in modern society, a legitimacy as we look for new things, new ways of looking and new ways of doing things. The cultural-economic drivers of contemporary societies for the new, be it in new scientific knowledge, new technologies and gadgets, or cultural expression, have seen an increased focus on the integration of the arts, in their broader sense, into commerce. Both the arts and sciences are driven by curiosity and imagination, with the desire to explore the unknown. Curiosity aims to go beyond the familiar and to explore a space of new possibilities. It is, by definition, about the unknown; however, there is always the desire to tame the curiosity and imagination. Yet we must still be open to giving it free rein. Creative research in the arts often sits with these paradoxes – if research is the curiosity-driven production of new knowledge, it is inherently beset by uncertainties, since the results or outcomes, by definition, are unknown.

ARTS AND SCIENCES

The sciences and the arts are much more closely connected than their currently institutionalized forms may suggest; however, there are some very fundamental differences. Although the drivers are the same, the context for the research is often very different. Creative industries, especially regarding the arts, are deeply contextual and culturally constructed. This is not to say that scientific facts are not also contextual. Ludwik Fleck in *The Genesis and Development of a Scientific Fact* argues that every scientific concept and theory is culturally conditioned. He challenges the assumption that facts are there to be discovered through proper passive observation of natural phenomenon. Rather, he asserts that facts are invented, not discovered. Even scientific facts are **made** things. They are constructed from a deep narrative, a philosophy about the way that the world works, and we test against that theory. Bruno Latour in *We have never been Modern* redescribed the Enlightenment idea of universal scientific truth, arguing that there are no facts separable from their fabrication.

Techno-sciences, important as they are, are not alone in leading the direction for creative research. Artists have been quick to realize the artistic challenges offered by hybrid forms and the increased domain of ways of looking and translation that the arts can bring. Crossing the natural and the artificial domains they can add creativity to broaden the range covered by the techno-sciences.

GENERALIZATIONS FROM PARTICULARIZATIONS AND PARTICULARIZATIONS FROM GENERALIZATIONS

The cultural context of creative research in and through the arts plays an enormous role in our understanding of what happened and how we may learn from it. Case studies and narrative methods are usually an archaeological presentation and by nature become a synoptic presentation of events. The challenge for the researcher is how to maintain the complexity and contextuality of the situation in the narrative. Clifford Geertz's development of Gilbert Ryle's concept of 'thick descriptions' perhaps offers a way to explain not just behaviour, but also the context in which that behaviour takes place, holding onto the micro details of what is happening. The aim is to move away from a deterministic view of the world and to focus on issues of complexity and emergence – by focusing on the micro interactions that result in emergent macro patterns.

THE CHALLENGE FOR THE CREATIVE RESEARCHER

Due to the complexity and sociocultural nature of creative research, it requires a more eclectic approach to method. There seem to be two broad ways of ordering experience: the logico-scientific and narrative modes of thought, and although these are complementary, they are not reducible because they imply different assumptions of causality. So rather than separating research into these categories, the researcher needs to try to take a more reflective and reflexive approach to the study, by looking at how things, processes, industries, societies are formed, the processes and contexts from which they emerged.

It is this humanistic driver that should invigorate the research into the creative industries. This book provides a series of frameworks for consideration and implementation, dealing with issues of how one looks and develops objectivity in a subjective world, adding credibility and ethics to the process. As creative research develops a greater institutional framework, don't be afraid of the arguments and disagreements that will arise between researchers, methods and interpretations, it is all a key part of making sense of a complex world.

—Pradeep Sharma
Professor of Design and Innovation
Provost, Rhode Island School of Design

FOREWORD TO THE FIRST EDITION

When conducting research in and for the creative industries, there are a wealth of different possible research approaches that can be taken – reflecting the diverse nature of the disciplines (design, arts and crafts, advertising, architecture, fashion, film, music, TV, radio, performing arts, publishing and interactive software) and academic contexts (art schools, business schools and universities) involved. The result is that there are variations in the emphasis and approach taken to how students are taught to link theory with practice, and how they view and engage with the concept of 'research'. The need for understanding and awareness of a range of approaches is critical for anyone learning about and working with design, business and the creative industries today.

Research is a systematic process of enquiry. And design, by its very nature, takes a people-centred approach to problem solving. Currently, the idea of an explicitly defined, 'design research culture' is undergoing change, and in particular, the issue of how to more closely link design research in academia to design practice in industry is under scrutiny. Equally, there is a growing move to establish design and design management sciences previously developed. New models of enquiry appropriate to the interdisciplinary and collaborative nature of the creative industries are emerging in recognition of the fact that no single discipline operates in isolation within the creative industries. Due to the user-centred nature of the design process, the opportunity exists to take an inclusive rather than an exclusive approach to the creative research process, in a way that is invaluable as a method for facilitating new stakeholder conversations and people-centred, cross-disciplinary investigations.

—Kathryn Best
Author, speaker and educator in design,
strategy and systemic change

INTRODUCTION

The creative industries were defined in the UK Government's 2001 Creative Industries Mapping Document as 'those industries which have their origin in individual creativity, skill and talent and which have a potential for wealth and job creation through the generation and exploitation of intellectual property' (https://www.gov.uk/government/publications/crea-tive-industries-economic-estimates-january-2015/creative-industries-economic-estimates-january-2015-key-findings and the definition has been maintained in the 13th of January 2015 updated official statistic on the Creative Industries). The creative industries – architecture, advertising, art, theatre and performing arts, design, film, computer games and multimedia, publishing, music, media, radio and television – make up an increasingly important element of economic activity in the United Kingdom, Western Europe, the United States and Asia. In the UK, the creative industries have become a major economic force, accounting for over 7 per cent of the economy. With a growth rate that is double that of the economy as a whole, the creative sector is a vital source of employment and business development. Countries such as China and South Korea are now positioning their creative industries as priorities for strategic growth, while in the United States and across Europe, the level of competitive challenge is rising significantly. The creative economy is another categorization, which includes the contribution of those who are in creative occupations outside the creative industries as well as all those employed in the creative industries. The creative industries, a subset of the creative economy, include only those working in the creative industries themselves (and who may either be in creative occupations or be in other roles, such as finance).

In its Creative Economy Report of 2008, the United Nations Conference on Trade and Development (UNCTAD) introduced the topic of the 'creative economy' in the world economic and development agenda, describing it as 'an emerging concept dealing with the interface between creativity, culture, economics and technology in a contemporary world dominated by images, sounds, texts and symbols.' The UNCTAD emphasizes how the creative industries 'are among the most dynamic sectors in the world economy providing new opportunities for developing countries to leapfrog into emerging high-growth areas of the world economy' (p. 7) and asserts that 'creativity and knowledge are fast becoming powerful means of fostering development gains' (Creative Economy Report, 2008).

In November 2015, Nesta published that the EU's creative industries employed 11.4 million people in 2013, accounting for 5 per cent of the EU workforce (https://www.nesta.org.uk/blog/creative-europe-measuring-creative-industries-eu). The three largest creative industry workforces in the EU are those of the countries with the three largest workforces, with German creative industries employing 3.1 million (5.8 per cent of its workforce), the UK's creative industries employing 2.3 million (7.9 per cent) and France employing 1.4 million (5.5 per cent of the workforce).

However, in relative terms things look different. Sweden has the highest proportion of its workforce (8.9 per cent) employed in the creative industries, followed by Finland (8.2 per cent) and then the UK.

Sweden also has the highest proportion of its workforce employed in the creative economy (12 per cent) compared to 9.5 per cent in the UK.

This emphasis on the buoyancy of the creative industries has been mirrored in the education sector with the creation of courses linked closely with the requirements of the creative industries. Being a mainly visual discipline, research methods used within the creative industries must take this into account, and yet also be both rigorous and valid within other disciplines.

This book is designed to show you how to work within the research process to produce both undergraduate- and postgraduate-level research proposals and dissertations. Each phase of a research project is addressed in the order in which it will be undertaken and within the context of the creative industries. Research is rarely undertaken in a linear process and this book explains why this is the case, offering alternative yet robust frameworks. Guidelines help you to assess the kind of researcher you are and show you how using different philosophical perspectives will influence your research. You will also discover how to choose and frame a research question for your project. The book will guide you through the process, giving realistic, practical and relevant support while you research and write up your creative industries dissertation.

Research can be enjoyable as well as rigorous and valuable; and research is blooming in the creative industries. It is now possible to learn from examples that stem directly from a creative background rather than those that have been borrowed from other disciplines. Research is embedded in the daily life of designers and creators – it is not separate from it. We 'research' which university course we want to take or where to go on holiday. In our professional life, we research the needs for a new product or a design concept. The way in which we make sure that our proposed choices are based on accurate information is, in fact, research. Research in the academic sense is a refinement of what we do in our daily lives. These research processes can take place simultaneously, and can be linear or iterative, but we usually end up basing our understanding and decisions on them. This book explains how these processes can be used and demonstrates the value they have for your future career within the creative industries.

AIMS OF THE BOOK

Creative Research: The Theory and Practice of Research for the Creative Industries, second edition, aims to promote understanding of the role of research in the creative industries and to emphasize the importance of research as a way of validating creativity. It is a guide for students of design, design management, architecture, marketing, media communications, arts practice, humanities, social sciences and business studies, as well as for practitioners. This second edition has widened its focus by looking at both undergraduate and postgraduate projects. This book also examines the requirements of both written and practical design projects. The book begins with an overview of research methods and is then followed by four parts.

Defining the research problem

Part One: Defining the research problem looks at the preliminary stage of research where research projects and initiatives are created. The focus is on identifying and creating the ideas from which a research proposal can be written. Part One guides the reader through research philosophies and research approaches, and discusses the implication of different philosophies and methods on the process and outcome of the project.

Part One also investigates the skills required in creating a conceptual research framework and understanding the value of teamwork and autonomy. The relationship with, and the role of, a project supervisor is discussed relative to guiding design decisions and developing the verbal, visual and written communication skills necessary to achieve an effective exchange of ideas and information.

Managing the research design

Part Two: Managing the research design looks at the stage of research where research projects and agendas are developed. The focus of this stage is demonstrating how research projects in creative fields can be both rich and vibrant yet credible to other disciplines. To help identify the challenges that will be faced when starting a research project, examples of creative research projects from a range of disciplines are provided.

The thoughts of leading academics are presented, exploring alternative research techniques and outlining the strengths and weaknesses of the approaches. Also included is an exploration of the skills necessary to manage time, develop networks and facilitate the research process.

This stage is about developing the responsibility to manage research agendas and projects.

Managing the research process

Part Three: Managing the research process looks at the stage of the research process where you actually undertake primary and/or secondary research. The focus is on the process and practice of managing research projects, including the decision making involved on whether you have gathered enough data or whether you have to alter your research plan.

Evaluating the success of the research project allows positive feedback to inform and guide your project to a valuable conclusion.

Part Three also investigates the skills required when managing creative projects, such as interview skills, and the written and verbal communication skills necessary for effective research and documentation. This stage is about how to undertake your research and manage the opportunities and constraints that emerge as a result of data collection.

Managing the research

Part Four: Managing the research looks at the stage of research where sense needs to be made of what has been discovered, and the findings related back to the original research intentions. Do they tell a believable story when communicating the research?

Part Four also investigates the skills required to analyse both qualitative and quantitative data and looks at ways of successfully presenting a project. This edition has more detail on the newer and up and coming quantitative and qualitative methods.

Real-life findings and results stages are presented, as are discussions with leading academics on the value of analysis and the influence of design.

This stage is about undertaking the analysis of the collected data and knowing how to communicate those findings and results.

CONTEXT

The role of research in the creative industries has a diverse background. Research methods have been borrowed from the fields of visual research, sociology and management. This section of the book begins with an overview of the field of research within the context of the creative industries, and then goes into detail about the stages involved in undertaking a research project within this field. It also investigates the skills required in creating a conceptual research framework, and highlights the importance of understanding the value of teamwork and autonomy. We also examine the boundaries between the creative and cultural industries.

THE NATURE OF RESEARCH

We constantly try to understand our environment and how our world appears to our senses. We tend to do this in three ways: experience, reasoning and research. This means that sometimes we know what is happening because we've had experience of it before, sometimes we can reason why it is happening and at other times we need to find out by searching for information. We know that these ways of understanding are not separate in real life, but often overlap. And when we try to make sense of what is happening, in our day-to-day life we depend a lot on experience and the value of our experience, which should not be underestimated.

Experience is valuable within research because it gives us a source from which we can devise our hypothesis or research questions. However, we need to recognize that experience has limitations too, if we are attempting to find out the ultimate truth about a phenomenon.

WHAT IS RESEARCH?

In our everyday life, we come across the word 'research' on a daily basis. When we watch a television programme that discusses levels of employment or factors in the economy, research normally provides the data upon which the report is based. When advertisers refer to users' opinions on the results of using a product, research normally provides the data upon which the claims for the product are based.

Many of us criticize such uses of data because it can be difficult to understand how these claims are made and what processes and analysis the researchers have actually undertaken. This makes it hard for us to evaluate how accurate the information really is.

It is perhaps all too easy to collect facts without having a clear purpose or objective, to list the facts we have researched without evaluating or interpreting them, or to use the word 'research' just to get ideas

THINK BOX

Research is the systematic investigation into and study of materials and sources in order to establish facts and reach new conclusions.

- Systematic: research needs to be systematic. A definite set of procedures and steps should be followed. Completion of a number of stages in the research process is essential if the most accurate results are to be recorded.
- Organized: research must be organized, structured and methodical. It is a planned procedure, not a spontaneous one (even though the plan can change from time to time). It is focused and limited to a specific scope.
- Question: research is focused on relevant, useful and important questions. Without a question, research has no focus, drive or purpose. However, realizing the importance or relevance of your findings is arguably one of the most important factors.
- Answer: whether it is the answer to a hypothesis or even a simple question, research is successful when we find answers. Sometimes the answer is no, but this is still an answer.

Figure I.1

The key components of a research project include a combination of critical reflection on the theory, critical reflection on yourself and what you have done, and critical reflection on the practice of undertaking the project. The relationships between these three factors are then analysed: theory with self, self with practice and practice with theory.

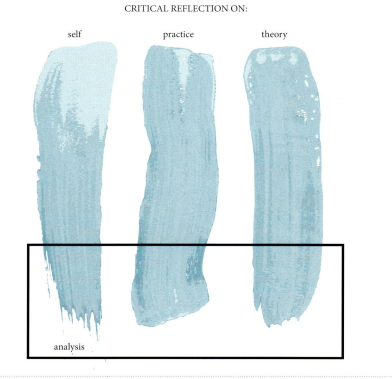

CRITICAL REFLECTION ON:

self   practice   theory

analysis

context

Figure I.2

This diagram gives you an idea of the cyclical nature of research. Research is an iterative process, so although the arrows in the diagram show the cyclical nature of research you can go back and forward from one stage to another to achieve clarity and understanding in your project.

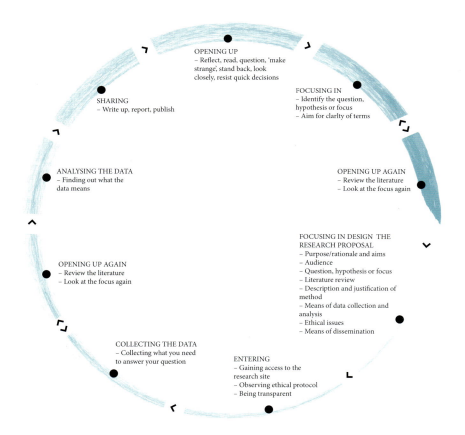

OPENING UP
– Reflect, read, question, 'make strange', stand back, look closely, resist quick decisions

FOCUSING IN
– Identify the question, hypothesis or focus
– Aim for clarlty of terms

SHARING
– Write up, report, publish

OPENING UP AGAIN
– Review the literature
– Look at the focus again

ANALYSING THE DATA
– Finding out what the data means

FOCUSING IN DESIGN THE RESEARCH PROPOSAL
– Purpose/rationale and aims
– Audience
– Question, hypothesis or focus
– Literature review
– Description and justification of method
– Means of data collection and analysis
– Ethical issues
– Means of dissemination

OPENING UP AGAIN
– Review the literature
– Look at the focus again

COLLECTING THE DATA
– Collecting what you need to answer your question

ENTERING
– Gaining access to the research site
– Observing ethical protocol
– Being transparent

noticed. In order for our audience to find our research credible, believable and relevant, we need to ensure that our research presents a systematic and organized way of finding answers to significant or pertinent questions.

Research is not always straightforward. There may be stages in the inquiry where you may not be quite sure what you are looking for; or, having found something that you were not looking for, you will then need to find out how important or relevant this finding is. Sometimes, this can prove to be the most exciting aspect of research.

There is nothing like looking, if you want to find something. You certainly usually find something, if you look, but it is not always quite the something you were after.

— J.R.R. Tolkien

THINK BOX
What do professional researchers do?

On the next page is an example of a published research project, Crowdfunding Good Causes, by Jonathan Bone and Peter Baeck (2016), which clearly states the aims of the research and explains why it is relevant. The research is honest, stating what has and has not been achieved as well as detailing what may need to be improved. This can give other researchers an indication of what they can pick up on in future research projects. It also provides an excellent source of pertinent, up-to-date research ideas for students. Crowdfunding is increasingly used to fund design start-ups and individual design projects, so by finding out about the opportunities and challenges we can use this information to set up our own crowdfunding.

CROWDFUNDING GOOD CAUSES

This research was based on interviews with UK crowdfunding platforms and a survey of more than 450 charities, community groups and social entrepreneurs and explores opportunities and challenges in crowdfunding for good causes.

Key findings

- Crowdfunding makes up less than 0.5 per cent of giving in the UK, but has significant potential to fund projects with a social purpose, from community events, campaigns and movements to restorations, gardens and playgrounds.
- Opportunities in crowdfunding, in addition to funding projects that would otherwise struggle to access finance, include many potential non-financial benefits such as the potential to boost volunteering, increase transparency, more experimentation and new ways of combining campaigning and fundraising to increase awareness on social issues and needs.
- The main challenges are a potential negative impact on equality and participation in projects, too much focus on short-term initiatives rather than long-term projects. While it is a potential new source of finance the report also highlights that crowdfunding is hard and there are significant limits to what can be raised.
- When asked about the reasons why they were yet to use crowdfunding, two in three charities, community groups and social entrepreneurs reported not having the skills and capacity to set up and run a crowdfunding campaign.
- Forty-three per cent of charities, community groups and social entrepreneurs reported that they were likely to use crowdfunding in the next 12 months.

While there has been a rapid growth in crowdfunding in the rest of the economy (e.g. making up 12 per cent of new loans to small businesses and 15 per cent of the market for seed and venture-stage equity investment) the report estimates that crowdfunding for good causes makes up less than 0.5 per cent of giving in the UK.

This study explores opportunities and challenges in crowdfunding for good causes and how more charities, community groups and social entrepreneurs can be supported to make the most of crowdfunding. This was achieved through a combination of interviews with crowdfunding platforms focusing on projects with a social purpose, a review of existing literature on crowdfunding for these types of projects and a survey of more than 450 charities, community groups and social entrepreneurs to understand their perception, awareness and usage of crowdfunding.

Recommendations of the report

Charities, community groups and social entrepreneurs should

- try and set up at least one crowdfunding campaign
- join up fundraising and campaigning teams to run crowdfunding campaigns
- curate a group of projects on a pre-existing platform or develop a customized crowdfunding platform (particularly relevant for larger organizations or networks).

Grant funders, social investors and other supporters should

- invest in crowdfunding skills and capacity building
- integrate crowdfunding into existing funding schemes and programmes through match funding
- support transition from crowdfunding projects to developing sustainable organizations
- set up referral schemes from grant funders and social investors to crowdfunding platforms
- test and measure effect of crowdfunding.

Source: 'Crowdfunding good causes', Nesta, 6 June 2016, http://www.nesta.org.uk/publications/crowdfunding- good-causes

THE NATURE OF RESEARCH WITHIN THE CREATIVE INDUSTRIES

The creative industries are often considered to be those industries working with art, entertainment or media, for example, the fashion industry, the movie industry or publishing. Perhaps the best-known usage of the term 'creative industries' derives from the UK's Department for Culture, Media & Sport (DCMS), which began developing strategies for the creative industries in 1997 (www.gov.uk/government/publications/creative-industries-mapping-documents-1998). In the UK approach, the creative industries are those requiring 'creativity and talent, with potential for wealth and job creation through exploitation of their intellectual property' (Higgs, Cunningham and Bakhshi, 2008; DCMS, 2001). In the UK definition the word 'culture' is not mentioned although there is undeniable cultural content in the output of most of the creative industries. In most continental European countries, on the other hand, there is an inclination towards using the word *culture*. Notwithstanding the diversity of these conceptualizations of the creative economy, most lead to the same collection of industries making up the creative sector, many of which were mentioned in the introduction to this book. Some classifications may include industries like sport (presumably on account of its cultural connotations) or software (because writing any sort of computer program requires creativity). But by and large the various conglomerations of industries described as creative or cultural in different parts of the world look very similar. Within an international framework, the cultural industries are defined by UNESCO as 'industries that combine the creation, production and commercialisation of contents which are intangible and cultural in nature; these contents are typically protected by copyright and they can take the form of a good or a service' (www.unesco.org/new/en/santiago/culture/creative-industries/).

However, the definition used within this book encompasses all forms of cultural production where design and trends, as well as goods and services related to artistic or entertainment value, play an important part.

The creative industries are characterized by the generation and exploitation of intellectual property. Their origin lies in the intellectual capital of those having an idea that they want to develop. However, an idea or product not only has to be creative but also needs to be recognized by others as having intrinsic value. It has to possess cultural capital. In order for our research to be successful and relevant within the creative industries, we need to be aware of the intellectual, cultural and social capital by which it is sustained.

There are many interrelated disciplines within the creative industries, and practitioners tend to draw on the knowledge that is developed both within the creative industries and from disciplines operating outside of them. Knowledge from marketing, management and finance are drawn on as well as processes and concepts from product design and graphic design, for example. After all, the names of these disciplines represent boundaries that are artificially drawn; however, in reality they are bound with common threads of knowledge and practice which run across each discipline.

Designers and 'creatives' are very busy people and tend to work within industries that demand a quick turnaround of projects and adherence to strict deadlines. This is as true at the strategic end of design as at the operational end. Research for practitioners therefore moves more towards being seen as possessing a particular benefit or use, and this is usually a commercial one. This is not necessarily one of profit, but one of fulfilling certain industry or discipline requirements.

This is one of the areas that designers and practitioners have in common, as research also tends to have a practical application, and normally the findings from research of this nature would be applied to a project or plan. The consequence is that, in the creative industries, research outcomes can be far reaching, as they may be transdisciplinary in nature, and as such may also potentially have a practical application.

Design research is about understanding real people in the context of their everyday lives and then using what we learn to inspire our work. This loose definition may conjure up a narrow set of methods, but at IDEO, we're broad in our approach: Design research here is not any one thing, and it's informed by the passion and skills of our teams as much as any organizational process.

– Dan Perkel: IDEO

CATEGORIES OF RESEARCH

Research can fall into several categories. The first is where a research question is set and then answered by the research process, although there may not be any requirement to use these findings for any specific purpose.

Question >> Answer

The second category is where the research has a practical requirement and involves collaboration between researchers. Such research would result in the generation of knowledge, which would then be applied to a practical situation.

Question>>Answer>>Use

The third category involves people in the research and examines the social consequences and human interconnections of the area under investigation.

Question>>Answer>>Effect

We could therefore be faced with a situation where we are advancing knowledge, proposing creative design solutions, solving human problems and examining the social implications of what we are doing – all this is dependent on both the purpose and the context of your work. Research needs to serve the concerns of practice as well as theory. It needs to serve the needs of the international community as well. Culture is a driver of development, led by the growth of the creative economy in general and the creative and cultural industries in particular, recognized not only for their economic value but also increasingly for the role in producing new creative ideas or technologies, and their non-monetized social benefits. The main themes of proposed research within the creative industries, which were recently identified by UNESCO in their Creative Economy Report (2013), are explored on pages 153–155.

INTEGRATION AND DISINTEGRATION: THE IMPACT OF DIGITAL TOOLS AND DISTRIBUTION, AND COLLABORATION AND OUTSOURCING RELATIONSHIPS

Value chains within the creative industries are changing radically, partly due to new digital technologies and tools, online distribution and opportunities for outsourcing creative services.

New design and modelling tools offer actors in this chain a level of experimentation previously unheard of. We have a lot to learn about these tools; for example, how they can be used with more traditional methods and how they have the power to reduce creativity and innovation. The internet distributes content directly to the market, which can remove intermediaries, and although the advantage is clear for digital products, it also extends to physical services, such as books and clothing. Our demand for specialized niches can now be met as never before.

Questions arise from this, concerning the fragmentation of markets and audiences and how this may affect mass consumption. Strategies being used currently include collaboration and outsourcing to manage the cost of creative projects; yet although the management of risk and coordination remains at the forefront of project management this can sometimes be challenging as the industry remains one that is based to a great extent on personal networking relationships.

The issue still remains that research is needed to inform decisions on whether to create or buy in the new age of creative services.

UNDERSTANDING HOW INNOVATION CHANGES BUSINESS MODELS AND MARKETS

There are growing trends in the areas of consumer experience, and in the producers and services associated with digital technologies. The creative industries are constantly changing and the direction and rules relating to these changes are not yet clear. New business models are in a stage of experimentation and modern strategies are not all proving to be effective. Research is needed to make sense of what is happening and how this ultimately affects the industry.

THE CREATIVE PROCESS AND ORGANIZATION

Research has begun to unravel the practices, tools, structure and artefacts that are used to stimulate the creative process. The environment within which creativity is practised is another focus of research involving the organizational structure, workflow, people and their associated networks, all of which may have an impact on creativity. We also need to examine how this environment can be widened to bring in creative ideas, and, consequently, research is needed to understand this somewhat ephemeral area.

MANAGEMENT CAPABILITIES AND SKILLS

Not all fields within the creative industries have a formal management career path with relevant training structures in place, and therefore practising managers are not necessarily prepared for the changes that innovation can bring. Systematic research is needed on the complexity, financial stability and working conditions of the industry.

SMALL FIRMS AND GROWTH

Many of the businesses within the creative industries are small- to medium-sized enterprises and many are 'lifestyle' businesses, which are sometimes criticized by some people as unwilling to upscale. However, there are difficulties associated with growth within the creative industries, and these associated barriers to entry need to be researched in conjunction with the gatekeepers of the industry. The role of intermediaries in the industry is likely to change over time because of wider environmental trends, and research is needed to track these changes and to evaluate their impact.

The above concerns have been previously highlighted and documented in a conference paper entitled 'Management Research Priorities in the Creative Industries: A Consultative Review' (Sapsed et al., 2008), which presents an indication of the nature of research today and tomorrow within the creative industries.

The creative economy is not a single highway but a multitude of different local trajectories found in cities and regions in developing countries

THE IMPORTANCE OF RESEARCH WITHIN THE CREATIVE INDUSTRIES

It is useful to set some conceptual and theoretical boundaries to our working definition of the creative industries at this point. The creative industries have been discussed alongside the cultural economy. What are the creative industries and what do practitioners do within the creative industries?

The term 'creative economy' was popularized in 2001 by the British writer and media manager John Howkins (2001), who applied it to fifteen industries extending from the arts to science and technology. The idea is a very broad one as it embraces not only cultural goods and services but also toys and games and the entire domain of 'research and development'. Therefore, while recognizing cultural activities and processes as the core of a powerful new economy, it is also concerned with manifestations of creativity in domains that would not be understood as 'cultural'.

The term 'cultural industries' traces its roots back to earlier work in the Frankfurt School in the 1930s and 1940s, which decried the commodification of art as providing an ideological legitimization of capitalist societies and the emergence of a popular culture industry. By the early 1960s we began to recognize that the process of commodification does not always or necessarily result in the breakdown of cultural expression. Indeed, often the contrary may be true, for industrially (or digitally) generated goods and services clearly possess many positive qualities. In the 1980s the term 'cultural industries' no longer carried these negative connotations and began to be used in academia and policy-making circles as a positive label. This referred to forms of cultural production and consumption that have at their core a symbolic or expressive element. It was also propagated worldwide by UNESCO in the 1980s (see Girard and Gentil 1983, ch. 5). Its scope is not limited to technology-intensive production as a great deal of cultural production in developing countries is crafts-intensive.

The term 'creative industries' is applied to a much wider productive set, including goods and services produced by the cultural industries and those that depend on innovation, including many types of research and software development. The phrase began to enter policy making, such as the national cultural policy of Australia in the early 1990s, followed by the transition made by the influential DCMS of the UK from cultural to creative industries at the end of the decade.

The sector comprises a large variety of creative fields, from the heavily industrialized, such as advertising, marketing, broadcasting, the film industry, the internet and mobile content industry, the music business, print and electronic publishing, and video and computer games to those less industrialized, traditional fields of the visual arts (painting and sculpture), the performing arts (theatre, opera and dance) and museums and library services. Other creative activities include the domains of craft, fashion, the design industry, and also architecture, cultural tourism and even sport.

THE CULTURAL AND CREATIVE INDUSTRIES

The cultural and creative industries have also been captured in various 'concentric circles' diagrams. One of the earliest and best known is that of David Throsby, presented below:

- [The creative industries are] driven by business for which the creation of new content and intellectual property is a central activity.

- Creative businesses are ideas-based, in terms of both product/service development and business practice.
- Creative businesses seek to develop new markets as much as to serve those that already exist.
- The sector is predominantly made up of small to medium sized companies (SMEs) such as advertising and entertainment. These work within complex supply chains to provide products and services on which other sectors depend.
- The sector thrives when located within 'creative clusters'; it is dependent upon informal networks through which creative ideas flow.

VALUE TO THE ECONOMY

The creative industries already represent a leading sector of the economy in the Organisation for Economic Co-operation and Development countries, with an annual growth rate of between 5 and 20 per cent. The sector is increasingly important for the knowledge-based economy, as it is knowledge and labour intensive and fosters innovation; it therefore has a huge potential for the generation of employment and export expansion.

'"Society and economy" is changing, driven by the rise of human creativity, which becomes a key source of competitive advantage. The rise of the "creative economy" is drawing the spheres of innovation (technological creativity), business (economic creativity) and culture (artistic and cultural creativity) into one another, in more intimate and more powerful combinations than ever' (Florida, The Rise of the Creative Class, 2000, p. 201).

'Lying at the crossroads between the arts, business and technology, the creative industries can be defined as 'those industries that have their origin in individual creativity, skill and talent and which have a potential for wealth and job creation through the generation and exploitation of intellectual property' (UK Creative Industries Task Force, 1997).

GROWTH IN THE INDUSTRY

The explosion of the sector might be explained as the result of a series of factors. One possible reason is that the increase of work productivity resulting from the rapid development of new information and computing

technologies has led to the development of new spheres of consumption, both in knowledge-related and leisure activities. Secondly, the growth of complexity and uncertainty in social and economic life, the drive of innovation and economic competitiveness and the issue of wealth creation all call for answers to complex issues, widening the working parameters of researchers who strive to develop knowledge or simply ideas.

Within this approach, research activity is being placed more and more within the same parameters as the arts and culture, contributing to the creation of the so-called new creative economy. According to Richard Florida (2004), creative professionals represent a significant part of the economy in developed countries. The core of that part is represented by those fields with the economic wherewithal to create future ideas, new technology and original creative content: science and engineering, architecture and design, education, the arts, music and entertainment.

TECHNOLOGY

Technological challenges occupy a central place in this debate, in relation to issues such as changing the industry's value chain under digital coding, thereby highlighting the need for new business models. There is a challenge implicit to developing content for new digital technologies as a future locus of art consumption, or for new distribution channels, including mobile online content and ad hoc device networks. Besides the technological challenges presented, issues such as cultural diversity and the circulation and exchanges of cultural products on the internet are among today's pressing debates. The influence of innovation on patterns of consumption represents another important research issue. New patterns of consumption, determined by the rise of the 'new creative class', are considered to have an increasing influence on both local and regional development.

RANGE OF ACTIVITIES

The creative industries include practitioners from a wide range of activities who generally work in small organizations. The knowledge they draw upon to inform their practice and theory tends to come from other disciplines. Practitioners tend to be very busy and are unlikely to set up a research project unless they can see a commercial advantage to doing so. Research undertaken in this industry usually has to have a practical consequence. This means that action will be taken as a result of the research. The research is therefore transdisciplinary, and by drawing on knowledge from a range of disciplines it enables us to gain a rich insight that would not otherwise be available. This research tends to first develop ideas and then relate them to practice, and so may lead to a stock of relevant and practical knowledge directly relevant to the field. Research can also generate theory, which will then relate to and inform practice.

THEORY AND PRACTICE

Research in the creative industries tends to use both theory and practice, and the research problem at hand will interact between both of these worlds. There has been some debate about how rigorous the nature and quality of research is in the newer fields within the industry, for example software and digital as these are still emerging. In order to be rigorous a method has to be consistent and have well-defined steps to follow and these need to be established as new sectors develop.

It has been argued that research in the more traditional fields, such as economics, history or science, is of a higher quality as the rigour in research methods used in these fields has been well developed and tested. There is also the question of how research can be both theoretically and methodically rigorous while also having a practical application.

It could be argued that research in the creative industries needs to produce findings that will advance both knowledge and understanding, but that will also address the issues and practical problems that evolve for practitioners within the creative industries.

SUMMARY

This section has explained the importance of research within the creative industries and has given an indication of some areas that have been defined as potentially worthy of future research projects. These suggestions could help you to base your potential research in an area that is pertinent, up to date and well sited in your field of study within the creative industries.

Design research both inspires imagination and informs intuition through a variety of methods with related intents: to expose patterns underlying the rich reality of people's behaviours and experiences, to explore reactions to probes and prototypes, and to shed light on the unknown through iterative hypothesis and experiment.

– Jane Fulton Suri, IDEO

THE PRACTITIONERS: RACHEL COOPER ON CREDIBILITY IN CREATIVE RESEARCH

This section aims to illustrate the value of academic research both as a resource for your research project and as a tool for the creative industries to apply to practical strategic and operational management. This section uses a published statement in www.designcouncil.org from Rachel Cooper, who is distinguished professor of design management and policy at Lancaster University. Her research interests cover design management, design policy, new product development, design in the built environment, design against crime and socially responsible design. She was also founding editor of *The Design Journal* and founding president of the European Academy of Design.

RACHEL COOPER ON *THE DESIGN JOURNAL*

I wrote the first editorial of *The Design Journal*, published by Gower, 'Design Research Comes of Age', in which I said that design research had, to date, existed in niches, and had been disseminated under various guises such as engineering, CAD, management, and art and design; indeed the very nature of design research had been debated. Since that first issue of the journal we have, with Gower and then its partner company Ashgate, continued to publish a broad spread of double blind refereed papers from a range of international authors representing a vast array of design disciplines. Originally, many colleagues were concerned that the coverage was too broad, and that in design one needed to focus. However, the longevity of the journal is evidence to the fact that, while other journals came and went, the philosophy of the original editors has paid off

and been part of a vanguard driving design research across and beyond its narrow disciplinary confines.

RACHEL COOPER ON THE ROLE OF ACADEMIC DESIGN RESEARCH

Academic design research is research conducted primarily by higher education institutions into a variety of topics and issues concerned with design. Its emergence, since the 1960s, followed the recognition of the increasing complexity of design problems and the need to develop tools and methods. Design research grew significantly from the early 1990s as UK government research funding provided new opportunities to researchers.

Introduction to academic design research

The overall aim of design research is to develop an accessible, robust body of knowledge that enhances our understanding of design processes, applications, methods and contexts. Often, this knowledge helps to define best practice and workable methods in dealing with design and design-related problems. It therefore has considerable potential for improving our use and management of design.

Design research embraces a wide range of disciplines, research inquiries and methodologies. These include the following:

- Theoretical studies in design which aim to develop a science of design and provide conceptual frameworks for design inquiries.

- Design discipline-specific research such as industrial design, fashion and textiles and interactive design, which may have a specific technical or product focus, and can include materials and process research.
- Research into usability, applied ergonomics, ethnography and other studies which aim to develop methods to bring design closer to user needs.
- Cultural and historical research which aims to better understand the role that design plays in our culture, and how individuals and communities interact with visual culture.
- Design pedagogy research which explores issues of learning and cognition.
- Applied research into design problem areas, such as crime prevention, sustainability, demographic change and healthcare, which aims to develop new methods for dealing with contemporary problems.
- Design management research which examines how design can be managed in the context of new product development, branding, environmental design and economic competitiveness.

Design research is cross-disciplinary, and often inter-disciplinary. Design departments are responsible for much design research. However, since the 1980s there has been growing interest in design from the social sciences, psychology, marketing and other management areas. This has led to a rich culture of design research.

Academic research is 'open source'. Central to the academic approach is that research problems, methods and findings are made fully transparent and accessible. This enables research to be built upon and applied by others. While some contract and consultancy research is often restricted in terms of its dissemination, the bulk of design research is published using a range of methods and media. These include research conferences organized by "learned societies" or research networks (e.g. The European Academy of Design) usually themed on a specific topic. These combine presentations of work in progress and fully completed research and provide a forum for discussion. Published proceedings of full papers and abstracts represent an important resource for design researchers and users of design research, and provide a means of developing an international community of researchers in the following specific disciplines:

- Refereed journals, which publish research papers that have been peer reviewed by specialists. Some are cross-disciplinary (e.g. *The Design Journal*) while others are more specialized (e.g. *Design Management Journal*). Journals represent a rigorous source of research methods and findings.
- Books, which provide detailed arguments and findings; they can lack the immediacy of conference and journal papers, but provide in-depth coverage of research.

To summarize, design research needs to be

- Credible

To be credible the results of qualitative research need to be believable from the perspective of the participant in the research. From this perspective, the purpose of qualitative research is to describe or understand the phenomena of interest from the participant's perspective; it is the participants who need to legitimately judge the credibility of the results.

- Transferable

Transferability refers to the degree to which the results of qualitative research can be generalized or transferred to other contexts or settings. The qualitative researcher can enhance transferability by doing a thorough job of describing the research context and the assumptions that were central to the research.

- Dependable

The traditional quantitative view of reliability is based on whether the results can be repeated or replicated. The idea of dependability, on the other hand, emphasizes the need for the researcher to account for the ever-changing context within which research occurs. As the researcher, you are responsible for describing the changes that occur in the setting and how these changes affected the way the researcher approached the study.

- Confirmable

Qualitative research tends to assume that each researcher brings a unique perspective to the study. Confirmability refers to the degree to which the results could be confirmed or corroborated by others. There are a number of ways we can enhancing confirmability. The researcher can document the procedures for checking and rechecking the data throughout the study. Another researcher can take a 'devil's advocate' role with respect to the results, and this process can be documented. The researcher can actively search for and describe any *negative instances* that contradict prior observations. And, after the study, you can conduct a *data audit* that examines the data collection and analysis procedures and makes judgements about the potential for bias or distortion.

DESIGNING THE RESEARCH PROBLEM

Having outlined what research is and the context within which research is set in the creative industries, this section moves on to outline the issues and processes involved in defining a research project. This is the stage at which research projects are conceived; the focus is on identifying a problem to investigate in conjunction with reading the theory underpinning the problem you are considering researching and finding a research framework that is workable for your needs. This stage involves generating ideas and refining them.

CHAPTER 1
WHAT MAKES A GOOD RESEARCH TOPIC?

If you are doing a research project as part of your studies, one of the most important factors to consider is whether or not your idea will meet the requirements of the examining body. Consequently, you need to choose your subject with care and you must carefully check the details of the project you are planning against the assessment criteria.

INTEREST

It seems an obvious point, but your project should be something that you are genuinely capable of doing and it must be based on a subject that really interests you. You may be working on the project for up to six months or longer, so you need to be really enthusiastic about it – otherwise, it may very quickly become a chore rather than a pleasure. You need to link your research project to the relevant parts of your course and demonstrate how they inform your topic.

FOCUS

One of the attributes of a good research project is a clearly defined set of research questions and objectives. You therefore need to ask yourself whether or not your research questions will provide you with enough depth to give you a substantial project. If you have been given a research idea, perhaps by an organization with which you are working on an internship, you will need to ensure that your questions and objectives relate to that idea.

AVAILABLE KNOWLEDGE

Interest and focus, combined with a good knowledge of the available literature, will enable you to understand how you can gain new insight into the topic. Try to consider whether or not there is sufficient published knowledge in the field that you are considering working in. It is important that the issues you are considering researching are linked to a relevant theory. You also need to use the available literature to put your topic into context.

DATA AVAILABILITY

Some topics may be too large for you to complete in time, while others may not provide you with the focus or depth to meet the assessment requirements. You may have chosen a topic that is sensitive, such as the issue of housing for the homeless. Collecting the relevant primary data for such topics may prove difficult, so you need to reflect on how this might be resolved. You may also require additional finance for travel, or other resources to undertake your primary research and you will need to make sure that this is available before you begin.

CAREER GOALS

It is important to consider your own career goals. You can use your research project as an opportunity to pursue a particular subject or to focus on a particular industry. Your research project can be used to introduce yourself to potential employers and will demonstrate up-to-date knowledge of research and findings that are pertinent to your expertise.

Use this set of questions to ask yourself if you should proceed with your chosen topic:

- Is it feasible?
- Are you really interested in the topic?
- Do you have the research skills necessary to undertake the project you have defined?
- Can you do the research within the given time frame?
- Will the subject be up to date when the project is finished?
- Do you require additional finance to undertake the project and do you have access to it?
- Can you gain access to the data you need?
- Is it worth doing this project?
- Does the topic fit the specifications set by the examining body?
- Does the research topic contain issues that have a clear link to theory?
- Are your research questions and objectives stated clearly?
- Will your proposed research provide new insights into the topic?
- Will your findings be pertinent whatever the outcome?
- Is the research topic in line with your career goals?

CHAPTER 2

GENERATING AND REFINING RESEARCH IDEAS

Before you can refine your research into a research question or proposition, you need to generate some ideas. Have you ever wondered how creative artists, designers and inventors come up with their remarkable ideas? Even though idea generation may seem a mysterious and random process, there is a practical, simple method we can all apply to help us to increase our chances of having great ideas: by using connections. Any idea, no matter how small, is an association between previous, established ideas. These connections happen in our minds all the time – often spontaneously and when we are barely conscious of them.

FINDING CONNECTIONS

An interesting characteristic of these connections is their unpredictability. Many times, ideas are formed by associating two completely unrelated concepts, in unexpected or unusual ways. To create movable type, Johannes Gutenberg connected the idea of the wine press and the coin stamp. To create the concept of a mass-circulation newspaper, Joseph Pulitzer combined large-scale advertising with high-speed printing. Great ideas may even seem to be random at times – but that doesn't mean that there's nothing you can do to develop them. Mick Pierce, an architect working in Zimbabwe, was asked to design the largest building in Harare – without air conditioning. For inspiration, he turned to the termites of the African savannah. Despite temperatures dropping to as low as 6 degrees Celsius at night and soaring as high as 40 degrees Celsius (104 degrees Fahrenheit) during the day, termites are able to keep temperatures in their mounds at a constant

31 degrees Celsius (87 degrees Fahrenheit). By opening and closing a series of vents around the mound, the termites redirect air breezes and maintain a constant temperature. Pierce used exactly the same principles in his design for the building. Omitting the need for air conditioning units immediately saved the build millions of dollars, and the building now uses about 90 per cent less energy than any other building around it despite having a constant static temperature of about 22 degrees Celsius (71 degrees Fahrenheit). In early 2009 he designed an educational centre to encourage visitors to value water in Doha, Qatar. The solution was a large dome covering 5,000 metres squared with an eye as the crown. The Doha eye, modelled on the human eye with a lens and a retina, followed the sun in order to harvest energy to be turned into electrical power. The white-painted dome would collect dew at night at its perimeter, where it would run into a circular constructed *wadi* (a shallow valley) surrounding the dome. The dome was to be placed in a water park demonstrating the principles of salt water farming using groundwater, in which a water tower would act as an energy source.

The conscious generation of ideas is often the starting point for an innovation journey. There are many techniques to support idea generation; the most widely used one is brainstorming. Most companies do not see the generation of new ideas as a problem. The question tends to be how to generate quality ideas, and how to select which of these ideas are to be taken.

— Bettina von Stamm.

HOW TO CREATE A LOT OF IDEAS

Idea generation happens randomly, so having great ideas is not a task that can be approached directly. The only way to increase the likelihood of having great ideas is to increase the amount of ideas that you have at your disposal to form connections. Simple ideas are the raw materials for higher-level ideas. The more ideas you have, the more material your mind will have to associate and generate good ideas. Being prolific, then, is the key to having great ideas. There's no trade-off between quantity and quality; they are intrinsically linked and it is only through quantity that you get quality. If the best way to get quality ideas is by creating them from a vast pool of ideas, then we need to have as many ideas as possible. Here are some ways that can help you to develop a pool of ideas from which to start funnelling down to a narrower and deeper focus.

BRAINSTORMING

Brainstorming is a way for you to come up with many ideas in a short period of time, by working in a group. It's based on the way that your mind naturally works when you're being creative, and it is something that you can do intentionally when you need to create more options or ideas for your research project:

- Defer judgement: no criticism right now. Do you remember how people once said that flying was impossible? Don't be one of the naysayers. At some point, it is important to judge an idea, but don't do it while you're trying to generate ideas.
- Go for quantity: the more ideas you come up with, the more likely it is that one or more of them will be a great idea.
- Look for unusual or wild ideas: worry about how to make it work later, so look for as many 'crazy' ideas as you can – the wilder the better.
- Combine and build on ideas: 'piggyback' one idea onto another to create a new idea.

By using these principles when you look for new ideas or options for your project, you give yourself permission to come up with ideas that you might not otherwise pay any attention to, but that actually make sense when you tailor them, or add something else to them. Start with a problem that interests you and come up with ideas about how to research it: what is the problem? How does it connect with other contexts or problems? Before you start, tell yourself how many ideas you want to come up with – maybe thirty ideas if your problem is well defined or hundred ideas if you want some really bizarre ideas – and don't stop until you come up with that number. You may want to give a value to each idea and double the value for the next idea and so on. The aim here is to stretch for one more idea, because it may be worth a lot.

MOVEMENT LADDER

You can also use a movement ladder to generate ideas. This works well when you already have a good research idea but need some inspiration. You can use it to define your concept, by looking for the idea behind the solution you need. If your project concept is to research levels of motivation in designers in SMEs, the broader concept is not perhaps motivation, but the overall performance of the design organization. You then think about all the specific things that fit within this concept.

Figure 1.1 Laddder abstraction

I FEEL GREAT WHEN I'M WEARING ONE
Better looking
More presentable
Improve myself
Accessorize
quality
good design
different from others
LUXURY BRAND

Go up the ladder: What wider categories could it be an example of? Something to drink from, made of clay perhaps, a gift, if you chose to think of it as something to drink from and you laddered up you could ask what would be an example of this? It could be a small container, something to hold fluid.

If you ladder down and build on the concept of 'a small container' what are some examples of small containers? Perfume bottles, old ink bottles, plastic containers, milk bottles and so forth.

If you ladder up again and take the example of milk bottles you might think 'what are they examples of?' An answer might be recyclable containers. What are recyclable containers an example of? An answer might be water reduction, ecological policies and so forth.

In general laddering up towards the general allows you to broaden out towards new areas and laddering down allows you to focus on to specific parts of these new areas. If you alternate between the two it helps you explore a wide territory.

RANDOM WORD

The random 'word technique', originally devised by Edward de Bono as an aid to research, is another useful, fun and unique way to generate new ideas. Choose an object at random, or a noun from a dictionary, and associate that with the research concept you are thinking about. This technique is also known as the method of focal objects. For example, imagine you are thinking about how to improve Wikipedia. Choosing an object at random from an office, you might immediately spot a fax machine. Fax machines are becoming rare. People send faxes directly to known phone numbers. Perhaps this makes you think of providing ways to embed wiki articles in emails and other websites, as is done with YouTube videos. Does it stimulate other Wikipedia ideas for you?

You can use provocation by declaring usual perceptions out of bounds, or provide a provocative alternative to the usual situation under consideration. Prefix the provocation with the term 'X' to signal that the provocation is not a valid idea put up for judgement but rather a stimulus for new perceptions.

Alternatively, simply challenge the way things have always been done or seen, or the way they are, simply to direct your perceptions to explore beyond your current mindset. For example, you could challenge the convention of coffee cups being produced with handles; the challenge here is a directive to explore without defending the status quo. Handles exist because cups are usually too hot to hold directly, so perhaps coffee cups could be made with insulated finger grips; or tailor-made coffee cup holders similar to beer holders could be produced.

Suspend judgement and don't be overly logical with information at every step of the way. This allows for the formation of different patterns of thought and association. By generating alternatives and creating a quota of ideas, you can overcome creative blocks to formulating different ways of looking at things.

CREATIVE THINKING

Sometimes it is really difficult to come up with ideas for your research project. This section provides you with useful tools and techniques to stimulate your creativity and describes new and imaginative ways to come up with ideas. Creativity helps you generate ideas, but it does not replace logic and rationality in evaluating the feasibility of your design research ideas. Creative thinking provides you with a variety of ideas before you evaluate and select the idea with the most potential to develop into a project. Creative thinking techniques introduced in this section will support your thinking throughout your project.

HOW CAN I BECOME A CREATIVE THINKER?

Creativity is an ability to see things differently and to generate new forms. The following section introduces you to six techniques to bring out your creativity.

Issue exploration and problem solving generally work by splitting the thinking about an issue or problem into a series of stages. The three-stage version shown below works in a wide range of settings including those that are time pressured (Henry and Martin, 1987):

1. *issue exploration*
2. *idea generation*
3. *implementation planning*

There are sub-phases within each of these stages. For example, you may choose to map, clarify and reframe an issue in the first stage. This section discusses techniques you can use at each stage and phase. The techniques have been chosen because they tend to work with most people in most settings, do not take long and are easy to understand and facilitate.

You can use the creative approaches described here to work out how you might pursue opportunities for your research project, develop a vision, solve problems or implement plans.

You can also work creatively on issues by working with a small group of people who may agree to be participants in your project. Ways of exploring issues include considering possible and desired futures and clarifying the nature of the issue, by mapping and reframing. If you are clear about the nature of the issue, it may be sufficient to formulate a clear statement encapsulating what you want to address, give participants a quick chance to clarify anything they are unclear about and attempt to reframe it before starting to think about possible solutions. If the problem is large, unclear or embedded in a messy or politically sensitive context, it is worth taking time to clarify its nature and map out key elements before reframing. If you are exploring opportunities, it is worth considering possible ideal solutions early on. Considering a preferred future is often also useful when problem solving.

After reframing or mapping exercises, people may realize that the problem they originally intended to address is not the crux of the matter, and then proceed to look for solutions to a different issue from the one first raised. The simple techniques described below offer useful ways to explore and reframe issues.

Most problems, issues and possibilities merit some degree of clarification, if only a discussion about the elements involved. The *why?* technique offers one way of doing this.

IDEA GENERATION

1. Why?

Think of an issue, problem or opportunity that you would like to do something about. Ask yourself (or get someone else to ask you), 'Why does this issue matter?' Then ask again: 'Why does (whatever your answer

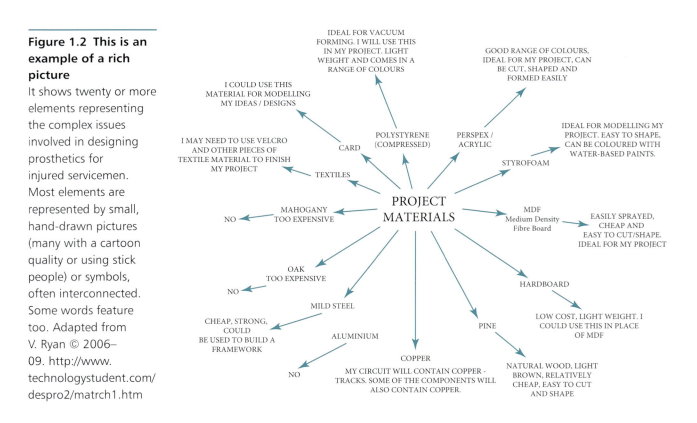

Figure 1.2 This is an example of a rich picture

It shows twenty or more elements representing the complex issues involved in designing prosthetics for injured servicemen. Most elements are represented by small, hand-drawn pictures (many with a cartoon quality or using stick people) or symbols, often interconnected. Some words feature too. Adapted from V. Ryan © 2006–09. http://www.technologystudent.com/despro2/matrch1.htm

was) matter?' Repeat this exercise several more times to go back a few more levels. Three or four rounds of questions are usually sufficient. The *why?* technique offers a way of probing the causes and assumptions that might not otherwise be considered and are often a good way of clarifying unclear briefs.

2. Mapping

Large, messy or unclear problems generally benefit from some kind of mapping exercise that lays out the elements and enables people to see how they relate to each other. Diagramming techniques like *rich pictures, mind maps, fishbone* and *causal mapping* are very useful tools in such cases (examples of which are searchable online).

If you prefer something more orderly and bullet-like you might be more comfortable with *force-field analysis*. As ever, some issues lend themselves more readily to some techniques than others.

If you are dealing with a really big issue that you are unclear about, you might find it helpful to start with a brainstorm or brainwriting exercise to check out what issues are involved before attempting any kind of diagramming. The brainstormed issues can be summarized on a *mind map* (described later).

Cause and consequences

People often find the *causes and consequences* technique particularly relatable. Proceed as follows:

1. Think of an issue you would like to explore.

Figure 1.3 Causes and Consequences
This diagram shows a central circle with various branches coming out of it. The branches above the circle are coloured blue and labelled 'causes' while the branches below the circle are coloured yellow and are labelled 'consequences'.

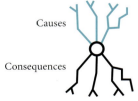

Causes

Consequences

2. In the centre of a large sheet of paper write down a key phrase or a few 'keywords' that summarize the nub of your problem within a small circle. (Keep the writing fairly small so there is ample space to add four levels above and below.)

3. Immediately, above this, write down what seem to be the most direct causes of this problem. Join these to the central problem by a line as shown above. (Keep the lines short to leave sufficient space for more levels.) Try to limit the number of immediate causes to three, four or five main ones.

4. Above each of these direct causes, write down what seem to be the most direct causes of each of these. (Restrict yourself to the main one or two causes of each.) Repeat this process several times so that you end up with a tree of causes of the issue, linked as indicated above. Three or four levels are usually sufficient.

5. Similarly, below the central issue, plot the direct consequences of the issue or problem, and then several tiers of the consequences of these consequences.

A *cause and consequence* map asks you to map out the 'whys' and 'so whats' of a particular problem or issue. The centre represents the original issue; the finer branches show the increasingly remote causes of the issue and the finer roots the increasingly remote consequences of the issue. You may end up with cross-connections, so that the tree becomes a network. This kind of exercise can be useful in planning policy documents. The consequence part can be useful in evaluating proposals. Eden et al.'s (1983) technique of cognitive mapping offers a more complex approach.

I wish . . .

Here is another method to drive your idea forward. Think of an issue you would like to do something about. Write down at least ten statements in the form 'I wish …', such as 'I wish we talked more often'. The ten statements should describe some of the things you would like to happen for you to take your chosen issue forward. It does not matter if they are sensible or crazy.

Take this to a second stage and choose two of the ten of your statements, selecting one as being most important and the other as most interesting.

Discussion

This offers a way of tapping into your vision of what you would like to happen. When you consider an ideal way forward, it will often direct your attention to very different areas from those you would consider when focusing on fixing the problem. Focusing on the important issue is what we usually do when we try to solve problems, but including a few suggestions that you rate as interesting often takes better account of tacit concerns. When using *I wish* in a group ask people to write up their wishes on a flip chart in turn and aim for at least twenty I wish statements.

If you are faced with a rather negative group of people you might like to ask them to list their *concerns* about the problem early on, as they may be unwilling to fully engage with more playful approaches, like I wish, until they have dumped their concerns. One way of doing this is to invite people to write their concerns on a big board, a bit like writing graffiti.

Multiple redefinitions

Think of your issue as a question and write it down in a few words beginning:

● How to …

Then complete each of the following sentences in turn:

● What I'd really like to do is …
● If I could break all the rules of reality I would …
● The issue could be likened to …
● A strange way of looking at it would be …
● But the main point is …

Then redraft your issue as a statement in the light of the insights gained:

● How can I …?

Discussion

These questions can be used as a means of opening up perspectives on the issue at hand.

It is virtually always worth spending some time considering different angles on the issue at hand. In my experience with reframing exercises, about 70 per cent of the time people realize that another angle or a completely different question is the one that ought to be explored, not the question they started with.

Other people's definitions

A variant, if you are exploring an issue with a group of people, is to ask each person to write down what they think the main issue is in the form: how to … . This usually works best if each person writes up their own 'how to …' statement rather than giving one person control of the pen. You proceed as follows:

1. The issue owner gives a bit of background and the group clarifies any uncertainties by asking questions about the nature of the problem. Avoid putting forward solutions at this stage.
2. The client and each group member write down their best attempt at summarizing the nub of the problem beginning 'how to …'. Write these on a large sheet of paper, such as a flip chart, so everybody can see and discuss them.
3. Finally, the client chooses or creates a final version to take forward for idea generation.

The group members act as consultants but their task is not to decide how they would tackle the issue, but to help the client settle on a perspective that is most helpful to them. Since the client has the last word, carefully phrased suggestions that are sensitive to the client's focus are likely to be more persuasive. *Dialectical approaches* illustrate some more complex ways of using other people's viewpoints.

IDEA GENERATION AND DEVELOPMENT

There are a number of different ways of generating ideas including classic listing, analytical and lateral thinking approaches. *Classic* techniques like *brainstorming* or *brainwriting* ask people to list ideas and use other people's perspectives to prompt new ideas. *Analytical* approaches consider many alternatives systematically. *Lateral* thinking introduces something unrelated to the issue to prompt different ideas. All of these approaches aim to produce a mass of ideas and to get to quality through quantity.

- Listing
- Lateral
- Checklists

Classic listing

Listing techniques like *brainstorming, brainwriting, nominal group technique* and *brainwriting* offer a means of generating a lot of ideas in a short period of time.

Warm-up

When facilitating a group session some people like to start idea generation with some form of warm-up to engage the group. One way of doing this is to ask the group to generate ideas about something like 'how many uses can the group think of for a cup?' This can ease the atmosphere. Another approach is to do something completely different, perhaps go for a walk outside or play a game. The theory is that such activities can energize a group. Some consultants believe this kind of diversion helps creative thinking; others manage fine without them, so their inclusion or otherwise is up to you.

Brainstorming

Brainstorming asks you to list as many ideas as you can think of that might address your issue whether sensible or crazy. Record every idea. Brainstorming emphasizes the importance of deferred judgement by forbidding all criticisms and put-downs during idea generation. If the group contains reserved or reflective people, *brainwriting* is often more effective at drawing them in.

If you think you have the obvious solution and/or have considered all the possible options it can be hard to relax enough to come up with the new ideas that might lead to a much needed new angle. One way around this is to purge all the obvious and sensible answers that immediately spring to mind via a quick brainstorm.

Some people like to sort and classify these initial ideas and then begin a second round of idea generation. For instance, you could try some of the lateral thinking techniques below, with a view to coming up with new examples to add to your map of classified ideas. For some people this two-stage approach (of generating ideas via brainwriting and classifying these on a mind map before moving on to use lateral thinking

techniques to come up with more ideas) clears the mind and leaves it more open to explore less obvious approaches. Others prefer not to cluster or classify ideas and choose favoured ideas more intuitively.

Brainwriting

Think of a question you would like solutions to. Ask a few colleagues or friends to spend a few minutes helping you come up with ideas.

1. Remind everyone of the agreed question and the principles that all ideas are accepted and no criticism is allowed.
2. Get each person to write down their ideas about possible solutions to the question. An easy way of doing this is get each person to write each idea on a separate post-it or sticky note. (The small or medium ones work best.)
3. Collect these ideas together. One way is to stick all the notes on a wall and group them into categories, naming each category on another sticky note in capitals. Another way is to list all the ideas on a flip chart or whiteboard. With the latter it helps to go round the group two or three times asking each person to give one idea in turn before allowing a free for all, so everybody has a chance to contribute.
4. If you have time, you can encourage people to build on other people's suggestions to come up with further ideas.
5. Continue until just after the flow begins to dry up, perhaps ending up with thirty plus ideas in a larger group.

Discussion

Research suggests that *brainwriting* produces a greater variety of different classes of ideas than brainstorming as people are less influenced by group-think at the start (Janis, 1972). It is almost impossible to take in a long list of ideas without grouping them in some way, so listing techniques are often coupled with a clustering or mapping technique to allow participants to get a better handle on the different classes of ideas that have been generated. These days the most common method is to stick the sticky notes on a wall and group related ideas together.

If the group includes anyone who finds it hard to come up with ideas on the spot, encourage them to use the *five Ws* checklists (see page 33) as this is a very good aid to idea generation.

Notebook

One way of gathering ideas on your own is to extend idea collection over a longer period. Carry a small notebook or smartphone around with you and get in the habit of recording thoughts or ideas relevant to the problem or issue immediately as they occur to you. In a similar way, some people keep a sheet of paper or smartphone by their bed to record ideas that come to them when they wake.

Nominal group technique

If you want to involve people who are geographically distant from each other, get everyone to email ideas; collate these ideas and send the grouped list of ideas back to participants. Ask people to add any further ideas they think of and return the amended list. Send the expanded list to all participants. You may also like to ask them to select their top five ideas.

Lateral thinking

Lateral thinking describes a range of techniques that can be useful in provoking radical thinking about an issue. These techniques take people on an *excursion* away from the problem as a way of getting to an area of thought that is remote enough from ordinary thinking to bypass unconscious assumptions and habits and provide a genuinely new perspective. They achieve this through devices like random jumps, distorting or transforming the topic or exploring analogies. Sometimes you can relate the reversed problem, analogy or random word *directly* back to the problem. Often you take an excursion away from the issue, noting ideas associated with the random input, for example, and then attempting to relate one or more of these back to the issue (forcing the connection if necessary) to show the original topic in a new light.

Random

Select a question or issue you want to develop ideas for. Pick a random word or object in a manner that suits you. For example, look around you and pick the first object you see or take a walk and bring back something that struck your attention, perhaps a stone or leaf.

Alternatively, get a book or magazine, close your eyes, open it, point your finger somewhere on the page and note the nearest noun or verb. Alternatively, call up a random internet page and pick a keyword to describe it.

Once you have a random word or object, forget your original question, and write down the first six to ten or so words you associate with the random word or object. Then pick one of the associations that most appeals and relate this back to the original issue. Then pick the association that seems least related to the issue under consideration and try and relate that back to suggest a new approach. For example, if the question was how to design a new chair and the random input was a light bulb, this might suggest a glass chair or human shaped chair or chair with a light attached.

The value lies in the thought you give to how the random stimulus can be made relevant to the issue. It may immediately suggest new way(s) of tackling the issue or you may need to make several links before getting to a usable new idea.

Discussion

It is often the most apparently distant associations that lead to fundamentally new ways of addressing the issue.

Weirdos

Brainwriting often produces some weird or unacceptable ideas that can be valuable as triggers for other more useful ideas, when used as starting points for provocative excursions. For instance 'kill my manager' is clearly out of the question. However, there may be many perfectly acceptable ways of removing their impact from the situation: perhaps the job could be taken over by some other manager, or they might be encouraged to move to another department. Alternatively, by considering the loss that would result if the manager were killed, you might begin to appreciate the manager's value.

Reversal

Reversing the sense of your topic is usually an excellent and fun way of coming up with new ideas on the topic. For instance, 'how to get on better with my manager' may be reversed to 'how to get on worse with my manager'. This might suggest throwing things at the manager, arriving late, not telling them about work that has not been done or telling him or her how difficult you find them. You can re-reverse these ideas to suggest new approaches.

Take the issue you want to do something about and reverse it. For example, if your issue is how to improve the perception of a brand, you could consider how to reduce the perception of a brand or create absolutely no brand recognition, for example. Either alone or with a few colleagues, friends or family, list at least ten ways you could achieve the reversed question. Then consider each in turn, re-reversing most of them to come up with new ideas.

Superheroes

Pick a hero or heroine, from Nelson Mandela to Adele, perhaps a famous sportsperson or cartoon character. Discuss what this person is like and how they set about things and see if this suggests a new way of tackling the issue at hand. This is usually a fun exercise. A variant is to pick an organization you admire and discuss how they set about things and what they produce, and then examine what new approaches that suggests. The organization can be from a different field to yours if you like.

Checklists

People who like systematic methods may prefer checklists to lateral thinking techniques. Checklists are also useful if you are working alone. Some remind you of a set of steps to go through; others give you factors to consider.

It is sometimes interesting to record which checklist item suggested which ideas, so that you can subsequently reflect on how particular new ideas emerged.

Five Ws and H

The who? what? why? how? when? where? checklist is a wonderful all-purpose back-of-an-envelope prompt for generating different angles and ideas on any topic.

Whenever you are stuck for ideas, think of each of the six words above in turn and try to relate it to your issue. Some people find it helpful to use this checklist when asked to come up with ideas in meetings. 'Who?' suggests something about the people, 'where?' the place, and so on. These questions prompt you to formulate new questions and ideas, and to think about what you have forgotten. For instance, if you are task oriented you may have neglected the 'who?' and if you are people oriented you may have neglected the 'what?' element.

Attribute listing

Choose a product or service you would like to improve. List various characteristics (or components) of the product or service (for instance its colour, shape, size, cost, parts, material and so forth) and think systematically about how each of these in turn could be changed and how all these possible changes could be combined. For example, if considering a bicycle, materials might lead you to consider manufacturing in plastic instead of metal, parts might lead you to consider a drum rather than a bell.

All these idea generation methods generate a mass of ideas and most people benefit from classifying, sorting and/or clustering the resultant ideas to make it easier to take them in. Classification may also reveal gaps and provide a platform to develop further ideas. Note that an alternative approach to creative thinking eschews classification in favour of using ideas as springboards. Here people rely on their intuition to determine which new idea is the one they should take forward. This approach works in more open and relaxed environments (e.g. advertising) and with highly creative people, but in a more conservative environment, people often seem to do better if they classify the ideas they have come up with first.

TABLE 1.1		
ATTRIBUTE LISTING (improving a torch by examining the positives and negatives)		
Feature	*Attribute*	*Ideas*
Casing	Plastic	Metal
Switch	On/off	On/off low beam
Battery	Consumable	Rechargeable
Bulb	Glass	Plastic

IDEA CLASSIFICATION

Mind mapping

Mind maps

Another method for generating research ideas is to use mind maps, which are visual diagrams with lines and bubbles representing ideas and the relationships between them. The core idea sits in the middle with related topics branching out from it. Ideas are further broken down and extended until your page looks like an impressionist painting of a spider colony.

Mind maps can be very useful because they are fast to create and no effort is wasted. Hierarchy and categorization are visually and clearly defined and rather than writing out lots of descriptive phrases, only the key ideas are represented. Symbols and diagrams can be included to illustrate ideas, enabling the mind map to be read at a glance. Mind maps can be used in three different ways within research projects, which we shall now explore further.

Mind maps allow you to brainstorm and get ideas from your head quickly down on paper. They lend themselves especially well to free association. By recording, then rapidly reviewing freely generated ideas, we can find connections and new relationships between concepts that we otherwise might have missed. Drawing your ideas is also ideal for remaining in a creative mode where more logical and rigid methods might take you off track.

As you listen to a lecture or read a book you can very quickly create notes using a mind map. You can use large branches for chapters or key points, with detail added from them. A whole book can be summarized on one page and it is remarkable how well you can recall the information later and use it in your research with only the map as a guide. You can also use mind maps to plan your project. In one diagram you can represent everything that needs doing – the relationships between tasks, for example (what has to be done before something else can be).

Mind mapping makes it easy to see at a glance which ideas have been covered and which have not and offers space to add in extra ideas. Mind maps can take quite a while to prepare. Some people like to leave a mind map on their office wall to grow over days or weeks.

To produce a mind map, do the following:

- Start in the centre with a small circle labelled with a keyword or two to indicate the nature of the topic.
- Use keywords to indicate three to six major categories of ideas. Branch each of these out from the centre.
- Split each branch into several sub-categories for variants on this theme and place the ideas as twigs in the appropriate place on each branch as indicated in Figure 1.4. Generally, three levels of main branches, sub-branches and twigs are sufficient to group ideas. Two levels of main branches and twigs are virtually always insufficient.

It helps to use a large sheet of paper placed in landscape position, print all words, use felt tip pens not biro or pencil and use short branches so there is plenty of space to add in new ideas. Many people like to use a different colour for each main branch.

Figure 1.4 Mind mapping process
This diagram shows three different mind maps, each in various stages of completion. The first shows a central circle with three different coloured branches coming out of it. One of these branches divides into two smaller branches at the end furthest from the central circle. The second mind map shows the same item but with an extra branch coming out of the circle. All four branches then divide into further branches. The third mind map is the same as the second but with the addition of three large circles that group commonalities.

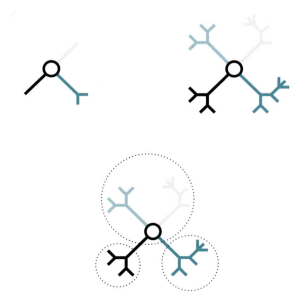

You can use 'balloons' drawn round clusters of ideas to reaffirm the existing classification or regroup the ideas.

These diagrams are very easy to take in, add to and remember, and can be used as an aide-memoire, and as a sorting and classification device. They are also useful for structuring reports and taking notes. See Buzan (1982) for more on this approach.

Another use of mind mapping is to reveal the pattern of material you have produced so that you see which particular angles have been emphasized and which have been neglected. You can then concentrate on filling in the gaps, inventing new tactics to meet a particular strategy, for example.

As a general principle, in problem solving it is a good idea to generate several different classes of ideas or strategies to introduce variety and stop yourself jumping to premature conclusions. Make sure the ideas really are different from one another – it won't help if your shortlist consists only of variations on the same theme.

IMPLEMENTATION

When it comes to implementing your plan, *help and hinder* offers a simple and very useful procedure that enables you to consider acceptance finding and action planning quickly. Many people find it useful when working alone or with others.

Help and hinder

1. Select a plan you are considering implementing.
2. Identify a few people and things (e.g. policy or resources) that might help and hinder you when implementing a proposed plan and note these on a matrix along the lines of the one below. It is important not to neglect the hindrances.
3. Underline what you see as the most critical of these factors, perhaps two of the helps and two of the hindrances. Some items may occur on both sides; for instance, a powerful senior manager would be an enormous help on your side, but could be a serious hindrance otherwise.
4. Think of ways of engaging the support of the key helpers and things (policies and resources, for example) and ways of getting round the key hindrances that could prevent the scheme going through.

5. Develop a specific plan of action, which indicates who will do what, when and where or a sequence of actions to be performed. Aim for a course of action you are definitely willing to undertake.

Discussion

Help and hinder can be used when you are working alone or with others. *Stakeholder analysis*, *force-field analysis* and *implementation checklists* cover some of the same ground. Obviously, there are many more sophisticated project-planning techniques.

Ideas association

You can also try ideas association techniques, by associating different ideas that are stimulated from a simple shape. Take a look at the symbol in Figure 1.5, for example.

Figure 1.5 What do you see?

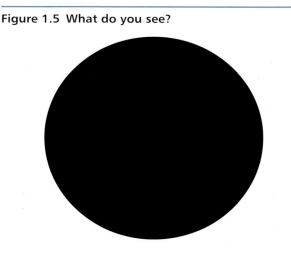

What do you see? A black dot? What else do you see? How about a very large full stop? What else can you think of? Here are some other ideas:

- An overhead view of a cup of black coffee
- A very dirty basketball
- An open sewer cover
- The pupil of an eye
- A passageway with no lights
- A black hole in space
- A bullet hole through the page.

Instead of accepting the first answer that comes to mind, try and go beyond it; be open to and create more ideas. This tool is practical when our normal automatic perceptions tend to keep us trapped 'within the box'. Thinking inside the box means accepting the status quo. Charles H. Duell, director of the US Patent Office, famously said, 'Everything that can be invented has been invented'. That was in 1899: clearly he was thinking inside the box! In-the-box thinkers find it difficult to recognize the quality of an idea because they routinely believe that an idea is an idea and a solution is a solution. In fact, they can be quite stubborn when it comes to valuing an idea. They are masters of the creativity-killer attitude such as 'that'll never work' or 'it's too risky'. They also believe that every problem needs only one solution; therefore, finding more than one possible solution to a problem represents a waste of time. However, thinking 'outside the box' requires different attributes that include

- A willingness to adopt new perspectives in relation to day-to-day events
- An openness to do different things and to do things differently
- Focusing on the value of finding new ideas and acting on them
- Striving to create value in new ways
- Listening to others
- Supporting and respecting others when they come up with new ideas out-of-the box thinking requires openness to new ways of seeing the world and a willingness to explore.

Out-of-the box thinkers know that new ideas need nurturing and support. They also know that having an idea is good, but that acting on it is more important.

Figure 1.6 Edward de Bono's Six Thinking Hats

'Six Thinking Hats' is a technique that allows you to separate thinking into six categories. Each category is defined with a coloured 'thinking hat'. By mentally wearing and then switching hats you can redirect your thought processes. Thinking techniques like these enable you to come up with creative solutions and organize your thoughts and ideas. Thus, the white hat, for instance, calls for needed or known information, the red for feeling or intuition and the black hat for judgement or why something may not work.

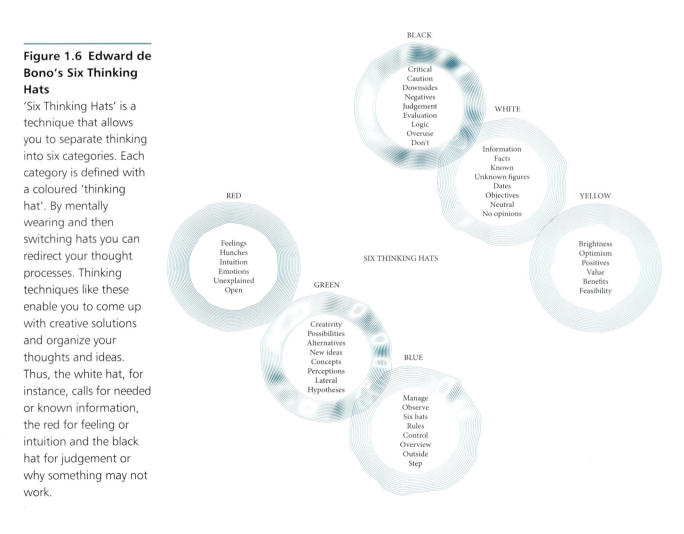

CHAPTER 3
TURNING IDEAS INTO RESEARCH PROJECTS

This section aims to show you how to funnel initial ideas down into a research framework for your research. The dissertation is intended to provide you with an opportunity to explore at length some aspects of theory, methods, knowledge or skills that you have been introduced to on your course. We will explore the four types of learning objectives – substantive, processual skills and concepts, methodological skills and processes, and self-knowledge – within this section. When you are planning your research project, you should think about the kind of learning you consider most suitable for you and your topic; first, you will be selecting a broad area of interest, such as workplace design, or a topic that draws together material from many areas. But you should also consider the type of learning that you want to focus on.

THINK BOX
Four types of learning objectives

Although one type of learning may be dominant in your project, you will probably be expected to address all four learning objectives. Whichever type of project you choose to do, remember that the primary aim is to enhance your own learning in an area of your choice. You may not be able to define these learning objectives very precisely and even if you do, they may change during the course of your project. However, try to reflect on the kind of learning objective that you are pursuing and revisit this from time to time during your project. Once you have defined your learning objectives, you can move on to selecting a topic.

1 Substantive

A substantive learning objective would be reflected in a statement such as: 'I wish to learn more about motivation amongst designers within the car industry.' Here you will seek to further your knowledge of the topic and explore relevant theory to it. One outcome of such an inquiry might be to rethink the concepts or models of practice involved. As such, the learning has substance as opposed to you merely learning about a process.

2 Processual skills and concepts

Processual skills and concepts reflect on problems and solutions – implementing techniques, concepts and models. This may lead you to a better understanding of potential barriers and problems involved in implementation, which could, in turn, inform how you approach other similar circumstances. This approach would be reflected in a statement such as: 'I wish to learn more about how to apply strategic design auditing in an organization.'

3 Methodological skills and processes

You may want to focus on the way in which research is undertaken by using methodological skills and processes. This type of learning focuses on the way knowledge is generated from data. An example of this would be reflected in the statement 'I wish to gain a critical understanding of how to research the perception of design, developing debates on how to collect data, and in particular gaining an understanding of subjectively meaningful emotions using focus groups'.

4 Self-knowledge

You might focus mainly on self-knowledge, expanding your thinking and reflective abilities in order to understand your own learning and actions: 'I wish to confront the area of project management, which is difficult for me, to inform myself how I might develop my personal organizational skills.'

SELECTING A TOPIC

Having reflected on your course and what has captured your attention, you have probably already selected a topic and generated many ideas around it. You may also want to think forward to your future career and to think about what will make you marketable. In addition, reflect on your strengths and weaknesses, on what is achievable for you and what resources you can easily draw on. When you have clarified these issues, you can move on to consider your research question. First, you need to be clear about what a research question is. It is the question around which you wish to have a conversation, build an argument and essentially answer. It frames your endeavour and it is the central point around which all your decisions and all your dialogue will revolve.

In order to define your research question, you need to refine the topic and develop the research questions by doing the following actions:

- Defining your topic area
- Defining the nature of your project
- Defining the issues that you will explore
- Analysing where relationships exist between the issues that you are exploring

The tricky part is to make sure that you don't get confused about your phenomenon of interest when formulating a specific research question. Although you will be interested in quite a few issues, you might end up having to let things go, otherwise you may end up with a project that is too big for you to tackle in sufficient depth within the period of time you have. You may find you need to focus on one question, rather than the four or five that you had initially considered. You may also find that the question you have defined is too big and needs to be focused in on even more. This is all part of the natural process of honing in on your topic, and you shouldn't be overly discouraged by this.

CHAPTER 4
IDENTIFYING AND USING THEORY

You may have an understanding of theory and practice that maintains *theory* is academic and abstract and is completely different with the *practice* of action and designing things and processes. However, your project will most likely involve focusing on and taking forward the theory–practice dialogue that has informed most of your design and creative studies to date. The theory–practice relationship within the framework of a research project is intended to ensure that the process is grounded in the real demands of managing a real issue. Your project is therefore intended to provide a sustained vehicle for exploring both the possibilities and the tensions of making use of theory within the day-to-day contexts of a career in the creative industries. Your choice of theory will depend on the issues you face in relation to different aspects of your project.

An individual's perception of the distinction between theory and practice depends to a large extent on their perception of theory. People have hugely different views on what theory is; there is, on the face of it, less ambiguity about what is commonly understood as management practice. We will not enter into a long debate about definitions of theory here – suffice it to say that your view of what theory is may differ to that of other students. You may want to begin to identify how you are going to use theory to inform your project. Before you do so, it might be helpful to think a little about the distinction between theory, tacit knowledge and theory-in-use.

Theory is what contains general conceptualizations that can be applied across many situations involving management, design and creation. As part of your studies, you will have engaged with different types of theory – it is typically what you read and are asked to engage with in an academic module. Consistent with a view that knowledge that is relevant to design practice is a great deal more than theory, you can use the term 'tacit knowledge' to describe knowledge formed through a combination of theory and practical understanding that guide daily actions. Therefore, let us assume that there is value in integrating theory and practice and that the theory you engage with as part of your studies will at least indirectly inform the way you go about your creative practice; it informs your tacit knowledge. Logically, it follows that theory-in-use is the tacit knowledge that is brought to bear upon actions. Theory-in-use is often intuitive or otherwise internalized but can be inferred from actual behaviour. If you could extract yours (or indeed someone else's), it would be an expression of how you see the world. Therefore, an extracted theory-in-use would tell us something about how we understand things to function, what we see as taken for granted and so on. It is this knowledge that influences how we act and behave.

The final aspect of your project proposal that you need to consider is evidence. The criteria for your project will probably require you to demonstrate your capability to find, analyse and provide appropriate evidence to

- support the initiative you are undertaking;
- inform the ways in which the initiative is decided upon, created and progressed;
- evaluate the extent of its success;
- identify what has been learned in the process.

There should be a general disposition towards securing and using evidence in these ways but you are normally not required to be an expert in the full array of approaches and techniques that are necessary for systematic research. The evidence that you choose to collect, analyse and draw upon will depend on the issues you face in relation to different aspects of your project.

that their offices are cold or the bus ride to college is uncomfortable) may be the symptoms of a deeper problem (such as low morale) rather than the problem itself. You need some ways of demonstrating that an issue is indeed as significant for the organization and yourself as you initially thought it was.

NEGOTIATING WITH COLLEAGUES/STAKEHOLDERS

You may have also begun to identify who the key stakeholders for your project might be. A stakeholder is someone who has an interest in and may affect your project. At some point, you may need to think about seeking their support for your initiative and in doing so you will need to supply some supporting evidence to secure their buy-in and to demonstrate the feasibility and the benefits of the initiative you are proposing. There may be stakeholders who are not that keen on your initiative and who may, therefore, seek to jeopardize any progress on it. It is prudent, therefore, to think very carefully about what kind of evidence would help you to communicate effectively

For the purpose of your project, there are two key areas that you need to consider: the initial diagnoses of the issues and initiatives, and negotiating with colleagues and stakeholders.

INITIAL DIAGNOSIS OF THE ISSUES/INITIATIVES

You may have already begun to identify some ideas for the focus of your project. When you identified these, you looked at not only your own role but also what is going on in the wider organization or environment. So the chances are that other key stakeholders apart from you will agree that the ideas you have identified are important and worth pursuing. Before you take any of these ideas forward, however, it is worth collecting or checking some facts to ensure that your understanding of the challenges, difficulties and dilemmas associated with the issues are in fact shared by others and that the initiative is indeed worth pursuing. So, for example, sometimes the things colleagues complain about (e.g.

with them. So, for example, if one of your stakeholders is the director of the company, can you get the facts and figures that are likely to gain their support? And if you can't get hold of any evidence that will help you persuade an unenthusiastic stakeholder then might you have to reframe your issue altogether? Incidentally, there may also be research/theoretical frameworks than may form part of your pool of evidence in the sense of helping you better articulate your initiative and perhaps demonstrate how challenges faced by your organization have been successfully dealt with by another organization in another context.

CHAPTER 5
UNDERSTANDING RESEARCH PHILOSOPHIES

Research philosophies relate to the development of knowledge and the nature of that knowledge. When you undertake research you develop knowledge in a particular field. This knowledge development can come about from answering a specific problem in a certain context. The research philosophy you adopt means you are accepting assumptions about the way in which you view the world. These assumptions will underpin your research strategy and the methods you choose as part of that strategy. The philosophy you choose to adopt will be influenced by practical considerations, but will also be influenced by your particular view of the relationship between knowledge and the process by which it is developed. If you are concerned with facts, such as the resources needed in a product manufacturing process, this is a different view on the way research will be conducted than if you are concerned with the feelings and attitudes of the designers towards their design managers in the same product manufacturing process. Your research strategy and methods would differ in both these circumstances but so, too, will your view on what is important and useful in either context. In this section we examine three major ways of thinking about your research philosophy: ontology, epistemology and axiology.

ONTOLOGY, EPISTEMOLOGY AND RESEARCH DESIGN

Ontology and epistemology are two different ways of viewing the research philosophy. Ontology can be defined as the science or study of being and deals with the nature of reality. In simple terms, ontology is associated with a central question of whether social entities need to be perceived as objective or subjective. Accordingly, objectivism (or positivism) and subjectivism can be specified as two important aspects of ontology.

The table below summarizes the ontology of four major research philosophies and how they relate to creative research:

Research philosophy	Ontology: your view of the nature of reality
Pragmatism	External, multiple view chosen to allow you to answer the research question.
Positivism	External, objective and independent of social actors.
Realism	Objective and exists independently of human thought and belief in existence (realism), but interpreted through social conditions (critical realism).
Interpretivism	Socially constructed, changeable and multiple.

Identification of which ontology you are using at the start of the research process is very important, as it determines the choice of the research design. This identification of ontology is not explicitly part of your research project, but understanding where you are positioning your work in terms of ontology helps you choose a research design that will be effective. You are more likely to find the type of data you need to gather evidence and critically evaluate it for your proposals of change.

Epistemology, on the other hand, is a theory of knowledge, especially with regard to its methods, validity, and scope and the distinction between justified belief and opinion; epistemology is the study of the nature of knowledge within a field of study. Defined narrowly, epistemology is the study of knowledge and justified belief.

The *Routledge Encyclopedia of Philosophy* defines epistemology as

> one of the core areas of philosophy. It is concerned with the nature, sources and limits of knowledge. There is a vast array of views about propositional knowledge, but one virtually universal presupposition is that knowledge is true belief, but not mere true belief. For example, lucky guesses or true beliefs resulting from wishful thinking are not knowledge. A central question for epistemology is: What must be added to belief to convert it into knowledge?

An example of this might be that you believe that management can only be learned through practice and that theory contributes very little to it. This is not knowledge – it is a belief: it becomes knowledge only when you seek to explore it through research (formal as well as informal).

Following on from this, epistemology poses some core questions:

- What are the necessary and sufficient conditions of knowledge?
- What are its sources?
- What is its structure?

And finally, last but not least: What are its limits? As the study of justified belief, epistemology aims to answer questions such as, How are we to understand the concept of justification? What makes justified beliefs justified? Is justification internal or external to one's own mind? Understood more broadly, epistemology is about the creation and dissemination of knowledge in particular contexts.

MATCHING PARADIGMS AND METHODS

We have discussed how important it is to match paradigms with methods and data collection. Table 1.2 indicates the ways in which research methods cross-paradigm boundaries.

TABLE 1.2

PARADIGMS, METHODS AND TOOLS

Paradigm	Methods	Examples of data collection tools
Positivist	Quantitative (although qualitative can be used)	Experiments Tests Scales
Interpretivist/constructivist	Qualitative (although quantitative can be used)	Interviews Observations Document reviews Visual data analysis
Pragmatic	Qualitative and/or quantitative and mixed methods. Methods are matched to the specific questions and purpose of the research.	May include tools from both positivist and interpretivist paradigms. E.g. interviews, observations and testing and experiments.

This table suggests that it is the paradigm and research question that will determine which type of data collection and what analysis method will be most appropriate for your research project.

The theory you use may or may not be made explicit in the design of the research, although it will usually be made explicit in your presentation of the findings and conclusions. The extent to which you are clear about the theory at the beginning will make it easier to structure the design of your research project, for instance, whether your research should use the deductive process, in which you develop a theory and hypothesis (or hypotheses) and design a research strategy to test the hypothesis, or the inductive process, in which you would collect data and develop theory as a result of your data analysis. In as much as it is useful to attach these approaches to different research philosophies, deduction owes more to positivism and induction to interpretivism.

The next two sections explain the differences between these two approaches and the implications of these differences to your research choices.

DEDUCTION: TESTING THEORY

Deduction involves the development of a theory that is subjected to a rigorous test. There are normally five sequential stages through which deductive research will progress:

1. deducing a hypothesis (a testable proposition about the relationship between two or more concepts or variables) from theory;
2. expressing the hypothesis in operational terms (i.e. indicating exactly how the concepts or variables are to be measured), which propose a relationship between two specific concepts or variables;
3. testing this operational hypothesis;
4. examining the specific outcome of the inquiry (it will either tend to confirm the theory or indicate the need for its modification);
5. if necessary, modifying the theory in the light of the findings. An attempt is then made to verify the revised theory by going back to the first step and repeating the whole cycle.

DEDUCTION

Deduction possesses several important characteristics. First, there is the search to explain causal relationships between variables. It may be that you wish to establish the reasons why students are not using the new outdoor seating in a university. After recording the number of times the seating was used on different days, by how many students at a time and in varying weather conditions, it occurs to you that there seems to be a relationship between use, the numbers of students and the weather conditions. Consequently, you develop a hypothesis that states that lack of use is more likely to be prevalent among individuals rather than groups and in poor weather conditions.

To test this hypothesis you decide to collect quantitative data. (This is not to say that deductive research may not use qualitative data.) It may be that there are important differences in which the outdoor seating is arranged in different parts of the campus. Therefore you would need to employ a further important characteristic of deduction approach: controls to allow the testing of hypotheses. These controls would help to ensure that any change in use was a function of weather and group size rather than any other aspect of the outdoor seating such as location. Your research would use a highly structured methodology to facilitate replication, which is an important issue to ensure reliability. *Replication* is a term referring to the repetition of a *research* project, generally with different situations and different subjects, to determine if the basic findings of the original study can be generalized to other participants and circumstances.

In order to pursue the principle of rigour, deduction dictates that you, in the role of researcher, should be independent of what is being observed. This is easy in this example because it only involves the collection of usage data. It is also unproblematic if a postal or online survey is being conducted, although the high level of objectivity this suggests appears less convincing when you consider the element of subjectivity in the choice of questions and the way these are phrased. An additional important characteristic of deduction is that concepts need to be operationalized in a way that enables facts to be measured quantitatively. In this example the obvious one is usage. Just what constitutes usage would have to be strictly defined: usage for one hour or more or just a few minutes? In addition, what would constitute the student using the seating or the 'group'? What is happening here is that the principle of reductionism is being followed. This principle holds that problems as a whole are better understood if they are reduced to the simplest possible elements. The final characteristic of deduction is generalization. In order to be able to generalize statistically about regularities in human social behaviour it is necessary to select samples of sufficient numerical size. In this example, research at a particular university studying one design of outdoor seating would only allow you to make inferences about that university and that range of seating; it would be dangerous to predict that usage by students was dictated by weather conditions.

INDUCTION: BUILDING THEORY

An alternative approach to conducting research in a university about student use of a new range of outdoor seating would be to go to the university and interview a sample of the students and facilities managers about their experience of using the seating. The purpose here would be to get a feel of what was going on, so as to understand better the nature of the problem. Your task then would be to make sense of the interview data you had collected by analysing those data. The result of this analysis would be the formulation of a theory. It may be that there is a relationship between absence and relatively short periods of employment. Alternatively, you may discover that there are other competing reasons for usage that may or may not be related to the types of student groups or weather conditions. You may end up with the same theory, but you would have gone about the production of that theory in an inductive way: theory would follow data rather than vice versa as with deduction.

Research using induction is likely to be particularly concerned with the context in which such events were taking place. Therefore the study of a small sample of subjects might be more appropriate than a large number as with the deductive approach, and you are more likely to work with qualitative data and to use a variety of methods to collect these data in order to establish different views of what is happening.

WHY THE CHOICE THAT YOU MAKE ABOUT YOUR RESEARCH PROCESS IS IMPORTANT

First, it enables you to take a more informed decision about your research design, which is more than just the techniques by which data are collected and procedures by which they are analysed. It is the overall configuration of your research project involving questions about what kind of evidence is gathered and from where and how such evidence is interpreted in order to provide good answers to your initial research question.

Second, it will help you to think about those research strategies and approaches that will work for you and, crucially, those that will not. For example, if you are particularly interested in understanding why something is happening, rather than being able to describe what is happening, it may be more appropriate to undertake your research inductively rather than deductively.

Third, the knowledge of the different research traditions enables you to adapt your research design to cater for constraints. These may be practical, involving, say, limited access to data, or they may arise from a lack of prior knowledge of the subject. You simply may not be in a position to frame a hypothesis because you have insufficient understanding of the topic to do this.

COMBINING RESEARCH CHOICES

So far we have given the impression that there are rigid divisions between deduction and induction. But this is not the case. It is sometimes advantageous to combine deduction and induction within the same piece of research.

As you can see from the case study of Hayley, it is possible to combine both research approaches and sometimes this can also be advantageous. The deciding factors about whether your research will be inductive, deductive or a combination of both depend on the nature of the project. If the subject

DEDUCTIVE AND INDUCTIVE RESEARCH

Hayley decided to conduct a research project on office design in her organization and its effects on the stress levels of employees. She considered the different ways she would approach the work were she to adopt either a deductive approach or an inductive approach. If she decided to adopt a deductive approach to her project she would have

1 to start with the hypothesis that employees working in a closed office design are less likely to experience stress;

2 to decide to research a population in which she would have expected to find evidence of stress, for example a sizeable office with a large number of employees;

3 to administer a questionnaire to a large sample of employees in order to establish the extent of stress and the levels of stress experienced by them;

4 to be particularly careful about how she defined stress;

5 to standardize the stress responses of the employees, for example days off sick or sessions with a counsellor.

On the other hand, if she decided to adopt an inductive approach she might have decided to interview some employees who had declared they felt stressed at work. She might have been interested in their feelings about the events that they had experienced, how they coped with the problems they experienced and their views about whether the office design affected levels of stress. Either approach would have yielded valuable data about this problem. (Indeed, both may be used in this project, at different stages.) Neither approach should be thought of as better than the other. They are better at different things. It depends where her research emphasis lies.

At this point you may be wondering whether your research will be deductive or inductive.

There are a number of practical criteria. Perhaps the most important of these is the nature of the research topic. A topic on which there is a wealth of literature from which you can define a theoretical framework and a hypothesis lends itself more readily to deduction.

With research into a topic that is new, and a lot of interest is being shown in it, and on which there is little existing literature, it may be more appropriate to work inductively by generating data and analysing and reflecting upon what theoretical themes the data are suggesting. You will need to consider the time you have available. Deductive research can be quicker to complete, albeit that time must be devoted to setting up the study prior to data collection and analysis. Data collection is often based on 'one take'. It is normally possible to predict the time schedules accurately. On the other hand, inductive research can be much more time consuming and last longer as you take more time to collect data.

you are investigating already has a lot of published research from which you can define a proposition, then a deductive approach may be more suitable. If the subject is new, with little published research, it may be more suitable to explore the subject using an inductive approach to generate data and to reflect on the themes that emerge from it. Time is also a key issue, as deductive approaches can be quicker to complete and time schedules can be more accurately predicted. Inductive research can take more time as data emerges and the time needed for data collection can be more difficult to predict. You may also want to consider your own preferences and the preferences of those evaluating your work before you come to a decision about which approach to adopt.

SUMMARY

This section has put research philosophies, paradigms and methods into the context of your research project. You should now be able to work out how to match the paradigms with the methods. When you are reading academic papers you can work out what paradigms and methods authors are using and how this influences the way they carry out research and the type of results they get.

In this section, three core approaches to reflecting on research philosophy will be considered: epistemology, ontology and axiology. Each contains important differences, which influence the way we think about the research process:

- Epistemology is the study of the theory of knowledge, including its nature, scope and limitations.
- Ontology is the philosophical study of the nature of being or existence.
- Axiology is the study of quality or value, and is often concerned with ethics and values. These three ways of research will vary depending on your choice of philosophical perspective.

Figure 1.7 Layers of research

Developing new knowledge when conducting research is made easier when following a structured approach, which will enable you to tackle your project in sequential stages and so be more manageable.

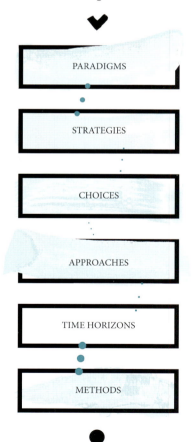

ONTOLOGY

Ontology is concerned with the nature of reality. This raises assumptions about the way the world operates and the commitment held to particular views by researchers. Two aspects of ontology exist: objectivism and subjectivism. Objectivism represents the position that social entities exist in reality external to social actors concerned with their existence. Subjectivism holds that social phenomena are created from the perception and consequent actions of those social actors concerned with their existence. One might argue that design is objective and might take an objective stance by saying that designers perform similar roles and are subject to job specifications and procedures to which they must adhere – they are part of a formal organizational structure, therefore their actions can be measured.

The subjectivist view holds that social phenomena are created from perceptions and the subsequent actions of social actors, and are therefore in a constant state of revision. This follows from an interpretivist stance that it is necessary to explore subjective meanings motivating social actors in order to understand them. In the case of clients of a design company, it would be your job as researcher to understand the subjective reality of the clients, and to understand their motivations and actions in a meaningful way.

AXIOLOGY

Axiology is concerned with values, including aesthetics and ethics, but it also includes the process of research. The role that your own values play in the research process is important if you wish your research to be credible. You may opt to write a statement of your own values in relation to the topic you are studying – this will heighten your awareness of any value judgements you may make when drawing conclusions from your own research.

RESEARCH PARADIGMS

A paradigm can be thought of as a lens through which we view the world. Different lenses necessitate different assumptions about the nature of the world and the ways in which we should attempt to understand it. There are many different lenses that exist for viewing and understanding the world, and the following section presents a simplification of a complex and constantly shifting set of boundaries that define the current paradigms. Although there is a great deal of diversity and overlap between the range of perspectives that can define paradigms, a distinction can be made between current approaches based on the physical sciences, such as the 'positivist' paradigm, and alternative paradigms such as constructivism, interpretivism, critical theory and phenomenology. One difference between these two paradigm clusters involves their views on the existence of a social world which is separate from the physical world. The list of recognized paradigms includes positivism, realism, interpretivism, objectivism, subjectivism, pragmatism, functionalism, radical humanist and radical structuralist. Some of these paradigms are discussed in this section, because they are relevant to the creative industries (though not exclusive to them).

Before discussing some of the different paradigms available to you, to assist you in your research, it is worthwhile to briefly touch upon how your research paradigm fits within your dissertation as a whole. Perhaps the clearest introductory way to do that is by thinking of your research as an onion.

You will see in the illustration below that the identification of the research philosophy is positioned at the outer layer of the 'research onion'. Accordingly, it is the first topic to be clarified in the research methodology chapter of your dissertation. This figure represents a standard research onion model.

Positivism

As a philosophy, positivism is in accordance with the empiricist view that knowledge stems from human experience. It has an atomistic, ontological view of the world as comprising discrete, observable elements and events that interact in an observable, determined and regular manner. Individual cases are subsumed within hypotheses about general laws of nature, and there is an assumption that human beings and human societies are subject to laws in the same way that the natural world is.

Positivism holds that all phenomena should be understood through the employment of a scientific method. It aims to create a theoretically neutral language of observation by stripping hypotheses and theories of subjective content. It is deterministic, de-emphasizing free will, emotion, chance, choice and morality; it posits a conceptual division between 'fact' and 'value', in which only empirically verifiable ideas essentially count as 'knowledge' or 'truth'. Positivism rejects universal or objective grounds for values, and argues that they can be justified only on arbitrary, normative, technical or utilitarian grounds. It authorizes recommendations for social reform on the basis of truth claims and certainty. Positivism also theoretically presupposes that scientific texts reflect or mirror a reality that exists outside the text and that a truth corresponds with this outside reality. This presupposition of representationality coincides with the paradigmatic contention that language is a neutral tool used to present clear and definitive meanings that capture essential truths.

Interpretivism

A positivist approach is in stark contrast to interpretivism, which does not aim to report on an objective reality, but rather to understand the world as it is experienced and made meaningful by human beings. This is not to say that social constructionism holds that things mean whatever the person interpreting them thinks they mean. Interpretivism rejects objectivism, but it is not a subjectivist philosophy either. The world is 'waiting to be discovered' or 'loaded with meaning' for social constructionists. That is, the world and things in it are seen to be important participants in the meaning-making process. They give something essential of themselves to the conscious subject so that what we come to learn or understand is not simply another subjective account of a phenomenon, but rather an account that essentially reflects significant qualities of both our culture and of the phenomenon. This conception of the interplay between a conscious, meaning-making subject and the objects that present themselves to our perception is what characterizes interpretivism. It is also the key point of argument for hermeneutic, structuralist, post-structuralist and postmodern thinkers.

Interpretivism is associated with the philosophical position of idealism, and is used to group together diverse approaches, including social constructionism (also referred to as simply 'constructionism'), phenomenology and hermeneutics; approaches that reject the objectivist view that meaning resides within the world independently of consciousness. Social constructionism and positivism share the broadly empiricist understanding that knowledge arises as a direct result of our experience of the world. However, they disagree about the extent to which we can say that an independent or objective reality exists. For positivists, there is something objectively real about the world, although we can only know it through experience. Positivists aim to put aside subjective perception in order to offer objective observations; but for social constructionists, this is impossible because things don't mean anything until the meaning-making subject interprets them.

An interpretive approach to research, however, is not simply a question of faithfully representing the meanings that arise from people's experiences in order to understand them. With a phenomenological approach, we encounter an intrinsic wariness of the beliefs and practices handed down to us by our culture and an exhortation to penetrate beyond received versions of the world to get at something more 'authentic' that lies within human experience. Phenomenologists seek to distinguish between something that is culturally inherited and, as a result, perhaps one-dimensional, predictable or 'stale', and something of human experience that is appositely 'authentic', 'rich' and 'fresh'. Within contemporary social science discourse, we sometimes learn about the importance of self-reflexivity within interpretive approaches. This is the idea that the research reflects the identity of both the researcher and the research subjects. In the name of self-reflexivity, researchers may choose to foreground their research discussion with descriptions of their personal motives, background and relationship to the research context. Or they may emphasize that the knowledge produced by the research represents the unique interaction of the researcher and the research subjects, with perhaps limited generalizability of the research findings, as a result. This kind of claim leans more towards subjectivism, or more precisely constructivism, than social constructionism.

Social constructionism also emphasizes the socially mediated nature of interpretation and aims to offer an insight with broad social relevance. For instance, interpretive research may aim to represent a different culture on its own terms in order to facilitate effective cross-cultural communication. However, research that aims simply to capture or retell individual subjective accounts has been criticized as 'indulgent navel-gazing', as a 'naive' form of subjectivism that reproduces everyday cultural understandings without subjecting them to critical analysis and without offering anything new or useful. This is not to say that social constructionists and phenomenologists should never incorporate reflection on their own experience within their research writing. On the contrary, researchers' experiences can provide useful and often compelling research evidence if it helps us to better understand the context or phenomenon under study in a way that has relevance for others. Within social constructionism, the researcher would reflect critically upon received understandings within their own and others' experience, and would actively engage in the production of new meaning.

Constructionism

Constructionism (also called social constructivism) challenges the objectivist stance of positivism. It is the epistemological view that all knowledge (and therefore all meaningful reality) is dependent on social actors being constructed through interaction between themselves and their environment, which is developed and transmitted primarily within a social context. Constructionism recognizes the existence of a reciprocal and interdependent relationship between objects in the world and social consciousness. It posits that there is no essential meaning to be found within objects or the world that exists independently of consciousness. All things depend upon humans to create meaning about them.

On the other hand, objects are not completely irrelevant to the meanings that are constructed about them. While context gives rise to different meanings about the same object, the object – with all its particularities – crucially participates in the meanings formed of it. Constructionism accepts multiple interpretations of an object, none of which is objectively 'true' or 'valid'. Constructionism emphasizes the cultural and institutional origins of meaning. It is not that individuals make sense of phenomena in the world on a case-by-case basis. Culture brings some things into view and endows them with meaning, and leads us to ignore other things. Culture provides the lens through which we view phenomena. There is no distinction between the construction of physical and social realities. Both are social constructions. Constructionism is not the same thing as constructivism. Constructivism emphasizes that one individual's meaning is as valid and worthy of respect as any other individual's meaning.

Phenomenology

Phenomenology is a response to the social constructionist observation that our meanings are shaped by enculturation, or the process by which an individual learns the traditional content of a culture and assimilates its practices and values. It calls for us to 'get back to the things themselves'; to arrive at new, more immediate meanings by allowing for a direct experience of the objects of our perception. It accepts the social constructionist understanding of the interrelationship between human beings and objects in the world, and seeks to offer a meaningful reflection on the nature of our world. It is a critical paradigm and calls into question what we take for granted in order to construct new understandings.

Symbolic interactionism

Symbolic interactionism originated in the work of George Herbert Mead (1863–1931) and is informed by the philosophy of pragmatism. It understands that both subjects and objects are constituted in the ongoing transaction of organism and environment (*The Cambridge Dictionary of Philosophy*, 1999) and sees society, or the exchange of significant gestures, as what makes individualism, consciousness and self-consciousness possible, and understands consciousness as being made possible via an internalization of significant gestures. It argues that children internalize social attitudes and institutions via role play, in which they act out the roles of 'generalised others' and relate them to broader social institutions. Symbolic interactionism holds that experience and social phenomena must be understood from the perspective of the role of the actor in any given situation.

As a research methodology, symbolic interactionism has developed within the field of ethnography, and both share the idea that any one culture is irreducible and incomparable. This research paradigm postulates that we can only comprehend a culture from within, by 'getting inside' how it sees the world through focusing on roles, cultural scripts, interactions between roles or actors, social rules or games, players and rituals. However, it also argues that human beings do not simply respond to social conditions mechanically or passively, but actively create, enact and change meanings and actions in a problem solving mode that reflects personal and social values. It has given rise to interactionist research including the dramaturgical approach (especially of Erving Goffman), game theory, negotiated order theory, labelling theory and grounded theory.

You may or may not be required to introduce a debate on philosophical paradigms for your research project. If you do, it will guide your project because you have chosen to accept a defined view of the world and an accepted body of knowledge.

RESEARCH STRATEGIES

There are several different research strategies available. These include experiment, survey, case study, action research, grounded theory, ethnography and archival research. Let's look at grounded theory.

Grounded theory

Grounded theory is associated with Barney Glaser, Anselm Strauss and Juliet Corbin and reflects the philosophical presuppositions of pragmatism and symbolic interactionism. It is an explanatory mode of interpretive research that tries to go beyond simply describing and attempts to generate theory from explanations of social processes. It rejects positivism's adherence to theory as the departure point for research. It seeks to exclude *a priori* theory, or other bias, using an inductive approach that builds theory up from experience. It draws upon positivist and post-positivist language and concepts (inductive, propositions, hypotheses) and explains events/conditions that are problematic or relevant to those it affects – asking 'what is happening here?' Grounded theory uses qualitative methods with a systematic approach to the collection and analysis of data. Grounded theory texts sometimes advise researchers to postpone the literature review until after the data has been collected. This advice needs to be interpreted in the social constructionist spirit intended. Grounded theory seeks to provide fresh perspectives, especially on areas of social life that have previously been explained within quantitative, positivist or highly theoretical paradigms. Grounded theory is not simply about presenting findings, a set of themes or a description of a phenomenon. It aims to produce systematic, explanatory theory founded in concepts that emerge from data, and is therefore a time-consuming, painstaking process that requires thorough immersion in the data.

CHAPTER 6
RESEARCH APPROACHES

Your research project will involve the use of theory even though that theory may or may not be made explicit in the design framework of the proposal. How much you know about the theory that relates to your project at the beginning influences whether your research should use the deductive or inductive approach or even a combination of both. A deductive approach will mean that you use a theory to develop a proposition and then design a research framework to test that proposition. An inductive approach means that you will collect data and develop theory as a result of the data analysis. A deductive approach is normally better suited to a positivist paradigm, and an inductive approach is normally better suited to an interpretive paradigm. The next section will look at the difference between these two approaches and will explore what these differences represent.

DEDUCTION

Deduction involves developing a theory that is tested and presents more of a scientific approach to research. There are five sequential stages to deductive research:

- Writing a testable proposition, which details the relationship between two concepts or variables
- Indicating how the concepts or variables can be measured
- Testing this proposition
- Studying the outcome of the research, which will confirm the theory or establish how the proposition needs to be modified
- If necessary, modifying the proposition and then repeating the process.

There are several important characteristics of deduction. First, there is a search to explain causal relationships between variables. For example, this could be to establish the reasons for employee turnover in the creative industries. If you examine the patterns of employee turnover, it may initially occur to you that there is a difference between the levels of turnover in different fields within the creative industries. Subsequently, you can develop a proposition that states that the level of employee turnover varies between two sectors of the creative industries, and that to test this proposition you will use quantitative data (note that this does not mean that you cannot use qualitative data with deduction).

In a deductive approach, the research needs to be independent of what is being observed; meaning that both you and your research need to remain objective. Your feelings and personal view of the world should not enter into the research. The research needs to be operationalized so that facts can be measured. Therefore, your terms need to be well defined. In the above example, this would mean accurately defining what you mean by 'the creative industries' and 'employee turnover'. Being reductive in this way makes it easier to understand the overall problem by breaking it up into bite-size chunks. The final stage in deductive research is generalization, whereby you need to determine that the sample that you take information from needs to be of a sufficient size to ensure that you can make inferences about a more general population.

> ### DEDUCTION
>
> Rule: All the sweets in this bag are red
> Case: These sweets are from this bag
> Result: These sweets are red

INDUCTION

You could use induction as an alternative approach to look at employee turnover in the creative industries. The purpose here would be to understand the nature of the problem and then make sense of data you obtain from, for example, focus groups. You would then form a theory based on the data that you have obtained. You may find that there may be a relationship between the sector of the creative industries and the level of employee turnover. Alternatively, there may be other reasons for the variance in employee turnover. The strength of an inductive approach lies in understanding the context within which the research takes place and not focusing on a cause-and-effect relationship. Not having a rigid methodology permits an alternative explanation of what is going on. A research project using an inductive approach is more likely to be concerned with the context in which the events are taking place and might mean that a small sample is more appropriate than a large sample. You are more likely to use qualitative data and a variety of methods to establish different views of the situation within an inductive approach. Why is the choice that you make between induction and deduction important? First, it allows you to make an informed decision about the research design. Secondly, it helps you to think about which choices and research strategies work best for you. Thirdly, knowledge of the different research traditions that exist allows you to cater for potential constraints, such as a lack of prior knowledge of the subject, limited access to data or your inability to design a proposition because you do not have sufficient understanding of the subject.

> **INDUCTIVE**
>
> Case: These sweets are from this bag
> Result: These sweets are red
> Rule: All the sweets in this bag are red

ABDUCTIVE REASONING

Abductive reasoning is a form of logical inference that goes from an observation to a theory which accounts for the observation, ideally seeking to find the simplest and most likely explanation. In abductive reasoning, unlike in deductive reasoning, the premises do not guarantee the conclusion. We can understand abductive reasoning as inference to the best explanation. You move from some observations to the best explanation of those observations. These ideas are really relevant to the creative industries and design in particular, but these abductive reasoning abilities are not unique to designers. Abductive reasoning is 'design thinking' but is not exclusive to designers as business people have always used this way of thinking. Design thinking applies the designer's crucial tool of abductive reasoning to the problems of business. In the design of business, Martin (2009) discussed in his model of design thinking a 'designer's sensibility'. Brown (2008) speaks of the ability to use an understanding of customers' needs (as well as technology and business factors) to move inwards and outwards in this funnel by iterating through many different heuristics and algorithms to ultimately imagine and then validate a way of solving this mystery. Intrinsic to this ability is abductive reasoning – making logical leaps to imagine what might be true in the future.

For example, a designer developing a new keyboard might study the use of keyboards used in the workplace. Typically, a designer will observe four or five users as those individuals conduct their work. The designer will ask questions of each user about their jobs and record details of their responses. The designer might also take photographs of the equipment being used, and probe for details about each item. The designer will then attempt to make sense of what he or she has learned. The goal is to find relationships or themes in the research data, and to uncover hidden meaning in the behaviour that is observed and that is applicable to the design task at hand.

> **ABDUCTION**
>
> Rule: All the sweets in this bag are red
> Result: These sweets are red
> Case: These sweets are from this bag

COMBINING RESEARCH APPROACHES

It is possible to combine several research approaches and this can be advantageous. The deciding factors about whether your research will be inductive, abductive or deductive, or a combination of some or all, is dependent on the nature of the project. If the subject already has a lot of published research from which you can define a proposition, then a deductive approach may be more suitable. Abductive reasoning typically begins with an incomplete set of observations and proceeds to the likeliest possible explanation for information you have. Abductive reasoning means we undertake a kind of daily decision making that does its best with the information at hand, which often is incomplete. If the subject is new, with little published research, it may be more suitable to explore the subject using an inductive approach to generate data and to reflect on the themes that emerge from it. Time is also a key issue, as deductive approaches can be quicker to complete and time schedules can be more accurately predicted. Inductive research can take more time as data emerges and the time needed for data collection can be more difficult to predict. You may also want to consider your own preferences and the preferences of those evaluating your work before you come to a decision about which approach to adopt.

FUNNELLING DOWN TO A PROJECT

Once you have chosen the focus of the area that you want to investigate and have determined the learning objective of your project, you will then need to identify the vehicle through which your research will take place. There are four different project vehicles for you to choose from that will be explored in the paragraphs to follow. Your project may not necessarily fit into one of these categories, but these ideal types are intended to give you some guidance at this stage.

Investigative hypothesis testing

When you derive a hypothesis or proposition from ideas introduced on your course, you test this using primary and secondary data. For example, 'the design of the watch face can increase the speed of the athlete using it'.

Aims:

- To learn through the analysis, testing and development of theory

- To derive one or more hypotheses
- To test the validity of the hypothesis by gathering data that is based on an appropriate sample

When to use this project style:

- When a topic area can generate suitable hypotheses that are tight and which imply specific causal connections
- When it is possible to gather data that will give evidence for or against accepting a hypothesis
- This style is applied to quantitative analysis, but not exclusively
- When you want to use questionnaire surveys based on theoretical hypotheses

The report would typically include the following:

- A word count
- A statement of learning objectives
- A review of the literature that clearly establishes the importance and relevance of the literature and the relevance of the hypothesis or proposition
- A clear statement of the hypothesis or proposition
- A thorough methodology explaining and justifying the sample frame and data-gathering instruments
- Findings that go beyond descriptive statistics
- Analysis that links the findings to the hypothesis or proposition and theory
- A concluding review that argues for the rejection or support of the hypothesis, areas for further possible examination and certainly a review of how the process and conclusions have informed your learning and understanding of the issue and topic – Normally, this type of project would involve the use of the analytical software SPSS, or other statistical packages

Applied context

This refers to when you carry out a piece of work for a 'client' in a real context using a theory or techniques that you have used on your course. For example, 'How can design be used to reduce injury during a car accident?'

Aims:

- To investigate a particular context or setting, or a specific problem or issue

- To work towards generating a suitable range of alternative actions, outcomes and possibly implementation
- To generate appropriate academic reflection and conclusions

When to use this project style:

- If you can see a specific need within the context (e.g. 'how design can be used to reduce injury during car accidents')
- If you wish to try/test out in practice the use of a particular technique or theory

The report would normally include the following:

- A word count
- A statement of learning objectives
- An explanation of the issue(s) to be addressed and why they are thought to be important
- A literature review that includes current practice in the area and that informs potential recommendations, relating your reading to your learning objectives
- A methodology chapter that explains how and why research was carried out in the organization
- A findings chapter that shows the outcomes or perhaps a client report
- An analysis that explains the findings and that lays the groundwork for recommendations and possibly implementation
- Recommendations for future action
- Conclusions that seek to generalize from the analysis and that draw out the links between the findings/ recommendations and current ideas in the relevant literature (discussions and conclusions about this should form part of your findings and conclusions)

Action learning

This refers to when you use or develop existing theory to carry out investigations in order to enrich your understanding of a practical work environment, for example 'A study of the skills required in the European fashion industry'.

Aims:

- To enrich your understanding of your own working environment

- To be based on a subject relevant to your course with an issue that is real and significant to you
- To use/develop existing theory by carrying out mini experiments
- To question action, and seek to rigorously develop more informed action as an outcome

When to use this project style:

- Where you have the possibility of incrementally exploring and changing your actions through involvement in a real, complex problem or issue over time
- Where there is a need to develop reflexive and critically examined action
- Where there is the possibility of discussing experience, thought, feelings and other people in an open way

The presentation of this type of project may vary with the issue or problem examined, along with actions taken by the individual over the course of the project. You will present your evidence to show that you have gone through a due process, including the appropriate gathering and understanding of theory, reported practice and other secondary information.

The project is likely to address a number of questions:

- What am I, or is my organization, trying to do?
- What is stopping us from doing it?
- What can we do about it?
- Who knows about the problems that have cropped up?
- Who can help us to solve them?
- What happens when proposed solutions are tried out?

Investigative theory building

At this stage of the project, you undertake interviewing, observing or interacting with participants in a real situation and then draw conclusions about it, for example, 'Personal perception of designer brands and how they influence identity'.

Aims:

- To take an inductive approach that gathers data and generates theory from it

- To explore empirical questions systematically
- To draw conclusions from an analysis of the attitudes, opinions, dialogue, views and findings of your research subjects

When to use this project style:

- When there is a lack of clarity about the issues to be studied

- To establish a greater understanding of how research participants perceive their situation / reality
- To understand multiple perspectives on a situation
- Where there is good access to the research participants, who will be willing to spend time with the researcher, and who will 'open up'.

THINK BOX
Deductive, abductive or inductive research?

Fred decided to conduct a research project investigating the impact of introducing issues of fair trade on fashion design brands and how this was likely to affect fashion brand purchases. He considered how he would approach his work if he used either a deductive or inductive approach.

If he introduced a deductive approach, his work would be likely to

- start with a proposition, such as potential purchases of fashion design brands were likely to increase if fair trade was introduced;
- research a population within which he would expect to find evidence of the increase in purchases due to the introduction of fair trade;
- design a questionnaire to be administered to a large group of potential purchasers in order to discover the impact on purchasing with the introduction of fair trade policies;
- provide carefully defined definitions of 'fair trade' and 'fashion design brands'.

However, if the research project were undertaken using an inductive approach instead, he might

- start with a focus group of potential purchasers to discuss fair trade and fashion design brands and the links between the two;
- he may go on to focus on the participants' perception of and feeling towards fair trade issues and fashion design brands;

- he may then go back to the literature to gain further insight on various issues.
- Having gained further insight from the literature, he might then decide to undertake semi-structured interviews with a select group of participants.

While if this was an abductive research project, he might approach his research in this way:

Designers work in extremely dynamic environments and, in these circumstances, belief formation and belief justification becomes more complex. Given Fred's experience in fair trade and design brands and a given set of criteria he could make a diagnosis of the situation using a best explanation of the issues. For example, if Fred wanted to design a new fashion brand featuring fair trade he might study the use of fair trade in other product brands. He might go and see four or five users of fair trade brands. He would find reasons for using the brands and record details of their responses. He would then return to the design studio. In the privacy of his natural work place, he will attempt to make sense of what he has learned. The goal is to find relationships or themes in the research data, and to uncover hidden meaning in the behaviour that is observed and that is applicable to the design task at hand. He would then make a creative leap to make sense of what information he has found out.

Any of these choices would yield valuable data. The three approaches can be used at various stages of a project. Neither approach is 'better' but rather will result in different type of information so the choices depend on the type of information Fred would want to obtain.

CHAPTER 7
ETHNOGRAPHY AND DESIGN ETHNOGRAPHY

ETHNOGRAPHY

Ethnography is a research methodology originally developed and used in various social sciences, such as anthropology and sociology. Its literal meaning is 'description of people'. The origin of the methodology lies in the late nineteenth century, when academics ventured out to less-known peoples to study cultures, human behaviour and social relations. One of the founders of modern social anthropology, Bronislaw Malinowski, changed the focus from a prescriptive approach by stating that ethnographers should investigate the social context from the points of views of those they are observing, rather than imposing their own cultural believes upon them. Many other influential researchers, such as Clifford Geertz and Margaret Mead, have followed along these lines and developed the field further.

Nowadays ethnography has extended into studying urban and industrial societies and the research methods have also evolved from participant observation to include more interaction, conversation and co-creation.

Typical ethnographic research employs three kinds of data collection: interviews, observation and documents. This in turn produces three kinds of data: quotations, descriptions and excerpts of documents, resulting in a narrative description. This narrative often includes charts, diagrams and additional artefacts along the continuum that help to tell 'the story'. Ethnographic methods can give shape to new constructs or paradigms, and new variables, for further empirical testing in the field or to move on to more traditional, quantitative social science methods.

While particularly suited to exploratory research, ethnography draws on a wide range of both qualitative and quantitative methodologies, moving from 'learning' to 'testing' with the focus being on learning, while research problems, perspectives and theories emerge and shift. Ethnographic methods are a means of focusing on localized points of view, households and community knowledge, a means of identifying significant categories of human experience from a close but also personal perspective. Ethnography enhances and widens topdown views and enriches the inquiry process by tapping into bottom-up insights. Consequently, this generates new analytic insights by engaging in interactive exploration of what can be subtle areas of people's difference or similarity. Through such findings ethnographers may inform others of their findings with an attempt to derive, for example, policy decisions or instructional innovations from such an analysis.

ETHNOGRAPHY AS METHOD

Ethnography refers to social research that has most of the following features:

a. People's behaviour is studied in everyday contexts, rather than under experimental conditions created by the researcher.
b. Data are gathered from a range of sources, but observation and/or relatively informal conversations are usually the main ones.
c. The approach to data collection can be unstructured in the sense that it does not necessarily involve

following through a detailed plan set up at the beginning. The categories used for interpreting what people say and do are not either presupposed or fixed. This does not mean that the research is unsystematic but rather that initially the data are collected in as raw a form, and as wide a front, as feasible.

d. The focus is usually a single setting or group, of relatively small scale.

e. The analysis of the data involves interpretation of the meanings and functions of human actions and mainly takes the form of verbal descriptions or explanations, with quantification and statistical analysis playing a subordinate role at most. As a set of methods, ethnography is not far removed from the sort of approach that we all use in everyday life to make sense of our surroundings.

All social research methods have their historical origins in the ways in which human beings gain information about their world in everyday life. Cultural anthropology is the study of culture – the behavioural tendencies we develop throughout our lives. Culture is the name we give to those learned personal characteristics that are shared with the groups to which we belong.

Anthropologists can provide three basic things:

- An antidote to the problem of ethnocentrism
- A conceptual framework for understanding what culture is
- A methodology for doing semi-structured research

Ethnocentrism is the inability to see the point of view of someone from another culture.

Given the international focus design can have it is likely that the users you are designing for belong to a different culture. The problem with ethnocentrism is obvious when you are designing for people who belong to a culture you are not familiar with but even in designing for a friend the very activity of product development distances the designer from the user. This is where cultural anthropology is useful because it involves learning to see things from someone else's point of view.

While ethnography often includes a description of the activities and practices of those studied, it is more importantly an attempt to interpret and give meaning to those activities.

DESIGN ETHNOGRAPHY

Design ethnography aims to understand the needs of people and future users of a design for a product or service, with an aim of going into depth on the everyday lives and experiences of the people a design is being created for. The aim is to enable the designer/creator and the design team to identify with these people; to build up an empathic understanding of their practices and routines, and what they care about. This enables the designer or design team to work from the perspective of these users on new designs, which are relevant for users in their daily lives. We can use this understanding to work on idea generation, concepts development and implementations.

Design ethnography explicitly aims to generate materials that communicate the insights from the research to a wide group of stakeholders, to make sure that the foundations for the design process are well understood and accepted. Design ethnography is purposefully not an expertise outside of the creative process but rather it is within the design process. It has a place right in the middle of it, just like the other specific expertise that exists within design and is about facilitating empathic conversations between users, clients and designers, as well as other experts and stakeholders involved in the design process. Design ethnography is firmly within the realm of design thinking and embodies the design process. The results from design ethnography facilitate that focus and language by offering a firm reference point that connects all the disciplines involved: the people they are ultimately developing the services for. This is relevant not only during the design stage but also during implementation. The level of detail of the ethnographic research can vary greatly between research projects and depend on time, budget and experience. In small-scale projects it might be just a few days; in large-scale projects it can take several weeks. Design is an inter-discipline where T-shaped people collaborate. The concept of T-shaped people was introduced to the design and innovation field by the design consultancy IDEO (Kelley, 2000). The idea behind the metaphor is to indicate that most professionals have both a deep expertise in a given field and a broad understanding of other fields they encountered for their work. In strategic and innovative projects, as many design projects are, various T-shaped people with different backgrounds and roles are working together as part of the same team.

Design ethnography is part of the deep expertise that contributes to the design discipline. The combination of a general understanding in the top ends of the Ts and the additional deep expertise in the bottom ends of the Ts leads to valuable collaborations that trigger successful new service concepts and ensure their effective implementation.

During the early stages of the design research process the researcher can trigger and document empathic conversations with the people who will be ultimately using and delivering the services. During the analysis stage that follows the methods are focused on clustering and probing the research data to discover relevant and inspiring insights. The methods used during the development stage contribute to idea generation, concept development, co-creation, prototyping and validation.

The empathic conversations between the various people and parties involved require both a sensitive attitude and a strong, visually engaging approach. The research activities and materials need to be well designed, in order to get people involved and elicit useful and inspiring results. And the subsequent new designs need to be researched again, to make sure that

the final results will be further improved in an iterative process.

Holism

This emphasis on natural settings derives in part from a belief that particular behaviours can only be understood in the everyday context in which they occur. To remove a behaviour from the larger social context is to change

Figure 1.8 Meaning is in context

Sum of the parts equals the whole

Can't reduce the parts and retain the meaning of the whole

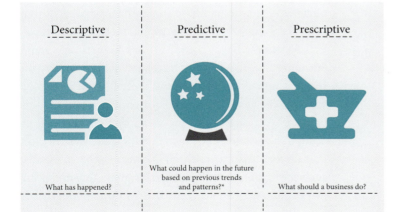

Descriptive — What has happened?

Predictive — What could happen in the future based on previous trends and patterns?*

Prescriptive — What should a business do?

Figure 1.9 Evaluating analytical options
Based on fieldwork ethnographers develop a descriptive understanding of the life of a group studied. Ethnographers describe how people actually behave not how they ought to behave. This distinction is illustrated above. Descriptive is what has happened, predictive is what could happen and prescriptive is what should happen. The orientation towards the descriptive should mean that researcher using ethnography assume a non-judgemental stance about the behaviour they are studying. Maintaining such a non-judgemental stance is sometimes referred to as cultural relativism, the notion that other people's behaviour should not be judged by the standards of some other group.

it in important, nontrivial ways. This concern with how particular behaviours fit into the larger whole is often referred to as holism. Holism is therefore a way of analysing an individual's behaviour by observing it as a whole. The aim is to look at the whole picture because if you take the picture apart it will be distorted. Take this picture, for example: the phone at the bottom has been taken apart and reduced into many small pieces. You could look at these parts individually to see what shape and size and function they have; however, it no longer looks like a mobile phone. In the top picture we can clearly see the picture is a phone and so can understand how all the pieces work together.

The key aspect of adopting ethnography in design is to ultimately understand more of the user's perception of the object, environment, system or service the user is engaged with. The goal is to see people's behaviour on their terms, not yours. While this observational method may appear inefficient, it enlightens us about the context in which users would interact with a new product and/or the meaning that product might hold in their lives. There are various methods we can use to obtain and use knowledge in an ethnographic project.

Ethnographer → Designer

A trained ethnographer is asked to study the work practices of a group of employees working in a bank. The insights from this study might then be transferred to designers through written reports and oral presentations. The designers would then have the task of identifying the relevant aspects of the reports in order to produce concepts for a redesign of the banks interiors. Because of differences between the language and perspectives of ethnography and design and because the ethnographer is likely to have little knowledge or appreciation for the immediate concerns of the designers, this is not a simple task. Making the findings of an ethnographic study useful for day-to-day design concerns becomes a major undertaking.

Ethnographer ↔ Designer

An ethnographic study is undertaken with the aim of finding out about the work practices of a group of employees working in bank. This is part of an office redesign project. The research team consists of ethnographers and designers. In this case the insights

and understandings, in part, would be embodied in the experiences of the designers who were first-hand participants in the study. Active involvement by designers in the field work and in constructing interpretations of the work activities at the bank helped focus the ethnographic study on issues more central to the design task and made the interpretations more relevant to the design.

Ethnographer ↔ Designer
        ↕User↕

The bank refurbishment project is undertaken by a team of ethnographers, designers and users. The understandings and insights derived from the study did not need to be written up into a report but instead were reflected in a co-designed office refurbishment design proposal. User partnership in developing and evaluating the scheme in relation to current and imagined work activities was assisted in the designers' participation in workshops and the designers brought their knowledge of interiors and technology constraints and opportunities to the collaboration. The success of the project was evaluated on the basis of how well the proposed design supported the work activities. In this scenario the ethnographer adopted, in part, the designer's orientation of seeking to understand human behaviour insofar as it enabled the design of the proposal to better suit to the needs of the users.

Rapid ethnography

Given the time constraints on industry-based design projects, many of the ethnographic methods employed by designers have come to be known as 'rapid ethnography'. This method has enabled designers to gain insights into users' activities in daily life but also keep up with the fast-paced needs of commercial business practice. Although this may mean that commercial or academic pressures can mean that less time is spent with participants than a traditional ethnography demands, such participation still enables designers to gain access to people's worlds and helps them to understand their situations. This understanding is then translated into the realm of a commercial or academic project business with the design of better products, services and environments that are more tailored to meet people's needs. The strength of the rapid ethnographic approach is that it gives voice to the users who remain at the forefront of the design solutions.

Why is ethnography relevant to design?

Ethnography is relevant to design for several reasons:

1. It allows the researcher to gain insight into the user's environment. Sometimes researchers can have little knowledge of the particular environment and by gaining this knowledge it will enable them to produce a design solution that better reflects the user's environment.

2. It stops researchers from using their own worldview on a situation and enables them to focus on the worldview of the users which will enable the design solution to reflect the users and not the designers.

3. Designers can create products or services when the possible uses are unknown. Such situations might be described as design in search of an application. Some understanding of the work in which potential users are engaged can help identify possible uses and refine the original design.

4. To better understand the context of use of the design it is inextricably linked to the conditions of the user's environment, so design that is tested in a more traditional way fails to capture important nuances.

5. Ethnography enables the researcher to provide a more comprehensive representation of the design for the user. When designing radically new designs, users often are unable to give meaningful responses to queries about how they might use such a product or services. They need to be provided with a way of envisioning and experiencing the design in the context of their own work practices before they can contribute to such a discussion. To create the context for such a discussion and to be useful partners in the joint exploration of the relation between work and technology, designers must have some understanding of the user's work.

6. Ethnography enables the researcher to shift design from a single objector task focus in order to account for a more holistic understanding of outside influences on the users. Simply, focusing on a single task or the tasks of the single user ignores how the work of one individual connects with that of many others.

The ethnographic approach, with its emphasis on native-point-of-view holism and a social context, provides a unique perspective when it comes to understanding users' activities. The ethnographer is interested in understanding human behaviour as it is reflected in diverse communities of people and the designer is interested in designing products or services that will support the activities of these communities. The challenge is to develop ways of merging these two different focusses. When ethnographers develop an understanding of human behaviour it generally requires a period of field work where the ethnographer becomes immersed in the activities of the people studied. Typically, fieldwork involves some combination of observation, informal interviewing and participation in the ongoing events of the community. Through extensive contact with the people studied, ethnographers develop a descriptive understanding of the observed behaviour. Designers, on the other hand, are interested in understanding human behaviour so that it enables them to design product or services better suited to the needs of the users. Designers, therefore, spend more time testing and evaluating their designs in relation to users' needs and abilities and less on understanding the support behaviour. When designers do attempt to gain a clearer view of the users for whom they design, they traditionally have been limited in the ways such a view is acquired. Design ethnography provides an alternative methodology for designers to use, which gives them access to people's everyday practices as members of social groups and has the potential to result in more meaningful and relevant design.

CHAPTER 8
EMPATHY

We need to obtain a deep understanding of the person for whom you are designing and develop an empathy with them. One approach to this is to develop an empathy map to help you synthesize your observations of the situation and to enable you to draw out unexpected insights.

To do this you create a four-quadrant layout on paper or a whiteboard. You then, using post-it notes, populate the map by taking note of the following four traits of your user as you review your notes, audio and video from your fieldwork.

Although thoughts, feelings and emotions of the user can be guessed at this will not provide a sound platform of understanding to begin the creative process. However, you can add your notes on body language, tone and choice of words and this may help you understand your users' thoughts and feelings. Wherever possible confirm your interpretations directly with the users and incorporate their feedback.

We also need to identity 'needs' – which can be human, emotional or physical necessities. These 'needs' will help define your design. One way of ensuring you focus on the problems to solve and not leap straight to creating a solution is to remember that needs are *verbs* (activities and desires with which your user could use help), not *nouns* (solutions). You can identify needs directly out of the user traits you note, or from contradictions between two traits – such as a disconnect between what they say and what they do. You can then write these on your empathy map.

The next stage is to identify insights. Insights are a realization that you can leverage to better respond to a design challenge. Insights often grow from contradictions between two user attributes (either within a quadrant or from two different quadrants) or from asking yourself 'why?' when you notice strange behaviour. One way to identify the initial elements of insights is to identify 'tensions' and 'contradictions' as you work.

PROTOTYPING FOR EMPATHY

Designers normally test prototypes with users to evaluate solutions, but you can also gain empathy through prototyping, bringing forth different information than simply interviewing and observation might. Of course, whenever you test with a user you should consider both what you can learn about your potential solution and what you can learn about the person – you can always use more empathetic understanding.

But you can also develop prototypes or create situations specifically designed to gain empathy, without testing a solution at all (or even having a solution in mind). This is sometimes called 'active empathy' because you are not an outside observer; you are creating conditions to bring out new information. In the same way a solution prototype helps you gain understanding about your concept, an empathy prototype helps you gain understanding about the design space and people's mindsets about certain issues.

Figure 1.10 Empathy map

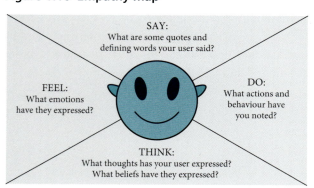

These empathy prototypes are often best used when you have done some work to understand the design space, and want to dig deeper into a certain area or probe an insight you are developing. Think about what aspect of the problem you want to learn more about. Then discuss or brainstorm ways you might investigate that subject. You can create prototypes for empathy to test with users.

Some ideas:

- Have your user draw something (for example, draw how you think about spending money, or draw how you get to work) and then talk about it afterwards.
- Create a game that probes issues you want to explore (e.g. you could make a simple card game which forces users to make choices related to your design challenge).
- Simulate an aspect of what users are going through to better understand it yourself (e.g. if your users plant seeds while carrying a baby, get a sling and carry ten pounds while planting seeds).

WHY INTERVIEW

In order to design or innovate for a user you need to understand a person's thoughts, emotions and motivations, so that you can work out how to design for their needs. By understanding the choices that person makes and the behaviours that person engages in, you can identify their needs, and design to meet those needs.

Ask why. Even when you think you know the answer, ask people why they do or say things. The answers can be surprising.

Never say 'usually' when asking a question. Instead, ask about a specific instance or occurrence, such as 'tell me about the last time you …'

Encourage stories. Whether or not the stories people tell are true, they reveal how they think about the world. Ask questions that get people telling stories.

Look for inconsistencies. Sometimes what people say and what they do are different. These inconsistencies often hide interesting insights.

Pay attention to nonverbal cues. Be aware of body language and emotions.

Don't be afraid of silence. Interviewers often feel the need to ask another question when there is a pause.

If you allow for silence, a person can reflect on what they've just said and may reveal something deeper.

Don't suggest answers to your questions. Even if they pause before answering, don't help them by suggesting an answer. This can unintentionally get people to say things that agree with your expectations.

Ask questions neutrally. 'What do you think about new films?' is a better question than 'Don't you think new films are great?' because the first question doesn't imply that there is a right answer.

Don't ask binary questions. Binary questions can be answered in a word; you want to host a conversation built upon stories.

Make sure you're prepared to capture. Always interview in pairs. If this is not possible, you should use a voice recorder – it is impossible to properly engage a user and take detailed notes at the same time.

DESIGN THINKING METHODS AND TOOLS

Design thinking is regarded as a system of three overlapping spaces – viability, desirability and feasibility – where innovation increases when all three of these aspects are used.

A large number of design research methods and tools can be used to facilitate the design thinking and innovation process.

The design thinking process consists of five stages: empathizing, defining, ideating, prototyping and testing. Empathizing relates to direct interaction with users. The ideation phase includes brainstorming and generating solutions, while the prototype phase implies rapidly making numerous prototypes. Finally, the test phase can also include the final implementation. From a design perspective, design thinking can be used to understand and create meaning and make sense of things.

Design thinking reveals a perspective that is deeper than the obvious benefits of the products and services offered to customers. It encompasses digging down to understand the behaviour, thoughts and attitude of users.

This section discusses six design thinking research methods. The criteria for choosing these methods lie in their visualization techniques and ability to enhance communication within multidisciplinary teams or individuals, but also because they are simple to use. These tools can also be used out with design thinking as effective research methods tools.

Personas

The persona method, which is an ethnographic method of data collection, can help identify the user's needs and desires. A persona is a user representation intending to simplify communication and project decision making by selecting project rules that suit the real propositions. Personas represent a 'character' with which client and design teams can engage and use efficiently in the design process. The method is used for the development of products and services, for communication and strategic design purposes, to reflect the human perspective of design thinking. Personas can be used during the empathizing or defining phases of design thinking.

Personas are a way to communicate and summarize research trends and patterns to others. It can provide a fundamental understanding of users. Personas can be used in a goal-oriented form of design process. They can also be used in conjunction with scenarios which are a form of strategy but in this context are written from the persona's perspective, at a more macro level, and articulate used cases that will likely happen in the future.

1. Personas: Defines who the story is about. The users' attitudes, motivation, pain points and goals.
2. Scenario: Defines when, where and how the story takes place. The scenario is a narrative that describes how the person behaves as a result of a series of events.
3. Goal: Defines what the persona wants or needs to do. The goal equals the motivation of why the persona has the need and what they want to achieve. When the goal is achieved the scenario ends.

This persona was created by interviewing a range of hillwalkers and also observing them hill walking. The designer then looked for and found patterns in the interviewees' responses and actions and used these to group similar people together. He then created archetypical models of those groups, based on the patterns found. Drawing from that understanding of the hillwalker he then went on to create a range of user-centred designs based on the needs of the personas.

Personas can be used for the following:

1. Build empathy
2. Develop focus
3. Communicate and form consensus
4. Make and defend decisions
5. Measure effectiveness

Build empathy

When you are working with a persona, you are examining the world through the eyes of the user in the persona, thereby internalizing the persona's goals, needs and wants.

Develop focus

Personas can help you to define who the product or service is being created for. Having this clear target visualized in one or more personas will help you to prioritize which users are more important than others. By defining who your users are makes it evident that you can't use one design solution for everyone.

Communicate and form consensus

More often than not, designers work on multidisciplinary teams with people with vastly different expertise, knowledge, experience and perspectives. Design students also need to work in a group on occasions. As a deliverable, the personas document helps to communicate research findings to people who were perhaps not able to be a part of the interviews with users. Establishing a medium for shared knowledge brings together all members of a team. When all members share the same understanding of their users, then building consensus on important issues becomes that much easier as well.

Make and defend decisions

Just as personas help to prioritize who to design for, they also help to determine what to design for them. When you see the world from your user's perspective, it becomes easier to decide what is useful and what is not. When a design choice is brought into question, you can defend it based on real data and research on users which is represented in the persona. This will show others the logical and user-focused reasoning behind the decision.

Measure effectiveness

Personas can be stand-in proxies for users when the budget or time does not allow for an iterative process. Various implementations of a design can be 'tested' by pairing a persona with a scenario, similar to how we test designs with real users. If someone who is play-acting a persona cannot figure out how to use a feature or gets frustrated, then the users they represent will probably have a difficult time as well.

Stakeholder map

A stakeholder map is a visual or physical representation of the various groups involved in a particular product or service, such as customers, users, partners, organizations, companies and other stakeholders. A stakeholder approach reflects the human and business perspective of design thinking. The interplay and connections among these various stakeholders can be charted and analysed for various purposes including, for example, the power of various stakeholders and the relationship between different stakeholders.

Customer journey map

A customer journey map describes a collection of touchpoints from the beginning to the end of a service delivery, as seen from the customer's point of view. A touchpoint is an instance or a potential point of communication or interaction between a customer and a service provider. The customer journey map helps the identification of chances for service innovation and problem areas for service improvement. The method touches on both the human and technical side of design thinking and is particularly useful in the empathy phase of design thinking.

Service blueprint

The service blueprint shows the steps and flows of service delivery that are related to stakeholders' roles and the process. Service blueprints show the actions between customers and service providers during a service delivery. It is a process-oriented method for the business and technical perspectives of design thinking shows all actions, including technical activities. A blueprint is useful to designers in the early innovation process, such as defining a phase, by showing the series of actions of both in-front tasks – actions that can be seen by the customer – and back tasks – actions that cannot be seen by customers, such as those among employees in the back office.

Business model innovation

Business model innovation is about exploring market opportunities; the challenge is to define what the business model actually is. The business model canvas is a visual way of handling a business model and related economic, operational and managerial decisions. Generally, a business model canvas describes the business logic of an idea, product or service in a simple and visual representation. The business model canvas mostly reflects the business perspective design thinking and can be effectively used in the ideation phase.

Rapid prototyping

The rapid prototype is a quick formation of visual and experiential manifestations of concepts. It can assist in determining which solutions are technologically possible. Prototypes can be created and quickly tested using this method. It can thus support communication in multidisciplinary teams in collaborative settings, such as workshops, by facilitating conversations and feedback regarding solutions for a particular product or service. Rapid prototyping is a form of research because by undertaking a prototype you will have a better idea of what is feasible and where the challenges lie in your concept. They can also generate quick ideas to immediately improve the design and obtain direct feedback.

Summary

Design thinking methods and research tools are a way of incubating ideas and creating innovative solutions both within teams and as an individual. Multidisciplinary teams, consisting of people with diverse competencies and backgrounds, are more likely to succeed in applying design thinking as they can be guided to combine methods and can transition from more- to less-reflexive practices. All three perspectives of design thinking are essential to design innovative solutions. Using human- and business-oriented methods, such as stakeholder maps, and as such leaving out the feasibility of the technology, can spark innovation. On the other hand, relying exclusively on business and technical tools does not help project effective decisions, especially as the user may prefer another path. Including the user's perspective and combining convergent and divergent design thinking methods and tools are therefore critical.

CHAPTER 9
MULTIPLE METHODS

The purpose of this section is to discuss the usefulness of multiple or mixed research methods, so that you can compensate for the inherent weaknesses within each method and provide a more complete understanding of the research problem by examining it from various perspectives. The choice of a specific research method is guided by the research question, the current state of knowledge regarding the research problem and the feasibility of employing a particular method. The use of different methods at various stages of a research stream can be viewed as a circular, iterative process whereby the results of subsequent research projects reinforce, augment and triangulate the findings from prior studies, or raise new questions to be addressed in subsequent studies. Two variations of the multiple method approach are suggested here:

- Use more than one method when conducting a single study
- Use differing methods to examine a phenomenon by conducting a coordinated series of studies

WHAT ARE MULTIPLE METHODS OF RESEARCH?

A mixed research method approach uses research tools from both qualitative and quantitative methodologies to answer a research question. If you are using a multiple methods approach, you can choose from the full range of methodologies at any point in the research process; from the purpose to the methods, from the sampling to the analysis, and ultimately also to the interpretation of your findings, too. Using a truly mixed methodology means that you may ultimately rely on a mixed approach throughout all stages of the process – but you can also choose to take this approach only for one stage of your research, if you prefer.

WHY CONSIDER MULTIPLE METHODS?

Every method of data collection has its limitations and is more suitable for one part of a question or proposition than another. If you use a variety of data-collection methods you can 'see' the responses from different perspectives, and by layering the data-collection methods you can work to the strengths and cancel out the weaknesses of some of them. Some situations are particularly complex. For instance, as you move through the research process, you may come to realize that your chosen method of data collection is not providing the insights that you require. If this happens, you will need to investigate what data collection tool might possibly provide them instead. Multiple methods are particularly suited to collaborative or action-research projects, in which the research may change direction as it is influenced by those with whom you are collaborating. It also allows you to explore questions and confirm responses to a research question and then confirm your theory in the same programme of research. If you seem to have contradictory results in your data analysis, continuing with a different research tool can give you the opportunity to explain these results.

DOES THIS CONTRADICT THE PARADIGM CHOICE?

Paradigms are social constructions that reflect basic belief systems or the worldviews of researchers, revolving around the notion of the creation of knowledge and how change can be accomplished. There is an ongoing debate concerning whether or not a particular methodology should be attached to specific paradigms. There is an established viewpoint

Figure 1.11 Connect the data
In exploratory sequential research, you would gather qualitative data to explore the problem and then quantitative data to try to explain the relationships found in the qualitative data. Exploratory research provides an initial understanding of an issue or a situation and is usually conducted because a research problem has not yet been defined.

Figure 1.12 Merge the data
Another option is to collect both quantitative and qualitative data and analyse them to provide the results.

Figure 1.13 Embed the data
Quantitative data can be embedded in a qualitative study and qualitative data can be embedded in a quantitative study. Qualitative data can help explain or build upon initial quantitative results.

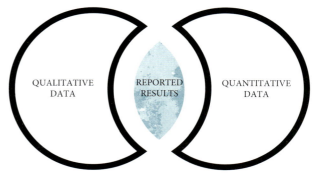

Figure 1.14 Single study
A single study may consist of qualitative and quantitative data collected over a period of time on one case. Changes can be made over time to the conditions to which the case is exposed.

that certain research tools fit in with the philosophical notions of certain paradigms. This in turn implies that quantitative and qualitative methods should not be mixed. From a mixed-method perspective, it can be seen as logical to mix methods when needed and to apply their findings to what is as yet an unknown reality. A mixed-method researcher could point out that paradigms are themselves socially constructed, are therefore changing and certainly not 'cast in stone', and that the relationship between paradigms and methodology is constantly evolving.

HOW DO YOU KNOW WHICH METHODS TO USE?

Data can be collected concurrently or sequentially. In an explanatory sequential research, you would collect quantitative data and then qualitative data to explain the quantitative results. The diagrams on above illustrate different sequences and processes in research design. The different design options need to be evaluated against your objectives and research questions in order to decide which will be most effective within a specific research project. This is an introduction to mixed-method design and involves philosophical assumptions that guide the direction of the collection and analysis of data. This approach considers the mixture of quantitative and qualitative approaches in the different phases of an evaluation process, and focuses on the idea that a mixed approach will provide a better understanding of and solution to the evaluation questions and hypotheses.

The different design options need to be evaluated against your objectives and research questions in order to decide which will be most effective within a specific research project.

Figure 1.15 Multiple study

In concurrent data collection, you would collect both quantitative and qualitative data at the same time and then try to look for similar findings. This demonstrates the circular nature of research and the way in which each research method is informed by and supports the other methods.

THINK BOX
Defining multi-method approaches

There is some confusion concerning the definitions that apply in multi-method research, which we shall explore below.

Multi-level, mixed-methods design

This is a design project in which qualitative data is collected at one level (by, for example, the designer), and quantitative data is collected at another level (by, for example, an organization) in a concurrent or sequential manner to answer different aspects of the same research question. Both types of data are analysed accordingly, and the results are then used to make inferences.

Multi-level, mixed-model design

This is a design project in which qualitative data is collected at one level (by, for example, the designer), and quantitative data is collected at another level (by, for example, an organization) in a concurrent or sequential manner to answer interrelated research questions with multiple approaches (qualitative and quantitative). Both types of data are analysed accordingly, and the results are used to make multiple types of inferences (qualitative and quantitative), which are pulled together at the end of the research.

Multiple methods design

This refers to design projects in which more than one research method or data collection and analysis technique is used to answer research questions. They include mixed-methods designs (qualitative and quantitative) and multi-methods designs (quantitative and quantitative or qualitative and qualitative).

Multi-methods qualitative study

This refers to design projects in which research questions are answered using two qualitative data-collection procedures.

Multi-methods quantitative study

This refers to design projects in which research questions are answered by using two quantitative data-collection procedures.

CHAPTER 10

THE PRACTICE: A RESEARCH-APPROACHED CASE STUDY

This abbreviated case study illustrates the debate we enter into when investigating which research philosophy to choose and the implications this will have on the outcomes of our research project. This is an extract from the author's unpublished PhD, 'Identity within the built environment', undertaken at the University of Strathclyde, Scotland.

ABSTRACT

This proposal focuses on choosing a research philosophy. The choice is between using an interpretive or action-research paradigm. Each will be examined within the context of the subject area: exploring the ways in which meanings are applied or constructed from symbolic artefacts in the organizational built environment. First, a concise review of the viewpoints of these philosophies with respect to the concept of interpreting symbolic artefacts is presented, evaluating the philosophies with respect to the assumptions made and questions posed. Second, a statement of ontological and epistemological positions adopted, discussing options for scope, research design, theoretical constructs, methodology and empirical study is presented. Finally, the proposal assesses the implications of using both paradigms and recommends using an interpretivist paradigm.

INTRODUCTION TO THE TOPIC

The physical aspects of an organization include a physical space that has been designed to meet certain functions. The strongest symbolic message an organization sends comes from its buildings and interiors, especially if the design of these is striking. Both the designed and non-designed aspects of the organizational built environment are clues to an organization's culture, and can also provide insight into its internal social structure and visual identity.

Purpose

The purpose of the research is to understand how meaning is applied or derived (descriptive) from physical symbolic artefacts in the organizational built environment by the occupants of that environment. The research will explore common aspects of interpretation and will assess the influence that interpretation of the designed built environment may have on its inhabitants.

ASSUMPTIONS

- People interpret physical artefacts differently
- There is an element of commonality in interpretation

INITIAL RESEARCH QUESTIONS

- How is meaning applied to or constructed from physical symbolic artefacts?
- What are the similarities and differences in interpretation of the same physical artefacts?

I have chosen to examine two research philosophies which both fall into the category of the phenomenological paradigm. Phenomenology is a qualitative paradigm concerned with understanding human behaviour from the perspective of the participants and focuses on meaning as opposed to measurement, and as such, is more sensitive to the qualitative issues contained in the research assumptions and questions.

RESEARCH DESIGN AND METHODOLOGY – INTERPRETIVE

The first stage of the research will comprise a review of the existing literature on symbolic artefacts and the organizational built environment, organizational culture and managing change. The primary research will consist of three stages:

- Descriptive research will consist of observation techniques to determine the attitude and the behaviour towards the symbolic artefacts.
- In-depth interviews with those observed, to establish the interactive application of meaning between the participants and the symbolic artefacts.
- Exploration of the specifics of the case study, including photography of the building and its inhabitants, interviews with the designer, participants and managers to examine intended meaning and their interpretations by the inhabitants. Patterns of data examined for emerging theory.

RESEARCH DESIGN AND METHODOLOGY – ACTION RESEARCH

Action research has change on the agenda. It is concerned with emerging or developing theory, but with a focus on eventually proposing change. Action research is designed to bridge the gap between research and practice (Somekh, 1995). Kemmis and McTaggart (1988) have defined action research as

> a form of collective self-reflective inquiry undertaken by participants in social situations in order to improve the rationality and justice of their own social or educational practice … and the situations in which these practices are carried out … . The approach is only action research when it is collaborative [and relies upon] the critically examined action of individual group members.

The other difference is that the inhabitants of the built environment have a sense of ownership of the research and can (because of their involvement) alter the course of the research. There is an emancipatory interest based on the notion of action researchers as participants in a community of equals.

Action research has not been chosen because the main aim in this project is interpretation of meaning and subsequent change is not an issue at this stage; although I recognize that by not involving the participants of the building in the control and ownership of the research, unknown aspects may remain uncovered. My main interest is to understand the way in which meaning is applied and to assess whether there are common areas of meaning to such an extent that assumptions can be made. This would inform designers involved in the design of a building and may inform strategic change practitioners. The spirit of this research is based on Geertz's methodology of examining 'events' in an ethnographic way. In this case, I have sought out two events. The pilot will focus on the move of a college from one building to a state-of-the-art purpose-built campus and the main research on the move of the Scottish Houses of Parliament to their new home in Edinburgh. I hope to apply the knowledge I gain from this to the concept of the designed organizational built environment.

The preferred paradigm is the interpretive paradigm, with action research being the second choice. These were initially chosen for consideration because the stated assumptions in the research proposal are qualitative, subjective and concern meaning.

CHAPTER 11
GERRY JOHNSON ON CREATING A FRAMEWORK

Professor Gerry Johnson is one of Europe's most highly regarded professors of Strategic Management. He is Professor Emeritus at Lancaster University Management School.

This section has been based on a live interview and a previously published interview and aims to explain how journal articles from different fields can be applied to the creative industries, either because of the knowledge they contain or because of the way in which they have been structured or written.

WHAT ARE YOUR RESEARCH INTERESTS?

'My research interests focus on management practices and processes associated with strategy development and strategic change, especially the role of political, cultural and cognitive processes. This has manifested itself in a number of research projects.' As a Senior Fellow of AIM I have also been involved in two major research projects. The first links to the interest in Strategy as Practice and examines the phenomenon of strategy workshops and away days. The second is concerned to understand the historic management processes that have contributed to the very few UK companies that have effected major strategic transformation in the last twenty years without the trigger of financial downturn. 'All of this work builds on the conviction that good quality research in management needs to combine both rigorous research methods and relevance to management and organizations. Most of my work has been undertaken as collaborative ventures with managers, takes form through teaching and teaching materials (including my

textbook) and is applied in consultancy work. As such, it is subject to the judgement of both academic peers and practitioners.'

WHY DO YOU THINK YOUR RESEARCH IS HIGHLY CITED?

'Our paper is highly cited as it fits within several different research conversations. First, it is a paper about sense-making and is, therefore, relevant to other research in this area. However, it is also a paper about middle managers and strategic change, and is therefore also cited by the growing body of work which explores the strategic role of middle managers. 'In addition, it is relevant to research in the recent field of Strategy as Practice. This body of work explores strategy as something an organization does, as opposed to something an organization has and, as such, puts the research focus on what it is that strategic actors in organizations actually do to deliver strategy.'

DOES IT DESCRIBE A NEW DISCOVERY, METHODOLOGY OR SYNTHESIS OF KNOWLEDGE?

'It doesn't describe a new discovery, but it does use novel methods in the form of research participants' maintained diaries and also through the use of focus groups. It is one of the few recent studies that track the implementation of strategic change on a real-time, longitudinal basis.'

HOW WOULD YOU SUMMARIZE THE SIGNIFICANCE OF YOUR RESEARCH IN LAYMAN'S TERMS?

'The significance of the research lies in that it shows:

- The important and active role that middle managers play in how strategic change actually develops on the ground.
- Whereas senior managers are usually credited with the meaning-making around change, in fact they become ghosts in the sense-making of others; rather than being active directors of change, they act more as agents of indirect infection, influencing organizational meanings through the presence of their actions and words in stories, rumours and gossip shared by others. Therefore, it is the actions, behaviour, gestures and language of peers, and their shared personal experiences, that have a more direct impact on middle-manager interpretations and change outcomes.
- The focus to date on vertical interactions between senior managers and others has obscured the importance of horizontal interactions within organizations.'

CONCLUSION

This section has illustrated the use that can be gained from reading high-quality published papers from adjacent fields as points of reference when constructing your own research framework.

For more about this, see Johnson G. et al., special issue of *Journal of Management Studies* 40(1), 2003; Balogun J. et al., 'Editors of Special Issue: Strategy as Practice', *Human Relations* 60(1), 2007; and the book, *Strategy as Practice: Research Directions and Resources*, by Johnson G. et al., Cambridge University Press, 2007.

THINK BOX
Design research in practice

Jane Fulton Suri is Partner Emeritus and Executive Design Director at IDEO. She is dedicated to sustaining and evolving design insight and inspiration. Jane has teased out some of the differences in design research.

Let's get more specific about what it actually means to conduct design research. Typically, research processes used in new product development combine multiple objectives into a single exploration.

A survey tool, for example, may be constructed both to seek out consumer insight about opportunities and to field a sample-size that enables statistical estimations of scale. Or a series of focus groups may be used to explore both the appeal of an early idea and the size of the potential market.

For known markets and offerings, this approach seems to work reasonably well. But in research for radical innovation, compromising the potency of a single research objective leaves important questions unanswered: we know what people say they want, but do their behaviours really support this? How can we use the best of our half-baked ideas to create a better, more integrated experience for consumers? How can we assess the likely size of an opportunity if we have nothing to directly compare it with? In research for radical innovation, there's great value in separating these objectives – distinguishing the types of questions we want to answer and creating appropriately-tailored tools to apply at different points throughout the innovation process. Design research addresses three different kinds of questions with respect to innovation:

- **Generative:** gaining insights and opportunities – research that provides human-centred insight, revealing new ways of framing opportunities and inspiring new ideas.
- **Evaluative or Formative:** learning and refining – research that provides continual learning throughout the process to determine the what, how, and to whom of the offering.
- **Predictive:** estimating potential – research that helps to estimate the scale and potential of an opportunity even when most variables are unknown.

Design research demands commitment from innovators to reach new levels of understanding about what matters to the people we want to connect with. For radical innovation, we need both evidence and intuition: evidence to become informed, and intuition to inspire us in imagining and creating new and better possibilities.

MANAGING THE RESEARCH DESIGN

This part of the book discusses managing the research design. This is the stage at which you make sure you are clear about what problem it is that you want to research, and confirm why you want to research this problem area, how relevant it is to the creative industries and, importantly, how you can do the research.

CHAPTER 12

DEVELOPING A RESEARCH DESIGN AND STRATEGY

How do you come up with the idea for your research project and ensure that it has a clear purpose? Probably, one of the most common sources of research ideas is general experience of practical problems encountered in your field. Many researchers in the creative industries come up with their ideas based on what they see happening around them. If you aren't directly involved in creative contexts, work with (or interview) people who are, in order to learn what needs to be better understood directly from the practitioners.

HOW TO FIND A PURPOSE

Finding a purpose for your research can be difficult. Many research questions throw up practical problems that may, at first, seem insurmountable. However, many of these practical problems can lead to extensive research efforts.

Another source for research ideas is the literature in your specific field. Certainly, many researchers get ideas for research by reading the literature and thinking of ways to extend or refine previous research. 'Requests For Proposals' (published by government agencies and some companies) describe problems that the agency would like researchers to address. These can be hugely useful as they often quite literally hand you an idea. Typically, the request describes the problem that needs addressing, the contexts in which it operates and the approach that they would like you to take in order to investigate the problem. You can, of course, think up your own research topic. It is natural that your ideas will be influenced by your background, culture, education and experiences – and this can make them even more interesting.

THE RESEARCH PROCESS

When you decide where you want your research to get you (that is, what the outcome of your research is likely to be), your research design is used to structure the research, as well as to show how each of the major parts of the research project, the samples or groups, and the research tools and analysis all work together in order to try to address the central research questions at hand. Understanding the relationships between designs and thinking about the strengths and weaknesses of different designs is important in making design choices. This section will discuss the major types of research designs and will give you some ideas about how to think about the design task, as well as providing examples of their use within the creative industries.

Definitions

Researchers who are attempting to answer a research question employ the research process. Though presented in a linear format, in practice the actual process of research can be less straightforward. This said, researchers attempt to follow the process and use it to present their research findings in research reports and journal articles.

Identifying the research problem

Research problems need to be researchable and can be generated from practice, though in such cases they must be grounded in the existing literature, unless you are using grounded theory. They may focus on local, national or international problems that need addressing in order to develop the existing research knowledge base.

Searching the existing literature base

A thorough search of the literature using databases, the internet, text and expert sources should support the research problem. This should be broad and in-depth, demonstrating a comprehensive search of the problem area. A critical appraisal framework should be used to review the literature in a systematic way.

Developing the questions and/or proposition

A more specific research question and/or proposition may be developed from the literature review. This will provide direction for the research, which aims to provide answers to the question or proposition.

Theoretical base

The research may employ a theoretical base from which to examine the problem, especially so at Masters level and in many research studies. In the creative industries, this might come from the fields of the visual arts, management, social sciences, psychology or anthropology.

Sampling strategies

Sampling is the method for selecting people, events or objects for study in research. Non-probability and probability sampling strategies enable the researcher to target data-collection techniques. These may need to be of a specific size or composition.

Data-collection techniques

These are the tools and approaches used to collect data to answer the research question or hypothesis – more than one can be used; most commonly, questionnaires and interviews are used.

Approaches to qualitative and quantitative data analysis

This component is more fully explored in the section on data analysis, but can involve qualitative and quantitative approaches, dependent on the type of data collected.

Interpretation of results

Results are interpreted in terms of how they answer the research question, and conclusions drawn. Implications for practice and further research are discussed, and the limitations of the research defined.

DESIGNS FOR RESEARCH

Much contemporary research is devoted to examining whether an action or manipulation causes some outcome or result. For example, 'How does the design of the built environment affect the productivity/creativity/innovation of organizational actors?' There are three conditions that need to be met before you can infer that such a cause-and-effect relation exists, as detailed in the paragraphs below.

Co-variation

This refers to changes in the presumed cause. For example, the design of the built environment must be related to changes in the presumed effect, which in this case is the productivity/creativity/innovation of organizational actors. If we change the design of the built environment in question, we should observe some change in the outcome measures, too.

Temporal precedence

The presumed cause must occur prior to the presumed effect. In this case, productivity/creativity/innovation must be measured before the building is refurbished.

No plausible alternative explanations

The presumed cause must be the only reasonable explanation for changes in the outcome measures. If there are other factors which could be responsible for changes in the outcome measures, we cannot be confident that the presumed cause-and-effect relationship is accurate. In the question concerning the built environment, we must ensure that it is, in fact, only the design of the built environment that has had an effect, and not issues such as the style of management or external economic forces.

This type of design, while robust, tends to look at the problem from a cause-and-effect point of view, which tends towards a positivist paradigm. Understanding the issues involved might lead to a more inductive approach – which is much less likely to be measurable and so also less likely to be generalizable.

DESIGN CONSTRUCTION

Most research designs, whether inductive or deductive, can be constructed from four basic elements, as outlined below.

Time

A causal relationship, by its very nature, implies that some time has elapsed between the occurrence of the cause and the consequent effect. While for some phenomena, the elapsed time might be measured in microseconds and, therefore, might be unnoticeable to a casual observer, we normally assume that cause and effect in the creative industries do not occur simultaneously. In a more understanding-, discovery-led approach, as indicated with interpretivism, time is also highly relevant and needs to be factored in.

The change or cause

The presumed cause may be a change made under the explicit control of a manager or leader in a specific context or the occurrence of some natural event or programme not explicitly controlled.

Observation(s) or measure(s)

Measurements or observations will be taken either at every same point in time in a design, or different measures or observations will be given at different times.

Groups or individuals

The final design element consists of the intact groups or individuals who participate in various conditions. Typically, there will be one or more change or cause and there may be comparison groups.

STRATEGY FOR DESIGN CONSTRUCTION

The basic elements of a research design need to be integrated with an overall strategy. Furthermore, you need to decide which potential threats to validity and credibility are best handled by design rather than by argument, measurement, analysis or preventative action. Although there is no best way to do this, it can be useful to work through the following stages outlined below:

- First, begin the designing task by setting forth a design that depicts the possible relationship between the cause (the built environment) and the effect (productivity/creativity/innovation of organizational actors).
- Second, you can deliberately overextend this basic design by expanding across time, change, observations and groups. In this step, the emphasis is on accounting for as many likely alternative explanations as possible using the design.
- Finally, you can then scale back this over-expanded version, considering the effect of eliminating each design component. It is at this point that you will face difficult decisions concerning the costs of each design component and the advantages of ruling out specific threats using other approaches.

There are several advantages to using this type of approach to design construction. First, you are forced to be explicit about the decisions that are made. Second, the approach is 'conservative' in nature. The strategy minimizes the chance of overlooking a major threat to credibility in constructing your design. Thirdly, you end up with a design which is tailored to your context. Threats which can be accounted for by some other, less costly, approach need not be accounted for in the design itself.

QUESTIONS TO ASK ABOUT YOUR RESEARCH DESIGN STRATEGY

While you are making decisions about how to construct your research design, it is important to have an end point in mind, some defined criteria which you want to achieve before accepting a design strategy. The criteria discussed below suggest the characteristics that might be found in good research design; however, it is still important that you individually tailor your own research design to your specific problem area rather than simply accepting a standard strategy.

Is it theory-grounded?

Your research strategy should reflect the theories being investigated. Where specific theoretical expectations can be hypothesized, these are incorporated into the design. For example, where theory predicts a specific effect on one measure but not on another, the inclusion of both in the design improves validity and demonstrates the predictive power of the theory.

Does it reflect the settings of the investigation?

Your research design should reflect the settings of the investigation. This can mean including the people who are working in that context, but also inter-group rivalry, demoralization and competition might be assessed through the use of additional comparison groups who are not in direct contact with the original group.

Is it feasible?

You need to be able to undertake the research. The sequence and timing of events need to be thought through as much as possible, even if you are using an inductive approach. Try to anticipate potential problems in advance. Where needed, you can incorporate additional groups or measurements in the design to overcome such problems.

Is it flexible?

Good research designs have some flexibility built into them. Often, this flexibility results from the duplication of essential design features. For example, multiple replications of a treatment help to ensure that failure to implement the treatment in one setting will not invalidate the entire study.

Is it efficient?

Good designs strike a balance between redundancy and the tendency to over design. Where it is reasonable, other less costly strategies for ruling out potential threats to validity are utilized. This is by no means an exhaustive list of the criteria by which you can potentially judge your research design. Nevertheless, goals of this sort will help you towards your final choice of design and do emphasize important components which should be included. To date, the development of a research methodology for use within the creative industries has largely meant adopting strategies from other disciplines instead. It is not surprising, then, that an emphasis on a few standard research designs has also occurred. Nevertheless, by moving away from the idea of design selection and towards an emphasis on design construction, you can gain much in the quality of your research.

CHAPTER 13
CREATING THE RESEARCH FRAMEWORK

There are some common elements to research projects, which can be used to shape the whole activity. Here, we will discuss the key potential stages of a general approach.

DECIDE ON A PROBLEM

A research project starts with a problem that you have defined within your broad area of interest. This could be along the lines of

- Indication of something hidden that might be revealed by your research
- The occurrence of an event for which there is no adequate explanation
- An apparent relationship between items not explained by current theories

In-depth research usually requires a lot of work and patience, including backtracking after you have gone off on a dead-end track. This means that you need to be highly motivated to stay on course. The problem you have defined needs also to appear to be solvable in the time allocated, with the skills and resources that you have available.

SETTING OBJECTIVES: LEARNING OBJECTIVES AND VEHICLE OBJECTIVES

Whatever kind of vehicle you choose, you will, of course, need to set yourself some objectives for what is to be achieved. It is important to be clear, however, that (except in the case of action learning projects) the vehicle objectives will be different from, though

integral to, the learning objectives. The greater part of the practical work on your project is likely to be devoted to achieving the aims of the vehicle. However, it is important to remember throughout that your learning objectives are the more important of the two sets.

In order to guide your work, you will need to set yourself some tentative objectives right from the start. Before you begin any serious work on your project, you should discuss both your learning objectives and your vehicle objectives with your supervisor. In the case of applied context projects, you will also need to agree the vehicle objectives with the client(s). If you are a sponsored student on the course, your sponsor may also need to be involved.

In this context, a few points are worth noting:

- Although you need to set objectives early on, you should not regard these as set in stone. At regular points during your project process, you should review the objectives and ask yourself whether these are still relevant in light of what you have learned so far. If you adjust the objectives, you may also need to adjust the methodology for the remainder of your work. It may be that the objectives you state retrospectively when you have completed the work may be quite removed from the way you thought about them at the start.
- You do not have to be successful in achieving the vehicle objective in order to pass the project, providing you demonstrate that you have learned from the experience of trying; often the greatest learning comes following a struggle in pursuing the vehicle objectives.
- It is essential to keep track of changes to your objectives and to the causes of these changes.

DEFINE A RESEARCH QUESTION OR HYPOTHESIS

The next stage is to formulate the research question. This creates focus and may require a significant thinning down of the original problem. If the problem starts out as being about global design, the universe and everything within it, then perhaps the research question should realistically be constrained to furthering understanding of some aspect of design, such as determining the impact of design on SMEs in northern France within product design.

Developing a hypothesis or a number of hypotheses involves converting the question into a predictive form and creating a null hypothesis by which falsification may be achieved. This can be used with a positivist paradigm.

THE LITERATURE REVIEW

The literature review is used to refine the topic by exploring the different facets of it and funnelling down into an area that will provide you with a deep enough focus on an area of interest. It is also used to find information about the context within which you will be potentially setting the project. By completing a critical review of the literature, you can map out what has and has not been achieved in the field of your chosen topic and then build up an argument which justifies your choice of project questions. You can then refine your research project methods and data-gathering techniques.

The literature review is your opportunity to demonstrate your ability to effectively criticize the literature, evaluating the strengths and weaknesses of a particular point of view, conceding the merits of some literature while rejecting others and focusing on the ideas and theories rather than the author. Naturally, you need to be aware of your own critical stance and be able to reformulate existing arguments to form a synthesis that will build your own argument. By critically examining the literature, you will develop the ability to identify any faults in an argument.

You could use the following structure for your literature review chapter:

- Define your terms
- Provide a brief overview of key ideas
- Summarize, then compare and contrast the work of key writers
- Narrow down to highlight the works most relevant to your research
- Consider these in detail – building your argument
- Highlight and define the areas (questions) you are going to look at in detail
- Lead the reader into the subsequent sections of your project which will explore these issues

MANAGING THE LITERATURE REVIEW

Whatever kind of project you design for yourself, you are expected to make use of relevant literature and to demonstrate your knowledge of this in the major project. Most projects will make some use of literature relevant to all four areas of learning identified earlier in the book. You may also need to make use of additional literature to inform your work on the project vehicle.

The main effort of your literature searching and synthesizing should, however, be in the area dictated by your learning objective.

When to carry out your reading and how to include it in your report is a matter for methodological choice (and, hence, discussion with your supervisor). For example, if you are concerned with theory deducing, much of your reading will have to be postponed until you are able to judge what kind of theory seems to be emerging from your data. On the other hand, if you are designing interview questions, you will probably need to base this design on your understanding of relevant literature in the area, and hence will need to do considerable reading at the start of your project. Most people choose to write up a separate chapter of their report reviewing the literature, but it is perfectly legitimate to thread it through the report on a continuous basis as it becomes relevant.

You can plan your literature review by deciding on a strategy for researching and writing your literature review. Either work backwards by tracking authors from recent key works and locate the work that influenced the more recent work or work forward from a seminal paper. A seminal paper is one which could be termed 'groundbreaking'. These are also papers that can contain a lot of references and citations of other work. You can

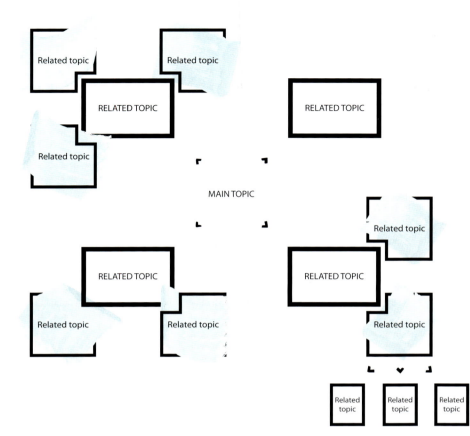

Figure 2.1 Literature review brainstorming
A literature review should discuss the ideas of others rather than develop your own. You should use the literature review to evaluate and discuss relevant key papers and show the interconnections between the topics as illustrated in the diagram. It can be used to demonstrate that you have a clear understanding of the topic and will guide and inform the research that you are going to undertake. It will also assist you in developing a clearly stated research question and in building an argument to discuss.

THINK BOX
Managing your learning

Each time you interact with your supervisor, your ongoing learning should be discussed. Your learning is central to the research process, and you should keep a learning diary throughout the duration of the research project, as this will help to determine your supervision needs and direction. The following headings might be useful:

- Date
- Event
- Learning
- Action

It may be helpful to keep an attachment to the learning diary of action planning, and the suggested headings for this process are:

- Goals
- Sub-goals

- Target completion dates
- Resources and methods
- Standards and feedback

Reflection on the knowledge you have gained should be evidenced in the final write-up of the project. It should be clear from your critical engagement with literature and other information sources how your ideas have developed and taken shape. Similarly, following on from your presentation of the methodology you have used, you should include a discussion of what you have learned from carrying out the approach you have adopted, and of how you could feasibly apply this knowledge in future. Your discussion of the conclusions you have reached should also reflect on the learning journey of the project and show how your ideas have developed in conjunction with your research practice, highlighting significant discoveries you made along the way.

see this from looking at database collections such as Athens and Proquest, which state the number of times that a paper has been cited in other works.

Take a note of the keywords used in your and other papers and this will help you to categorize the papers and information you have gathered together into relevant categories. Keep a note of the purpose of the papers that you have kept. Have you kept a paper because of its theoretical background, its research method and analysis or its results and conclusions of particular issues? You may have done so because of a combination of all of these, but it makes the information a lot easier to find at a later date if you have saved it in an organized manner. Try to avoid reading everything as this will take up a lot of your time and you may end up deviating from your chosen subject area.

If you take notes while you are reading, it will help you to keep track of your thoughts and of how you think it will relate to your project. If you keep the bibliographic details with your notes, it will save you a lot of time later on if you want to reference this work. There is nothing more frustrating than realizing that you haven't kept a note of the bibliographic details and that you'll need to spend valuable hours searching for them!

CLARIFYING YOUR METHODOLOGY

Once you have reached an initial sense of your learning and vehicle objectives, you need to think about how you are going to address these. That is, you need to think about the methodology and methods that you will use. You need to do this near the start of the project, and certainly before you do any detailed work on the project vehicle. You also need to do it to a fairly high level of detail. For example, if your project were to involve in-depth interviewing, you would need to clarify

- Who is to be interviewed, and why
- What questions are to be asked, and why
- How open-ended you would like the responses to be, and why
- How the responses will be recorded, and why
- How the recorded responses will be analysed and why
- How conclusions will be drawn from the analysis, and why

Data may also be gained from observation of naturally occurring events. In such situations, the researcher will try not to let their observation affect the data. There are two opposing ways of achieving this. First, you can be physically separated from the people being studied, so that you are not noticed (such as through the use of one-way mirrors or hidden cameras). Secondly, you can be so obviously present that people eventually ignore you and revert to natural behaviour (such as in reality TV shows).

Throughout the research process, you are expected to be methodologically aware; this means not only that you know what you are doing but also that you are able to provide the rationale for why you are doing it. For example, the design of interview questions should (normally) be based upon appropriate theory. Therefore, you will be expected to read and refer to appropriate literature.

Among the issues you may visit in the course of your thinking and discussion about methodology are the following:

- What addressing your learning objectives might mean in practical terms
- How to derive research questions, hypotheses or a project brief
- What reading and secondary research you should focus on and when
- How to identify, contact and talk to participants
- The design of your data-gathering approach or instrument
- Piloting
- What tools you will use to record and organize your data
- What methods you will use to analyse your data
- The synthesis of data and how to derive theory (or learning) from it
- Review and re-design of objectives, methodology and reading
- Project management (timetable, resources, review dates and so forth)
- Critical engagement with your methodology and results
- Learning review
- Alternative (creative) ways of writing up

As with setting your objectives, your methodology should be the subject of continual review and revision in the light of progress so far. You will have encountered many aspects of methodology during the earlier stages of your course and can expect to draw on some of these. Your courses will have provided a framework within which these and other tools may be used through introducing you to the main methodological processes. These include idea generation, literature search and the importance of theory, research/investigation design, analysis or evaluation of data/information, and critical, theoretically informed engagement with the data.

It is often the case that the 'reality' of methodological issues does not become fully meaningful until you actually carry them out; therefore, you should regard your courses as a starting point from which to explore them further. Discussion of each of these issues at the appropriate stage with your supervisor is essential. You should expect to revisit and revise the issues over time. You need to be methodologically aware to get the best learning from your project vehicle.

You need a methodology for addressing the learning objectives, as well as a methodology for addressing the vehicle objectives. In some cases, particularly in the case of action learning vehicles, it may be difficult to distinguish between the two. Once you have begun an investigation, you have already invested time in it. Conserve time where possible. You will discover that it is generally not rewarding to have to repeat work simply because you did not spend due time in advance planning how you were going to use (or analyse) the results of your investigation. In reality, there is never sufficient time to do the planning perfectly! But be as prepared as possible by ensuring that your project management is well structured and timetabled before you begin the serious work of your research. You will also find it helpful to keep a record of your actions in order to track your progress and log each stage of the research process.

THE PROJECT REPORT – A REFLECTION OF YOUR LEARNING

When you come to write up your research project, you may be asked to demonstrate that you have designed and implemented a process of learning exploration for yourself. Therefore, in your major project report, the learning objectives should dominate the vehicle objectives; the literature review should reflect the learning objective; the project methodology should reflect the learning objective; and the discussion and conclusions should duly reflect the learning objective.

For applied context vehicles, you will probably need to write a separate report for the client; you will probably wish to include this as a major chapter of your project report. The style of this should fit both the purpose and the client. For example, there is generally no need to include literature or a description of the organization in the client report. For investigative vehicles, it may be appropriate to write a separate investigation report. Note that it will not normally be necessary to include a lengthy description of the organization(s) which are the subject of the vehicle; a brief scene-setter which gives enough detail to interpret the remainder of your comments is all that is generally required.

The major project report must be equally accessible to, and interpretable by, the readers of it. Although you are ultimately writing the project for yourself, the rigour and integrity of your thought should always remain critical and central to it. Reflections on what you have learned may be made explicit and integrated in various sections of the report. Alternatively, you may have separate paragraphs designated throughout the report to deal purposefully with the development of your understanding and learning.

As with the structure of the report, the language you use should be carefully chosen. For example, in an action learning report, it may be appropriate to write in the first person, whereas in theory-deducing projects, the use of a third person may be more appropriate. There is no absolute rule and you should discuss the style of language that you will adopt for your report with your supervisor. In general, the language should be inspired by academic article writing (and possibly design writing) rather than journalistic or textbook styles. Your research will normally be presented in the following format:

- A word count
- Definition of a problem
- A statement of your learning objectives

- A review of the associated literature that informs the issues being studied through discussion of relevant concepts and practices, and which demonstrates a good understanding of the research area
- A methodology which explains and justifies the approaches taken and which deals with issues of rigour, such as triangulation
- An 'outcomes' chapter, which provides an analysis of the way in which the research subjects perceive their situation and their place in it. This includes a study of their roles, attitudes and beliefs. It normally begins by using their own language and then develops to a level of sophistication suitable to engage with the relevant theory and practice, and to relate to the learning objectives at hand
- A discussion which shows why your interpretation is interesting, links data to theoretical categories and explains how this understanding goes beyond treating the subjects' view as the only possible explanation of events
- Your conclusions should relate to how your thinking and understanding have developed

THE PRESENTATION OF ACTION LEARNING PROJECTS

The presentation of this type of project may vary with the problem or issue examined, as well as according to the actions taken by the individual. Evidence that you have gone through a process that includes both the appropriate gathering and understanding of theory, reported practice and other secondary information must be presented. That this has informed reflective action, and that some development – if only at the individual level – has occurred, must also be shown. In order to achieve this, it is sensible to keep a logbook recording notable experiences, key observations and your own personal development.

The project must involve action and implementation, as well as recommendations; and the transfer of learning into the workplace is paramount. The project is likely to address a number of questions:

- What am I, or my organization, trying to do?
- What is stopping us from doing it?
- What can we try to do about it?

Figure 2.2 The seven steps of the research project

This diagram shows what is involved in the research process. You don't always have to go from 1 to 7. You may find you move backwards and forwards from stages 1 – 7 as your work progresses.

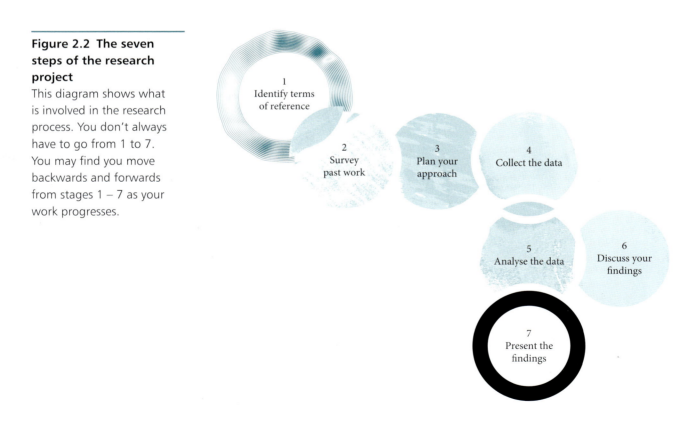

1 Identify terms of reference

2 Survey past work

3 Plan your approach

4 Collect the data

5 Analyse the data

6 Discuss your findings

7 Present the findings

- Who knows about the problems we are faced with?
- Who can help us to solve them?
- What happens when proposed solutions are tried out?
- The questions can be raised by individuals, or by people cooperating in a group or 'set' (to help with reflection and effective questioning)
- The planning evolves from the activity itself, rather than being predetermined; as such, the initial inquiry is likely to be refined – and potentially redefined – as the project progresses.

In order to structure this cycle of reflective action, the following four project steps can be set in place:

- Collect/Experience – observing and reflecting on the consequences of action in a situation
- Act/Understanding – forming and reforming understanding of a situation as a result of experience
- Planning – planning actions to influence the situation, based on newly formed or reformed understanding
- Action – acting or trying out the plan in the situation

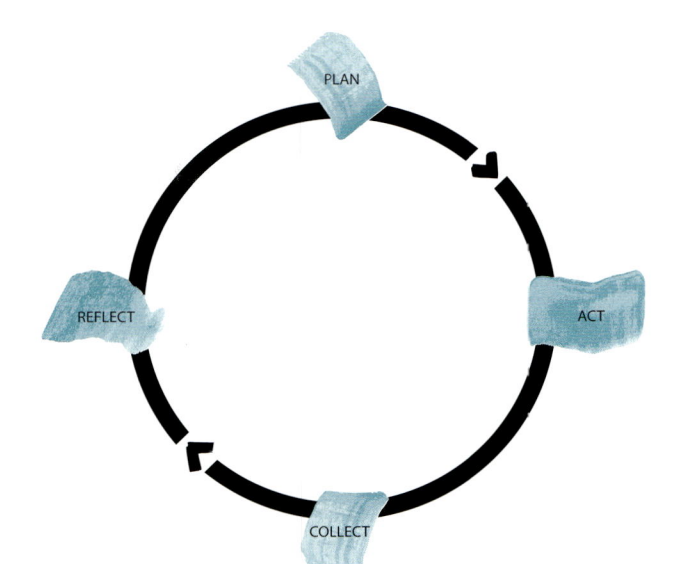

Figure 2.3 Action-research diagram
There are four basic steps in the action-research cycle: plan, act, observe/collect, reflect/ review. Action research is a form of inquiry conducted by researchers who wish to inform and improve their practice, their understanding and decision making in their practice, as well as to gauge the effect of their practice on the research.

CHAPTER 14

MAKING RESEARCH CREDIBLE: THE INFLUENCE OF ETHICS

Here are three more questions to ask yourself as a researcher. Reflect briefly on why you need to be asking these questions before looking at the explanations.

HAVE I GIVEN CONSENT?

It might appear odd to ask yourself the same question you are asking others but it is important you are fully informed and at ease with the research process. If participants make suggestions or ask questions that make you feel uncomfortable, ask yourself whether you consent to answer them. If not, then you can always decline.

IS MY IDENTITY CONFIDENTIAL?

This will depend whether you are a covert or overt researcher. If you are a covert researcher your identity will be hidden. If you have met participants and they consent to take part in the research, your identity is no longer confidential as they could potentially recognize you again. However, you have a right to keep some details such as contact details and other personal information confidential. You should always respect your right to privacy.

AM I BEING HONEST?

The data you are collecting and evidence you are gathering should be carefully analysed and accurately reported. You also need to be honest with yourself and ask if what you are saying and reporting is fair and truthful. Be honest about your own feelings and experiences in relation to your project.

Ethical principles exist to protect both the participants and the researchers, so remember to respect yourself as well as your research.

GAINING INFORMED CONSENT

As part of your research you will need to consider obtaining written consent using a consent form. A consent form is the written record of the decision of the participant to take part in the study. It is the proof of the communication between the researcher and the subject and is a signed document. A consent form should be accompanied with a participant information sheet. This provides an explanation of the study and what the participant is expected to do. Depending on the nature of the research the participant information will vary.

The principle of confidentiality in ethical research states that the identity of the participants must remain anonymous and the information they supply must be respected. This means that you must take steps to ensure that the data you collect remains confidential. Before you start collecting data you should give your prospective participant a full explanation of what will be done with their data. You should also provide a participant information sheet which clearly states how confidentiality will be maintained. In some cases participants may consent to their information being disclosed to others but you would still need to make sure the data is stored carefully.

The rights to confidentiality are also covered by law in most countries. The Data Protection Act (2018) came into effect on the 25th May 2018 and aims to modernise data protection rights in the digital era (see http://www.legislation.gov.uk/ukpga/1998/29/contents).

ETHICAL CONSIDERATIONS FOR DATA COLLECTION AND RESEARCH TOOLS

Ethical standards must be upheld when collecting data and you need to consider the measures that will be taken to protect the participants involved. You will choose to use certain research tools but as well as considering the paradigms and philosophies there are ethical advantages and disadvantages with each method. Some examples follow.

QUESTIONNAIRES

While designing questionnaires, care should be taken that all information gathered must be anonymous. The questions should be carefully written to avoid bias and should not give opinions or be misleading. Remember, participants have the right to not complete any particular items in the questionnaire and to withdraw at any point during the study.

INTERVIEWS

The main ethical issue to be considered is that of confidentiality – remember that an interview is a personal interaction and everything recorded needs to remain confidential to protect that person. You may also decide to ask someone to read and verify the data and the transcriptions. Ask yourself if they need to sign a confidentiality agreement? Remember to make notes as well to avoid misinterpreting what is recorded.

OBSERVATION

If you are using overt observation, it needs to be considered that the presence of an observer may be threatening or perhaps exert an influence on people's behaviour. You should only use covert observation in situations where there is no alternative as it is the violation of the principle of informed consent.

Research ethics are a crucial part of creative research. Ethics are a mix of common sense and professionalism. They are crucial to protect the welfare of the participants and the researcher and ensure the research has integrity.

Your research participants must have autonomy. This is the ability to have control over their decision making. If you make decisions on behalf of your participants, for 'their own good', you are acting paternalistically. This ignores a persons' autonomy and is disrespectful.

DECLARING YOUR INTENTIONS

This can be a tricky question and it leads back to the issue of your ethical responsibility. How much should you tell a colleague about your project before asking him or her your questions? There are several points to consider:

Is it fair to use someone's thoughts in a project when they weren't aware of what you were doing?

If they had known you were trying to do something they disagreed with, might they have given a different answer? Might you lose the sense of open and informal conversation if you indicate that there is a project lurking behind your 'innocent' question?

These are important questions of ethics and practicality. Seeking to balance the relative importance of each issue is not easy and will require some careful thinking.

With this in mind we also need to consider harm in terms of interviewing colleagues. Of course we do not intend to do harm to others but we do need to understand how this may inadvertently come about.

HOW IS 'HARM' DEFINED?

In terms of risk of harm, you have to think about

- **probability**: how likely is harm to occur?
- **severity**: how serious might the harm be?

Neither the probability nor the severity of harm is easy to estimate. Harm can be subjective: for example, distress, embarrassment and anxiety, which are clearly difficult to either predict or to control for. If researchers are to explain risks, and how probable and severe these might be, they need to listen to people's views about what worries them.

You will not be able to predict all the possible risks in your research. A simple question may cause upset for some participants for reasons that you could not know about.

Other typical harms caused by social research include inconvenience, time lost, intrusion, and boredom or discomfort. These may seem slight to you, but may be serious to the person concerned. People can feel wronged by research if, for example, they feel that they have been treated as objects, deceived or humiliated, or that their values have been disregarded. Research ethics are intended to prevent such problems.

HOW TO ASSESS RISK, HARMS AND BENEFITS

You can use the list of questions here as a starting point for reflecting on the possible risks, harms and benefits of your inquiry.

- Why do they matter?
- How widespread and how serious is the question being researched?
- If methods are being tested or compared, are they new methods or already widely used?
- What alternative methods might there be?
- What exactly will participants be asked to do? How much of their time will be needed? Will they be compensated for their time?
- What direct risks might there be to them? Intrusion? Distress or embarrassment?
- How likely and how severe might any risks be?
- How might risks be reduced? For example: rehearsing with respondents' ways of saying 'no' when they do not want to reply; assuring them that this will be respected and that they won't be questioned about why they refuse; or ensuring people who are worried or upset about the research can talk to someone about it afterwards.
- It can be useful to find out gently why people want to refuse. Does the research seem boring or irrelevant? Could it be improved with their help?
- How can people contact the researcher if they want to make further enquiries, or complain?
- Are there systems in place to review complaints and then possibly change research plans?
- How will the study's findings be used?
- If there are any hoped for benefits, what might these be?

STOP AND THINK

How will you recognize a potentially harmful situation?

How will you plan to overcome potential harm?

Your conversations with colleagues may not only be opportunities for asking questions but also for influencing them.

How do you decide whether to ask a question or push a particular agenda of your own? What if asking a question in a particular manner might help a colleague 'get it'? As is so often the case in this field, there are trade-offs between getting the very best information possible and achieving your work goals.

Another aspect of your on-going relationships is that you will need to be sensitive to your colleagues: without care, you can make interviews feel very demanding and even unpleasant for them. If the person you are asking questions of is also a friend, a colleague, a drinking companion, a confidant, a competitor. There is no way round this: you will always have to consider the implications of asking questions for your on-going relations.

SO HOW CAN YOU MANAGE THESE ISSUES?

Your management of your research project will be down to your own judgement of what to do. Perhaps the following questions will help you make those judgements:

Is getting a partial answer better than taking risks in order to get a 'perfect' answer?

Would you like another person to treat you as you propose to treat a colleague when asking them questions?

How do you balance a need to make progress with your project with a desire for better information?

SUMMARY

In this section you have explored ethics in terms of how harm is defined and what you need to take into account when planning interviews and conversations. In addition you have considered the various ways of gathering information by asking people questions and having conversations.

CHAPTER 15
YOUR RESEARCH PROPOSAL

Writing your research proposal is a vital part of the research project process. You may be applying for research funding and your proposal may go before a research committee, or you may be trying to ensure that you are appointed a particular academic supervisor. In either case, you will need to put a lot of time into preparing your proposal. Perhaps most importantly, writing your proposal will ensure that you are clear about what you are trying to achieve and how you are going to achieve it.

Usually, you would choose a subject for your dissertation because it really interests you and because you therefore, presumably, already know something about it. Often, the more you know about a subject, the harder it is to explain it to someone who has no knowledge of it. You may also find it difficult to imagine your work from the viewpoint of the reader. Writing down your thoughts and intentions will help you to organize your ideas into a coherent statement so that your supervisor can also understand what you are trying to achieve and can gain a good idea of how you are going to approach your research.

You also need to decide who your audience is for this piece of research. Who are you engaging with? Who is the reader, apart from the person who is supervising and grading your project, and what fields will you be drawing on?

Your proposal needs to be accepted and given approval for go-ahead in the same way that a proposal for a commercial client would. Although acceptance means that the proposal is satisfactory, it does not guarantee you success. But at least you have started your research journey knowing where you are heading and how you propose to get there.

BREAKING DOWN THE PROCESS

The dissertation-writing process can be broken down into six basic stages:

- Initial thinking about the project
- Attending a research methods class
- Writing a project proposal
- Obtaining a supervisor
- Carrying out your research project under supervision
- Submitting your project

Remember, the main purposes of the draft proposal are threefold: to help you to get started; to give your potential supervisor enough of an idea about your project to allow them to adequately assess whether they are willing to supervise it; and to provide an initial basis for discussion of the objectives and the methodology you are proposing to use.

HOW WILL YOUR RESEARCH PROPOSAL BE EVALUATED?

You should consider two main points. One is the extent to which the various components of your proposal fit together and make sense; and the second is whether or not the research can be carried out satisfactorily in the given time frame and with the resources that you have available to you.

AIMS AND OBJECTIVES

Now that you have selected your research topic, the next stage is to begin designing and planning your research project. You will normally express the main focus of your research project in terms of aims and objectives.

What are aims and objectives? An aim is a general statement, reflecting the intention or purpose of your chosen area of research. An objective is a specific statement relating to the defined goal/aim of your research. It is not uncommon to have more than one objective to satisfy your research aim, but for clarity these should be limited to three. The aim and objectives are interrelated. The aim refers to what you want to achieve, and the objective describes how you are going to achieve that aim.

Writing your aims and objectives

First, you need to consider exactly what you intend to achieve in your research. You need to be sure that what you intend to do is achievable in the given time frame. As we have so far discovered, the aim paints the background picture of your research. Useful ways of expressing your aims are by using verbs such as: investigate, assess, determine and identify. Once you have established your aim, the next task is to think about your objectives. Most of your objectives will be attitudinal or knowledge objectives, although there are other types.

Knowledge objectives usually encompass a level of understanding, problem solving and/or the ability to recall information, whereas attitudinal objectives usually deal with gaining information from a group of people relating to their attitudes. Attitudinal objectives allow for assumptions to be made, as well as for an acceptance of other (less conventional) views. For example,

- To review relevant literature to …
- To assess product user's opinions of …
- To make recommendations to …

Your objectives can determine the appropriate methodology to be used – cost analysis or focus groups/questionnaires, for example. Objectives have to fulfil the requirements of the aim. If you can plan out a realistic time schedule, it may help you to prioritize your objectives and prevent you from wasting time and effort.

You need to write both the aim and objectives clearly and precisely, as this will help to reflect your level of understanding of your research topic. In addition, the clarity of your aims and objectives will allow your reader to understand

- Who: your chosen subjects, units, goods or services
- Where: your research environment
- What: your factor of interest
- How: your plan to achieve your aim and objectives

Your project title

Give the title of your proposed project. Later, as you delve more deeply into your subject, you may wish to change the original title to more accurately reflect what your project is about.

Reasons for choosing your topic

Stating your reasons for choosing the subject will help both you and your supervisor to understand your motives and perspectives on the subject. You should explain why you feel the research you are planning to do is worthy of attention, as this should help you to work out whether it is sufficiently interesting to sustain you over the months that it will take you to complete the project.

Project learning objectives

Indicate what you expect your work to accomplish and the conclusions that you hope to draw from it. It is important to determine and state achievable goals at the outset. Confine your aims to what you really can accomplish in the time available and with the resources at your disposal.

Personal learning objectives

Indicate what you want to gain from carrying out the research and how you will know if you have achieved these aims. This is the more important set of objectives, which may alter substantially if you move to a new level of competence.

Sources of data

Indicate what information you need for your project, where you intend to get it and how accessible it is. Can you gain access to a company or organization(s)? What kind of data collection will you undertake?

Research question or hypothesis

The reasons for choosing the topic should lead smoothly into what seems a natural choice of research question or hypothesis. You can focus on a main research question (or hypothesis), and then subsidiary questions with learning objectives. Your learning objectives need to be precisely written and should have observable outcomes.

Relevant past studies

Inevitably, other researchers will have examined similar situations. Can you use their reports, monographs or textbooks to guide you? What do 'leading authorities' in your subject area have to say about it? You will need this information (a) to develop and support your own views, and (b) to demonstrate to your readers that you are aware of such previous work in your field. Always include references. This will help you to clarify where your proposal fits in relation to the published literature and the extent to which you understand the current literature.

Proposed methodology

By what methods do you intend to collect and analyse your data? This is probably the longest section in your proposal and should include ideas about and assessment of access to (client) organizations and/or other sources of data. This section includes details of how you propose to carry out the research and justify your choice of methods. Try to consider any ethical issues which may arise when gathering or using data and explain how you will adhere to any ethical guidelines.

Anticipated problems

What difficulties do you expect to have to overcome in conducting your project? Is it going to be hard for you to gain access to the information, either primary or secondary, which you will need? If so, what can you do about it?

Outline of chapters

Give a brief summary of the contents of each of your proposed chapters. This will provide you with an outline plan to work to. You may have to make some changes as you obtain more information, but it is useful to create such a framework at the outset.

Expected duration

How long do you expect to take to complete your project? Think about and state as precisely as you can: the overall timescale; the target date for completion of your first two chapters; other deadlines which you intend to set yourself; when you expect your final draft to be ready; and the target date for completion of your project. This will help you to decide whether your proposal can be achieved in the given time frame. It is worth remembering that no matter how carefully you plan this stage, you will probably take longer to complete each section than you had planned to.

References

You don't need a long list of references here, but include a few key literature sources that you have referred to and that have informed and helped you to focus on your proposal.

CHAPTER 16
MAKING RESEARCH CREDIBLE

By the time you have finished your research project, the research you have done, the results you have obtained and the findings you have reported on will all have taken you a lot of time and effort, so you want to be sure that your reader will believe what you are writing and that your research is credible. Good research design reduces the number of potential alternative explanations in response to the research question. There are other points to consider, however, and we shall explore these in further detail in this section.

> ## CREDIBILITY
>
> Is the research trustworthy?
> Is the research believable?
> Are the researchers' conclusions supported for its findings?

ARGUMENT

The most straightforward way to rule out a potential threat to validity is to simply argue that the threat in question is not a reasonable one. Such an argument may be made either before the primary research or after, although the former will usually be more convincing than the latter. In most cases, ruling out a potential threat to validity by argument alone will be weaker than the other approaches listed in the following paragraphs. As a result, the most plausible threats in a research project should not be ruled out by argument alone, except in unusual cases.

MEASUREMENT OR OBSERVATION

In some cases, it will be possible to rule out a threat by measuring it and demonstrating that either it does not occur at all or that it occurs so minimally as to not present a strong alternative explanation for the relationship in question. Consider, for example, a study of the effects of the design of an advert on subsequent sales of a particular product. In such a study, history (the occurrence of other events which might lead to an increased desire to purchase the product) would be a plausible alternative explanation. For example, a change in the local economy, the removal of a competing product from the market, or similar events could cause an increase in product sales. You might attempt to minimize such threats by measuring local economic indicators and the availability and sales of competing products. If there is no change in these measures at the onset of the advertising campaign, these threats would be considerably minimized. Similarly, if one is studying the effects of web technologies training on design students, it might be useful to speak to the students themselves to verify that they were not having any additional training to that provided in the study.

DESIGN

Here, the major emphasis is on ruling out alternative explanations by adding treatment or control groups, waves of measurement as well as observations.

Research objective	Appropriate design
To gain background information, to define terms	
To clarify problems and hypothesis, to establish research priorities	EXPLORATORY
To describe and measure phenomena at a point in time	DESCRIPTIVE
To determine 'causality' to make 'if-when' decisions	CAUSAL

ANALYSIS

There are a number of ways to rule out alternative explanations using statistical analysis. The plausibility of alternative explanations might be minimized using co-variance analysis. For example, in the study of the effects of the built environment on productivity, one plausible alternative explanation might be the status of local economic conditions. This could be statistical analysis, but it could be sufficient to discuss the economic conditions as an alternative explanation. Here, it might be possible to construct a measure of economic conditions and to include that measure as a covariate in the statistical analysis. One must be careful when using co-variance adjustments of this type; 'perfect' covariates do not exist in most social research within the creative industries, as they would inevitably involve human beings. The use of imperfect covariates will not completely adjust for potential alternative explanations. Nevertheless, causal assertions are likely to be strengthened by demonstrating that treatment effects occur even after adjusting on a number of good covariates.

PREVENTATIVE ACTION

When potential threats are anticipated, they can often be ruled out by some type of preventative action. If the programme is a desirable one, it is likely that the comparison group would feel jealous or demoralized. For example, you are able to put one section of organizational actors in a newly refurbished building, but the other section remains in the old run-down existing building. Several actions can be taken to minimize the effects of these attitudes, including offering the possibility of relocation to the comparison group upon completion of the study; or by using programme and comparison groups that have little opportunity for contact and communication.

The categories listed above should not be considered mutually exclusive. The inclusion of measurement, designed to minimize threats to validity, will obviously be related to the design structure and is likely to be a factor in the analysis. A good research plan should, where possible, make use of multiple methods for reducing threats. In general, reducing a particular threat by design or preventative action will probably be more effective than by using argument after the research project is completed.

TABLE 2.1

OUTCOMES OF YOUR RESEARCH

		Is the research relevant to a defined problem in your field?	
		YES	NO
Does the research follow a defined and justified research design?	YES	The results are relevant and credible	The result are not relevant but are credible
	NO	The results are relevant but not credible	The results are not relevant or credible

This table illustrates the overall credibility of your research project. This can be achieved with a simple check of whether or not you have followed a defined and justified research design; and by further checking the relevance of the defined problem to your field.

CHAPTER 17

THE INFLUENCE OF ETHICS

A number of ethical issues are likely to arise in both textual and visual research. This section discusses a number of key concepts that describe the system of ethical protections that contemporary research has created to try to protect the rights of research participants.

ETHICS, MORALITY AND LEGALITY

We all have a moral outlook, governing how we behave and how we determine what is right and wrong. Our moral outlook is shaped by our experiences and interactions with others. Nevertheless, society largely agrees on certain moral principles about right and wrong (such as justice and fairness), even though there is considerable disagreement about the application of these principles to particular circumstances and contexts.

Ethical approaches and frameworks are the application of key moral norms (or principles). Ethical behaviour in research requires that you, as a researcher, engage with moral issues of right and wrong. To do this, frameworks draw on ethical principles identified by the research community within which your project is situated. For the purposes of this discussion, ethics and morals can be seen as interchangeable.

The specific ethical issues that you will identify in your research are informed by your own moral understanding of ethics (so they can be understood as ethical issues or moral issues). You are likely to be able to identify some pertinent ethical issues before starting your research, but many are emergent and only become apparent once you are involved in the research project.

You need to resolve these issues in accordance with your moral beliefs, but also in ways that are in accordance with established ethical standards. Ethical decision making is also strongly influenced by ethical and legal regulation. You need to conform to legal regulation; and although ethical regulation does not carry such weight, you are generally obliged to comply

Figure 2.4 Principles

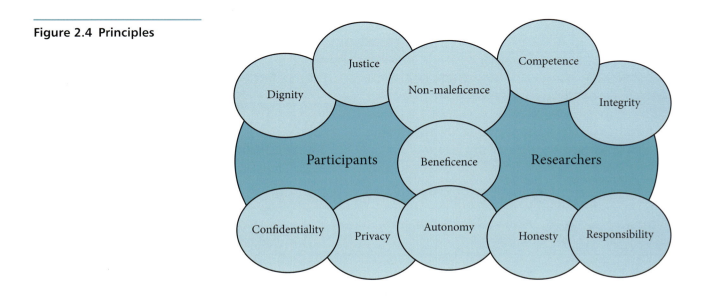

with ethical regulations and guidelines from your university. Conforming to ethical or legal regulation is not necessarily the same as conforming to ethical (or moral) behaviour; compliance with regulation in many contexts is often the minimum requirement and ethical behaviour demands more careful consideration of the issues involved.

POWER AND ETHICS

Within design research there is also the added burden of whether the principle of informed consent is always appropriate when dealing with the ethical implications of relationships with research participants in the field of design. Of course there are occasions when it is, if, for example, we ask fellow students to participate in our primary research but we are within a commercial setting. In that case the relationships between researchers and their participants are often characterized by a power imbalance that favours the research subject rather than the researcher.

Managers, perhaps your own manager, could have a high social status and may well be able to exert power in the organizational setting by defining access boundaries and setting expectations regarding output from a student project from which they may benefit.

As a design researcher you can often be in a weaker bargaining position, from which you must secure and may need to offer something in exchange (for example access to the data that has been gathered). The principle of informed consent can often make it difficult to gain understanding of groups that do not want to be studied, such as top designers or artists. An organization may also determine what may be considered to be a legitimate focus of study, by employing systematic screening devices that ensure their protection from the effects of research. This can be observed in relation to the increasing tendency for companies to ask researchers to sign confidentiality agreements restricting what information can be disclosed about them.

ANONYMITY IN ETHICS

When you are planning on setting up interviews you will need to consider that as a researcher in design you may face increasing pressure to protect the confidentiality

and anonymity of research participants in order to avoid harmful effects such as victimization. For example, in notes to contributors for some journals, authors are informed that they are required to protect the identity of research participants by 'using pseudonyms' and 'removing any information leading to identification of any of the individuals described in the study'.

Although confidentiality and anonymity are often treated as overlapping concepts, there are important differences between them; confidentiality relates to the protection of information supplied by research participants from other parties whereas anonymity involves protecting the identity of an individual or organization by concealing their names or other identifying information. The protection of anonymity is a particular issue for researchers in design because it is not clear from many ethics codes whether this ethical principle applies to the organization as well as individual research participants. If the organizational identity must also be concealed this has far-reaching implications since many design schools want to verify the identity of the organization as a means of confirming it as an illustration of realistic practice. The universal requirement to protect the identity of individual research participants also has implications for the type of research that can be done and the way findings are disseminated. An argument can be made for the lesser protection of the identity of certain individuals such as company leaders and politicians because their roles necessarily take them into the public domain. There may also be instances where research participants do not wish to remain anonymous because making their identity explicit is an important way of retaining ownership of their stories (Grinyer, 2002).

Many types of qualitative research do not enable anonymity during the data-collection stage: for example, in network studies the researcher must know who the respondent is in order to analyse their relationships with other respondents (Borgatti and Molina, 2003). The need for individual anonymity also has implications for what can be revealed about an organization. In a single ethnographic case study it is extremely difficult to protect the identity of individual research participants unless a significant amount of detail relating to the organization is changed. In some cases there may be a sound legal reason for making the organization unidentifiable, to protect the researcher, their employing university and the publisher from legal action (see Cavendish, 1982). However, sometimes the meaning of a case cannot adequately be conveyed without reference to its identifying features, including geographical location, corporate history and brand image.

To summarize, researchers in design have a responsibility to declare affiliations or potential conflicts of interest, including those relating to management consultancy that have a commercial value, or any private business interests that may potentially influence the outcomes of research.

ETHICS IN TEXT AND VISUAL RESEARCH

A range of approaches can help you to think through any ethical challenges you may be faced with. The most common approaches are consequentialist, non-consequentialist and principalist. A consequentialist approach is based on ethical decisions as consequences of specific actions. From this viewpoint, an action is seen as morally right if it produces the greatest balance of good over evil. Using a consequentialist approach, you would predict the outcome of a decision and decide on an action that you believe would result in the most beneficial outcome. For example, you might argue that it would be acceptable to undertake covert visual research if your findings could be seen as benefiting 'design against crime'.

> Ethics is knowing the difference between what you have a right to do and what is right to do.
>
> — Potter Stewart

If you use a non-consequentialist approach, you would argue that you only consider the end product of that action and not the consequences of it. If you adopt a non-consequentialist approach you might, for example, argue that it is morally right to keep a secret – even if the consequences of doing so may be damaging. Non-consequentialist approaches are related to principalist approaches, which are based on the principles of: respect for autonomy; beneficence; non-maleficence; and justice. Respect for autonomy relates to issues of voluntariness, informed consent, confidentiality and anonymity. Beneficence is concerned with the responsibility to do good; non-maleficence concerns the responsibility to avoid harm; and justice concerns the importance of the benefits of the research being distributed equally.

People using principalist approaches make ethical decisions on the basis of these specific principles. Each of these principles is viewed as important, but it is recognized that they may conflict with each other and that in such cases it is necessary to make a case for why one might need to be chosen over another. The principle of respect for autonomy may present considerable difficulties for visual researchers in relation to confidentiality and anonymity.

While the specific ethical approach that you adopt in your research guides your ethical decision making, it is recognized that research is contextual and that the specific dilemmas that arise are unique to the context in which your individual project is conducted. Some researchers have argued that decisions about ethical dilemmas cannot be reached by appeal to higher principles and codes, and that researchers have to approach each ethical challenge within the unique context in which they are working.

In a practical sense, this means that people should knowingly and voluntarily participate; and this is especially relevant where researchers had previously relied on 'captive audiences' for their participants (in universities, for example). Prospective research participants must be fully informed about the procedures and risks involved in research and must give their informed consent before participating. Ethical standards also require that researchers do not put participants in a situation where they might be at risk of harm as a result of their participation (harm can be defined as both physical and psychological).

You also need to protect the privacy of research participants. Almost all research guarantees the participants' confidentiality – they are assured that identifying information will not be made available to anyone who is not directly involved in the research. It may also be necessary to guarantee anonymity, which essentially means that the participant will remain anonymous throughout the study, even to the researchers themselves. Clearly, the anonymity standard is a stronger guarantee of privacy, but it is sometimes difficult to accomplish, especially in situations where participants have to be measured at multiple points in time (a pre-post study, for example).

Increasingly, researchers have had to deal with the ethical issue of a person's right to service. Good research practice often requires the use of a no-treatment control group – a group of participants who do not get the attention of the group that is being studied. But when that research may have beneficial effects, persons assigned to the non-attention control may feel that their rights to equal access to services are being curtailed.

ETHICS IN VISUAL RESEARCH

This section outlines the key ethical issues which visual researchers need to consider when undergoing research using photographs, film and video images. Prosser and Loxley (2008) have identified four different types of visual data: 'found data'; 'researcher-created data'; 'respondent-created data'; and 'representations'. Visual data includes photographs, film, video, drawings, advertisements or media images, sketches, graphical representations and models created by a range of creative media. It is because these media produce identifiable images that ethical dilemmas can occur. The issues identified relate to consent for the collection and dissemination of visual material, and to the importance of consent, both to participation and to the ways and forms by which the visual data will be used. Written consent for the use of images that identify individuals is preferable, as it provides an opportunity for study participants to see the visual data collected on them and to reflect on its proposed use.

It is important to consider carefully how research will be disseminated over the internet and researchers need to be cautious in making judgements about the well-being of online research participants. Caution is also advised in relation to covert research which, because of the ethical and legal issues it poses, is deemed as necessary only in 'certain circumstances'. Visual research is subject to a number of legal considerations that relate to both the taking of images (photos or film) and the use to which those images are subsequently put. There is a close relationship between law and ethics, but not everything that is legal is ethical. Frequently, law only sets the minimum acceptable standard. The

aspirations of ethical practice are higher and it can never be appropriate to defend proposed practice solely on the basis that it is legal.

CONSENT ISSUES

Informed consent is a central principle in ethical research. Researchers can easily hide from public view when taking photos; they can use strategies that conceal the subject of the photograph, or devices, such as a telephoto lens, that enable photos to be taken from a distance. Such covert or clandestine photography or film research is considered by many as both unethical and as intellectually limiting, given that it often only provides a very limited understanding of people's views and experiences, which are central to much visual research.

Although many visual researchers may not condone covert research, they might question whether it is always necessary to obtain consent from people who are the subject of photographs. If you are taking images of groups of people in public spaces, or at events, it is not practical, or indeed necessary, to obtain consent. However, when taking images of identifiable individuals (whether in public or private spaces), or of people in private spaces or organizations where people might reasonably expect not to be photographed or filmed, then it is polite and good ethical practice to seek consent, as well as being in the interests of obtaining good data. Visual researchers identify the importance of developing relationships of mutual trust with participants, so that images taken emerge from collaborations between researcher and participant and are jointly co-owned.

Figure 2.5 The fundamentals

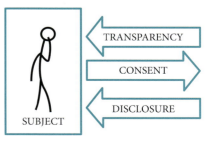

Consent means permission to take or make visual images, but also to use images subsequently. In the collaborative mode of working, consent to take and to use images entails the express agreement of the individual(s) concerned. Some researchers might view initial consent to cover both consent for making images and for their use; others might view these as things that have to be negotiated separately. In some cases, when visual data is being obtained for illustrative purposes, or when general, but not specific, consent has been given, a verbal request before photographing or filming may be appropriate.

This might simply entail asking if an individual objects to having their image taken and explaining the purpose of taking the image. In other situations, for example when conducting ethnographic work within a community, written consent (or consent recorded by some other means) after extensive discussion is necessary. This discussion should involve explaining the purposes of the research to participants in detail, the images that it is anticipated will be taken, the process of consent for obtaining and using specific images, and the plans for dissemination. Once detailed consent is obtained, researchers may still choose (with participants' agreement) to take photographs or film without participants' awareness so that 'natural' images might be obtained.

With the increase in ethical regulation, there has been a significant move to the use of signed consent forms for research participants. Signed consent forms are viewed as a means to safeguard researchers, to make issues of consent clear to research participants and to ensure attention to issues of copyright. However, using signed consent forms does not negate the necessity of explaining the research to potential participants and the reasons why their consent is being sought. Equally, signed consent does not give researchers the right to use images in unrestricted ways. Often, it is the case that consent forms are used at various different points during the research process as the need for specific visual data or the significance of particular images emerges.

THINK BOX
Issues of feasibility

Very soon after you get an idea for your research project, you begin to wonder whether or not you can do it. Is it feasible? This section discusses the issues that you will need to consider before starting your research project.

Rigour and practicality

There are several major considerations and many of these involve making compromises somewhere between rigour and practicality. To do a research project well, you may have to control the implementation of your project more carefully than you otherwise might. Or, you may have to ask participants lots of questions that you usually wouldn't if you weren't doing research. If you had unlimited resources and control over the circumstances, you would always be able to do the best quality research. But those ideal circumstances seldom exist, and researchers are almost always forced to look for the best trade-offs they can find in order to operate with the rigour they desire.

Is it feasible?

There are several practical considerations that almost always need to be considered when deciding on the feasibility of a research project. First, you have to think about how long the research will take to accomplish. Second, you have to question whether there are important ethical constraints that need consideration. Third, can you achieve the needed cooperation to take the project to its successful conclusion? Fourthly, how significant are the costs of conducting the research? Failure to consider any of these factors can mean disaster later on in the project.

CHAPTER 18

THE PRACTICE: A WELL-STRUCTURED RESEARCH PROJECT

This case study is an example of how a well-structured research framework can enable you to focus and achieve depth in your project. It is also an example of a project which uses only secondary data. This project used an extensive literature review to gather, analyse and synthesize material from various fields, achieving an in-depth critique of the literature and gleaning relevant material in order to answer the research question. This project demonstrates the extensive debates that take place about the use of different paradigms and methods, and how an understanding of the effects these debates have on research outcomes is an important part of the research process. This is an abbreviated version of Aly Rhodes' Masters-level dissertation.

CAN VISUAL COMMUNICATIONS CHANGE THE WORLD?

Can visual communications change the world? This is a complex question dealing with the philosophical, economic, political, social and personal, which aims to find a humanitarian position for graphic design. This investigation uses secondary data to investigate the broad range of issues that relate directly to the activities and strategies of graphic design. It focuses on the part that graphic designers play in the maintenance of consumerism and explores the phenomena of desire, wants and needs. It discusses political dissent that has arisen within the visual communications field; and explores strategic capability – most specifically, how the purpose of an organization determines its potential.

Corporate social responsibility practice shows that there is much to be gained from considerate design business. Social enterprise that focuses on social returns, not financial returns, offers alternative routes for graphic designers to marry personal values with career aspirations and concern for other human beings, by working collaboratively across disciplines to raise human potential.

Participatory design practices play a crucial role in this research as a way of empowering and facilitating social change. Communications design in particular has great political and social potential because of its ability to shape how knowledge and information is communicated.

When design is broken down to its lowest common denominator, and where human respect forms the basis of creative action, quality-of-life improvement for both individuals and communities is possible. The positive empowering changes that can be made in people's lives and the impact that these have in the world contribute to how we as humanity prosper.

BACKGROUND

This research inquiry is based on the current state of knowledge in visual communications, and relates to my chosen subject areas. Data presented here spans the last thirty years, but is mainly concentrated in the last ten. Most design research and practice has addressed design in terms of the added value that it can bring to business; through design thinking and processes that bring returns on investment. Alternatively, it is viewed in terms of style, artistic finesse or individual talent – how 'good' something looks.

PURPOSE

This research aims to explore graphic design from a humanist perspective. It attempts to show that the real value of visual communications is not commercial, nor to do with self-expression, but rather to do with how it can be used to facilitate quality-of-life improvement. Aside from this research being part of the fulfilment criteria for the academic programme, my main purpose was to expand my own personal knowledge, in order to better my theoretical understanding of an area within which I practise. To discover what other people think about visual communications and how/if they think it can facilitate, empower and change lives. Greater personal understanding will help me to refine my skills as a visual communicator, design director or manager.

KEYWORDS

Design participation, political and personal agency, user-, consumer- and people-centred/centred design, design democracy, popular and mass culture, social entrepreneurism/enterprise, ethical advertising.

ASSUMPTIONS

All human beings are born free and equal in dignity and rights. They are endowed with reason and conscience and should act towards one another in a spirit of brotherhood [or sisterhood]. (Article 1, Universal Declaration of Human Rights, 1948)

Communications design is a powerful tool due to the integral part it plays in all human relations.

A designed message … possesses great potential for affecting viewers … [it] can inspire a behavioural change … by generating knowledge, taking action or creating an experience. (Forlizzi and Lebbon, 2002)

While some people may have more talent than others, everybody has some ability to design.

Design, as a structured creative process, is an important competitive tool for firms in many sectors … . Design can enhance non-price characteristics,

improving quality and creating niche markets … formal design activities are also important for marketing, company image and brand loyalty. They can also impact on production costs and overall firm productivity … . Consumers benefit from greater variety and improved products and services. (DTI/BERR, 2005)

Design is a valuable business resource in meeting the demands of other businesses and consumers.

We are driven to seek happiness not by acquiring things that are useful, but by surrounding ourselves with signs that we are fulfilled. This is a situation perpetuated by the people who produce the objects [designers] … by adding meaning in the way they are advertised or shown in style magazines and celebrity features. (Davis and Baldwin, 2006)

An economic framework for the human condition is inadequate.

AIMS AND OBJECTIVES

The overarching aim of this research is exploratory. Since I was not aware of much research in my chosen area, I began searching to extend my knowledge. I have broken the question down into precise statements of intent to describe more specifically the areas of concern that I feel answer the research question. They require me to

- Uncover who constitutes the graphic design sector, what they do and how they fit into society and the economy
- Explore the difference between needs, wants and desires
- Investigate the extent to which visual communications meets a socially responsible agenda
- Look at graphic designers' personal and political reactions to the market, consumerism and social responsibility

LITERATURE REVIEW

I did an extensive literature review on the subject of value in graphic design, to discover criteria (other than purely financial), that visual communications can use to add value. My main findings were that

- In the management of design, the value that design offers is usually considered to mean financial value.
- Corporate social responsibility is a growing concern for design businesses.
- Design is already delivering to some extent on a socially responsible agenda.
- The form that corporate governance takes in turn shapes the way that strategy considers its stakeholders.
- Value concerns a range of behaviours and understandings that include individual morals, business ethics, state and universal laws.
- There has been some political reaction against consumerism by the graphic design profession, which has the support of major industry players.
- Participation is an excellent source of achieving appropriate design solutions.
- Socially inclusive design broadens accessibility and works to ensure inclusivity.
- Graphic design provides impressive social returns.

I have included some of the data found in that report in the literature review section of this research, along with additional data relating to the issues under investigation.

DESIGN

This investigation tackles the research question in an exploratory way. The issues related to my inquiry are presented as a literature review dissertation. Investigation is based on secondary data (books, reports, articles, video, websites and other online academic resources). Using these sources, I have attempted to show how theory relates to my argument and to recommend routes for improvement.

Until recently, there has been a distinct lack of philosophical writing about graphic design with specific regard to anything other than 'aesthetics, form and function' (Heller, 2006). I have used secondary data drawn from a small, but growing bank of knowledge to support my thinking.

My subject matter is complex, and cuts across many fields: ideology, design, consumerism, strategy

and social responsibility. I have looked to provide a broad and balanced picture of the current situation by presenting credible knowledge from reputable sources as, ultimately, doing so adds credibility to my own research.

I have been openly writing from day one of my inquiry. It has been an iterative process of refining and redefining. I have asked myself 'why am I doing this?' a thousand times. I took notes as I read the books and articles, ensuring that all citations and bibliographical details were accurately logged. I simultaneously searched, read, assessed, compared, analysed, wrote, categorized, made connections, revised and refined during my research. Throughout my investigations, I constantly asked myself questions about relevance, and about the strengths and weaknesses of the data that I found.

I also kept a diary of my own personal progress. It helped me to understand how I fitted into the whole scheme of (graphic design) things – and to frame the issues in my mind. I had long conversations with myself about how best to present the literature review. I eventually decided to present it in an order that I believe introduces each topic sequentially, in a way that best frames my argument. I believe that I have presented a thorough overview of current knowledge relating to my inquiry, which supports this investigation.

PARADIGM

A paradigm is a philosophical way of interpreting social data. Business and management research (tends to) use four paradigms from social theory, each of which indicates different ways of examining and explaining social phenomena in research. They are intended to clarify assumptions about how science and nature are viewed. By breaking the question down, the various elements can be successfully investigated using any of these paradigms. This inquiry cuts across radical humanist and radical structuralist paradigms because it looks to make sense of 'value-laden/subjective' data from individual sources to identify cultural and individual meanings; as well as exploring relationships and patterns of conflict/ dysfunction between the issues under investigation, and the frameworks within which they exist.

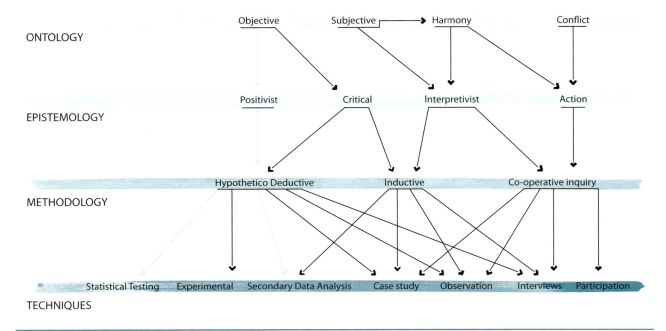

Figure 2.6 Research map

This diagram illustrates the interrelationships between ontology, epistemology and methodology and details the fundamental positions these are characterized by.

RESEARCH ONTOLOGY

Metaphysics is an area of philosophy that explores the big human issues. It deals with 'reality' principles beyond what empirical science can readily explain. Ontology, as part of metaphysics, is concerned with the way the world works and what makes things 'real'. It could be described as the study of 'being'. There are two commonly held views of reality, as outlined below.

Objectivism maintains that we, as individuals, exist within a reality that is external to and independent of us. Absolute laws and universal truths govern our 'being'. These 'natural' laws are considered fairly constant and reliable over time.

Subjectivism states that we create a world around us, through our perceptions and social interactions, which give meaning to reality. This view maintains that the world is in a state of constant flux, because that is the nature of individuals, and the contexts within which we operate.

Since these views are clearly in opposition, it is difficult to reason how either can provide the totality of knowledge and capture the entirety of such enormous questions as 'what is real?'. Nor can I say that I believe the truth is inside or outside of our own beings. I am inclined, therefore, to take a pragmatic view of how

reality is and assume that aspects of both perspectives can uncover valuable information. This is similar to Nietzsche's 'perspectivist' view. The wider the perspective, the broader the understanding.

RESEARCH EPISTEMOLOGY

So, what do I consider acceptable knowledge? What is important and useful in answering my research question? There are three main ways to answer these questions. I shall deal first with positivism.

Positivist views are generally held by natural scientists. It holds that reality is deduced from what can be readily shown to produce patterns and predictable behaviours, according to established laws. The truth is measured quantitatively, and labels are applied to individual elements and governing systems. Reality is represented by objects, facts and tangible data. This reality has a separate existence from oneself. Positivists take an objective viewpoint and this approach is considered as the least biased by 'science'. Research is based on observable and measurable reality.

Positivism asserts that only what you can see and touch is real. It uses existing theories to generate hypotheses for investigation. These hypotheses can be confirmed or refuted in the development of further theory. Positivism attempts to discover 'independent' and 'value-free' research, external to the process of data collection, so that replication of experiments can withstand statistical analysis. While 'independent, value-free' information is what I'm looking for, this is not really a suitable philosophy to use to investigate my question, as it does not offer a wide enough perspective. Cold, hard facts are not what I am looking to find.

Since social science thinking guides much of this research, I will look next at the possibility of using interpretivism to search for an answer to my question.

Interpretivism

Interpretivism takes the view that truth is constructed through an understanding of the meanings that individuals apply to phenomena in a socially constructed world. This view collects qualitatively and uses an inductive approach to theory. Unlike positivism, interpretivism believes that being able to generalize is not important, but that it is the context within which the phenomena occurs that demonstrates reality pertinent to each specific situation.

Reality is represented by subjective perception and the understanding of individual differences. Today, interpretive narrative is considered as equally relevant as positivist statistics. Interpretivism argues that insights into the complex world of business are lost in the generalized and rigid laws and theories of positivism. The researcher, often part of the data-collection process, aims to understand individual sense-making and our roles as 'social actors' in the world.

Interpretivism is based on phenomenological psychology and symbolic interactionism. Phenomenology is a humanist reaction to the dehumanizing techniques of behaviourism. The emphasis is on personal experience, not observable behaviour. It appreciates how each person's perception of the same experience is unique and that they determine individual expectations, attitudes, actions and reactions towards others (McKenna, 2006). Symbolic interactionism describes a continuous process of interpreting the world through others' actions, which affects our own meanings, actions and reactions. This philosophy can certainly lend understanding and meaning to my research question, since

its focus is human. However, since this perspective does not consider that which is beyond individual actors and their direct experiences in the world, it may be difficult to fully answer my question using only this paradigm. I believe that there is also something bigger, outside of human meaning or sense, which frames, controls and sets boundaries within which the social world and individuals exist.

Critical realism

Direct realism sees the scientific collection and understanding of data as developing from the belief that objects have an existence independent of the human mind (this is also true of positivism). This is in opposition to idealism, where the mind and its contents are believed to create the whole truth. In direct realism, 'What you see is what you get; what we experience through our senses portrays the world accurately' (Saunders, 2011). This perspective does not show the full picture though, as things are not always as they seem. Certainly, social and psychological factors cannot be 'measured' in this way.

Bhaskar (1989) states that we can only understand what is going on in the world if we understand the social structures that frame the phenomena which we encounter. The remainder – what we don't see – can be explained through social science theory (mental processing and social conditioning).

Critical realism believes that there are two steps to be taken when we experience the world. First, there is the sensory data that every object emits. Our experiences of this data produce individual interpretations. The second step involves the mental processes that we use to make sense of that data. Critical realists believe that both of these steps are essential to make complete sense of the world.

Critical realism recognizes the importance of the individual, group (including organizations) and society as impacting on the phenomena that we observe. It takes a view that entities (people included) are affected by the 'unseen' mechanisms in the bigger framework. Structures, procedures and processes interact to form our understanding. Causal mechanisms within this framework operate on social and real 'objects', and affect how things appear. I believe critical realism is the best epistemological outlook for this research.

APPROACH

The approach taken in answering the research question affects the process of the research. Considerations here are to do with whether theory is deduced or induced, or whether a combination of both is considered useful.

Deduction (posteriori – testing theory)

This is the approach most often used by positivists. Knowledge is gained from 'experience'. Predictions are made, hypotheses or proposals are shaped and experiments are conducted which attempt to prove or disprove. It is based on accepted scientific laws and natural patterns. 'The principle of reductionism is followed' (Saunders, 2011). Strict controls are used in an attempt to ensure that the same experiment can be repeated by anybody at any time, and achieve similar results. Deductive approaches attempt to generate truths that can be generalized, by deducing theory from results obtained. 'Deduction possesses several important characteristics. First is the search to explain causal relationships between variables. [And the notion that] in order to pursue the principle of scientific rigour … the researcher should be independent of what is being observed' (Saunders, 2011). My approach is deductive since I have set a question which presupposes that design can change the world, and I go about collecting information in ways that could be repeated by anyone, to find similar results.

Induction (priori – building theory)

This is an approach which sits in opposition to deduction. Here, theory is generated from investigation and no prior knowledge is required. Research is undertaken to 'make sense' of situations and phenomena. 'The result of this analysis would be the formulation of a theory' (Saunders, 2011). Theory follows data collection. It does not precede it. This form of research is particularly concerned with the context within which research takes place. It is a much more flexible way of generating knowledge than deduction.

GATHERING DATA

Research for this project began with investigations I undertook for a previous project. I used Athens to gain access to academic databases (tertiary sources). Generally speaking, there were no data access problems. However, there is a twelve-month delay in the release of some data. As a consequence, some of the most recent knowledge was unavailable through my university subscription.

Secondary data

Secondary data is a good information source as it is available in abundance. I have used secondary data to answer my research question. Some of the secondary data that I collected previously is used in this project. Secondary data can be drawn from a selection of sources, via tertiary indexes online and in libraries. Peer-reviewed journals hold the most credibility as they have a theoretical basis, and are evaluated by academic peers. They are published regularly so are current and easily accessible. Due to the rigorous approach of most academic inquiry, they are least likely to contain inconsistencies and inaccuracies. For the purposes of my research, I will use qualitative data as my main source. Qualitative data can come from printed sources: books, journals, newspapers, websites and interview transcriptions. It can also be drawn from unwritten material such as digital video, audio and imagery. One downside of printed materials is that they become outdated quicker than information that you can find on the web. Secondary data is generally of good quality, certainly of a higher quality than I could collect myself within the time frame available for this project. Investigations made over time by other researchers have allowed me to see how theory has developed with regard to my subject areas, and has been extremely helpful in shaping my understanding.

Tertiary data

The main tertiary sources I used through Athens were

- Blackwell
- Ebook
- EBSCO

- Emerald
- Gale
- JSTOR
- ProQuest
- Sage eReference
- Swetswise

AXIOLOGY

I acknowledge that this research is value-laden. First because its focus is human, and human beings are complex, value-ridden entities. Also, secondary data comprises many personal interpretations of the issues under investigation. And lastly, despite my best attempts to remain impartial, my own personal biases will inevitably play their part in interpreting and expressing that data.

ETHICS

Since I have not undertaken primary research, ethical issues are reduced as I did not have to consider the ethical treatment of participants. All data used was written by 'consenting' authors whose work already existed in the public domain. I have tried to ensure that all authors are represented fairly from their own perspectives. Where quantitative data is concerned, I have used credible sources and ensured accurate representation. Confidentiality was not an issue.

LIMITATIONS

I accept the limitations of this research in providing a broad overview of social phenomena. Due to the extent of the issues involved, it was difficult to delve too deeply into one particular area. For financial information, most data was drawn from the UK's Design Council. I feel, however, that this data is representative of the Western pattern of commercial design. Although I am working on a design-themed dissertation, I have decided not to use any imagery, as I believe it can create an imbalanced perception for the viewer – prioritizing some work over others of equal value and lending too much priority to imagery over narrative. I was over-enthusiastic in my data collection and note-taking and didn't keep a close eye on the word count. I was 'lost in a fog of data' (Berman Brown, 2006), which caused me editing problems about what to leave in and what to leave out. Unfortunately, some valid information was excluded because of word count restrictions.

CHAPTER 19
PRADEEP SHARMA ON THE CREATIVE INFLUENCE

In this section, Pradeep Sharma, provost at Rhode Island School of Design, discusses creativity and the creative influence. This section is based on a face-to-face interview and extracts from a paper. It gives a clear explanation of the creative influence and its value in studies of this nature. It can also be used to relate creativity to other fields.

WHAT ARE THE MAIN RESEARCH APPROACHES TO THE STUDY OF CREATIVITY?

There are generally four main approaches to creativity, which are dealt with individually or in combination. The first and oldest is the belief that creativity comes from God, and that we are empty vessels waiting for the Muse to pour the creative suggestion into us – the creative leap. The second tends to focus on natural abilities and personality traits, the effect of which is to encourage students to behave in certain pre-conceived ways. The third is socio-dynamic, which emphasizes the importance of the social and environmental factors surrounding the individual. Once again, the result is a tendency for students to behave in certain ways to encourage their own creativity. The fourth approach is the pragmatic generative approach, which encourages the use of new techniques.

HOW LONG HAVE WE BEEN STUDYING CREATIVITY?

The study of creativity has a long history; however, serious research into creativity, certainly from a

Western perspective, only really took place from the middle of the twentieth century. Many believe the trigger to be Guildford (1950), who in his APA Presidential Address challenged psychologists to pay attention to what he found to be a neglected but extremely important attribute in human behaviour – namely creativity.

The focus at the time was from a psychological and behavioural point of view. As knowledge and experience developed, other frameworks for research into creativity started to emerge. Prior to Guildford's plea, the earliest accounts of creativity were based on divine intervention. The creative person was seen as an empty vessel that a divine being would fill with inspiration. The individual would then pour out the inspired ideas. These mystical approaches dominated the study of creativity for thousands of years and still have a major influence today.

The psychodynamic approach can be considered the first major twentieth-century theoretical approach to the study of creativity. Based on the idea that creativity arises from the tension between conscious reality and unconscious drives, the psychoanalyst Sigmund Freud (1856–1939) proposed that writers and artists produce creative work as a way to express their unconscious wishes in a publicly acceptable manner. Later, the psychoanalytic approach introduced the concepts of adaptive regression and elaboration for the study of creativity (Kris, 1952). Adaptive regression, the primary process, refers to the intrusion of unmodulated thoughts in consciousness. These can occur during active problem solving, but often occur during sleep, intoxication from drugs, fantasies, daydreams or psychoses. Elaboration, the secondary process, refers to the re-working and transformation of primary processes through reality-oriented and ego-controlled thinking.

Soon after the emergence of the psychoanalytical approach, process models of creativity started to be developed. One of the earliest models of the creative process is attributed to Graham Wallas, based on the work of the mathematician Henri Poincaré. Wallas (1926) proposed that creative thinking proceeds through four phases.

The inclusion of incubation, followed by sudden illumination, in this popular model may explain why some people view creative thinking as a subconscious mental process that cannot be directed. Many other models further expanded on the theory of subconscious and uncontrollable events, and went on to present the theory that creative ideas emerge from a largely uncontrollable Darwinian process of random variation and natural selection.

In contrast to these models, Perkins (1981) argued that subconscious mental processes are behind all thinking and therefore play no extraordinary role in creative thinking. Just because we cannot fully describe our thought processes does not mean that we are not in control of them. Further, Perkins argues, just because random events play a part in some acts of creation, this should not be taken to imply that they are the only source of all of them. He coined the term 'ideate' to imply the subconscious and conscious generation of ideas. While some models still lean towards this magical process, the predominant models lean more towards the theory that novel ideas emerge from the conscious effort to balance analysis and imagination.

The systematic combination of techniques for directed creativity and techniques for analysis continues as a strong theme in several more recent models. In his APA address, Guildford (1950) proposed that creativity lies within all of us and can be measured with a psychometric approach, using paper-and-pencil tasks. Building on Guildford's work, Torrance (1974) developed the Torrance Tests of Creative Thinking. The predominance of the psychometric perspective is surprising considering the widely held belief that creativity is indefinable and un-measurable (Callahan, 1991; Khatena, 1982).

HOW CAN WE TEST FOR CREATIVITY?

Creativity tests tend to be of two types, those that involve cognitive-affective skills and those that attempt to tap a personality syndrome. The cognitive approach to creativity seeks to understand the mental representations and processes underlying creative thought. Finke, Ward and Smith (1992) proposed what they called the Geneplore model, according to which there are two main processing phases in creative thought: a generative phase and an exploratory phase. In the generative phase, the individual constructs mental representations that have properties promoting creative discoveries. In the exploratory phase, these properties are used to come up with creative ideas.

A number of mental processes may enter into these phases of creative invention, including the processes of retrieval, association, synthesis, transformation, analogical transfer and categorical reduction. Work in the social-personality approach has focused on personality variables, motivational variables and the sociocultural environment as sources of creativity.

Researchers such as Amabile (1983) and Eysenck (1993) have noted that certain personality traits often characterize creative people. These traits include independence of judgement, self-confidence, attraction to complexity, aesthetic orientation and risk taking. Proposals regarding self-actualization and creativity can also be considered within the personality tradition. According to Maslow (1968), boldness, courage, freedom, spontaneity, self-acceptance and other traits lead a person to realize their full potential. Focusing on the motivations behind creativity, a number of theorists have hypothesized the relevance of intrinsic motivation, need for order and the need for achievement, alongside other motives.

The most recent practitioner perspective has been taken up by pragmatics who have been keen to adopt a generative approach aimed purely at producing more and more ideas. This perspective has been of particular interest to business and management schools.

TOWARDS A SYSTEMIC VIEWPOINT

Most of the research into creativity has had the individual as its focus, and on how people can become more creative. In some reference frameworks, all the approaches and explanations have validity and there is plenty of data and evidence to support them. However, from an innovation point of view, they do not take into account the actual use or uptake of ideas.

More recent studies hypothesize that multiple components must converge for creativity to occur (Amabile, 1983; Csikszentmihalyi, 1988). Amabile (1983) describes creativity as the confluence of intrinsic motivation, domain-relevant knowledge and abilities, and creativity-relevant skills. The creativity-relevant skills include a cognitive style that involves coping with complexities and breaking one's mental set during problem solving; knowledge of heuristics for generating novel ideas; and a work style characterized by concentrated effort, an ability to set aside problems, and high energy.

Csikszentmihalyi (1988, 1996) takes a systems approach, choosing to highlight the interaction of individual, domain and field. An individual draws upon information in a domain and transforms or extends it via cognitive processes, personality traits and motivation. The field, consisting of people who control or influence a domain, evaluates and selects new ideas. The domain, a culturally defined symbol system, preserves and transmits creative products to other individuals and future generations.

Csikszentmihalyi (1996) further argues that if creativity is to have a useful meaning in management terms, it must refer to a process that results in an idea or a product that is recognized and adopted by others. The sole act of creation is not enough to be useful in a business sense. Creativity is not the product of single agents, but of social systems making judgements about the agent's offerings. The concept of creativity in a business sense has to be grounded in what the social system is willing to accept. It is therefore necessary for a creative idea or product to be accepted (Simonton, 1997).

Figure 2.7 The interaction of individual, domain and field
This diagram demonstrates how a systems approach can be adopted to show how individuals transform information in order to preserve and transmit new creative products to other individuals and future generations (Csikszentmihalyi, 1996).

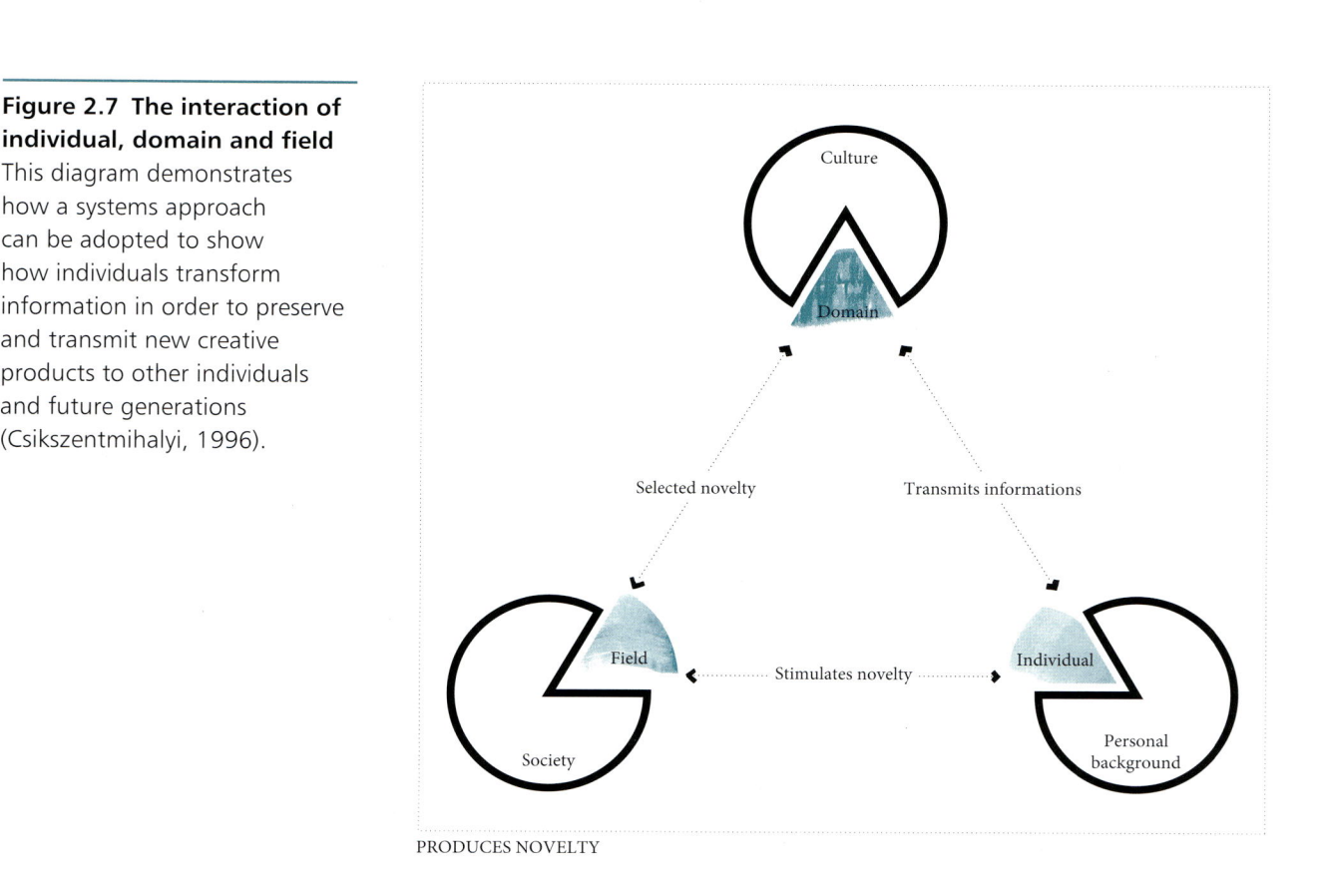

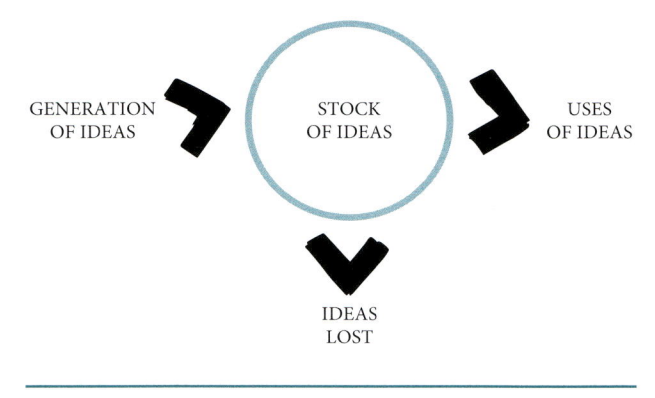

GENERATION OF IDEAS

STOCK OF IDEAS

USES OF IDEAS

IDEAS LOST

Figure 2.8 The design process gives form to ideas
This diagram illustrates how design is the process that gives form to ideas. The design process involves developing ideas into conceptual models and prototypes which may then be accepted or rejected by consumers and/ or society.

WHAT IS THE PURPOSE OF CREATIVITY?

If the purpose of creativity is to generate ideas, then we must not only look at the 'stock' of ideas but also where those ideas go and how they get there. For ideas to be used, they must be externalized and articulated to others for acceptance. Design is defined as the process that gives form to ideas. Hence, ideas are developed through a design process. In the process of design, ideas are generally developed into conceptual models, then prototypes, and later products which are accepted or rejected by the consumer/society. To complete the picture, these ideas, now embodied as products, diffuse into society where they go on to take on new meanings and functions perhaps different to those intended at the start of the design process.

WHY IS IT IMPORTANT TO UNDERSTAND CREATIVITY?

From a management perspective, an understanding of the dynamics at each stage is essential for innovation, especially if innovation is to be sustained over a period of time. For example, in terms of feedback, the use of ideas encourages creativity – nothing succeeds like success. Conversely, ideas getting lost, for whatever reasons, or not being captured, ignored or quashed is a

huge demotivator, which will also reinforce behaviour. The way that ideas are used is through a process of persuasion. Persuasion comprises the following components:

$$\text{Persuasion} = \text{communication} + \text{validation} + \text{acceptance} + \text{influence}$$

There are other factors which also come into play that have been omitted at this stage; these include timing, luck and so forth. Communication takes many forms and changes depending on at which stage it takes place. At the ideas/conceptual stage, the communication tends to be intangible and more metaphoric. It relies on the communication skills of the presenter, perhaps even on the theatre of presentation for the acceptance of the idea. At the prototype/ product stage, there is a tangible mediate in the form of a hard model which does a lot of the communication. When it gets to the product acceptance and diffusion stages, the communication changes once again to intangibles and storytelling. The validation and acceptance components include the traditional metric-based decision matrices, based on measurable facts.

However, they also have to take into account the intangibles, such as the vision and values of the people and the organization – what meaning does the idea have to those people? This starts to bring in concepts of mental models, capabilities, ethics and so forth. The influence component is about the sociopolitical nature of the decision-taking process. Generally, decisions are made not only about tangible facts but also on the basis of political issues, egos, politics and so forth. The fourfold division into self, others, things and systems is derived from the work of Boyatzis and Burgoyne on management competencies (Burgoyne 1989; see Figure 18, page 102).

Creativity looks at the aspects of knowledge creation with a study of the various perspectives on creativity. Teamwork or people management looks at the processes of knowledge sharing and addresses the issues covered above. Leadership, culture, vision, values, motivation and communication all form a major part of the curriculum. Technology looks at the tools and techniques for knowledge application.

It is believed that the teaching of creativity with an understanding of the supporting context or an

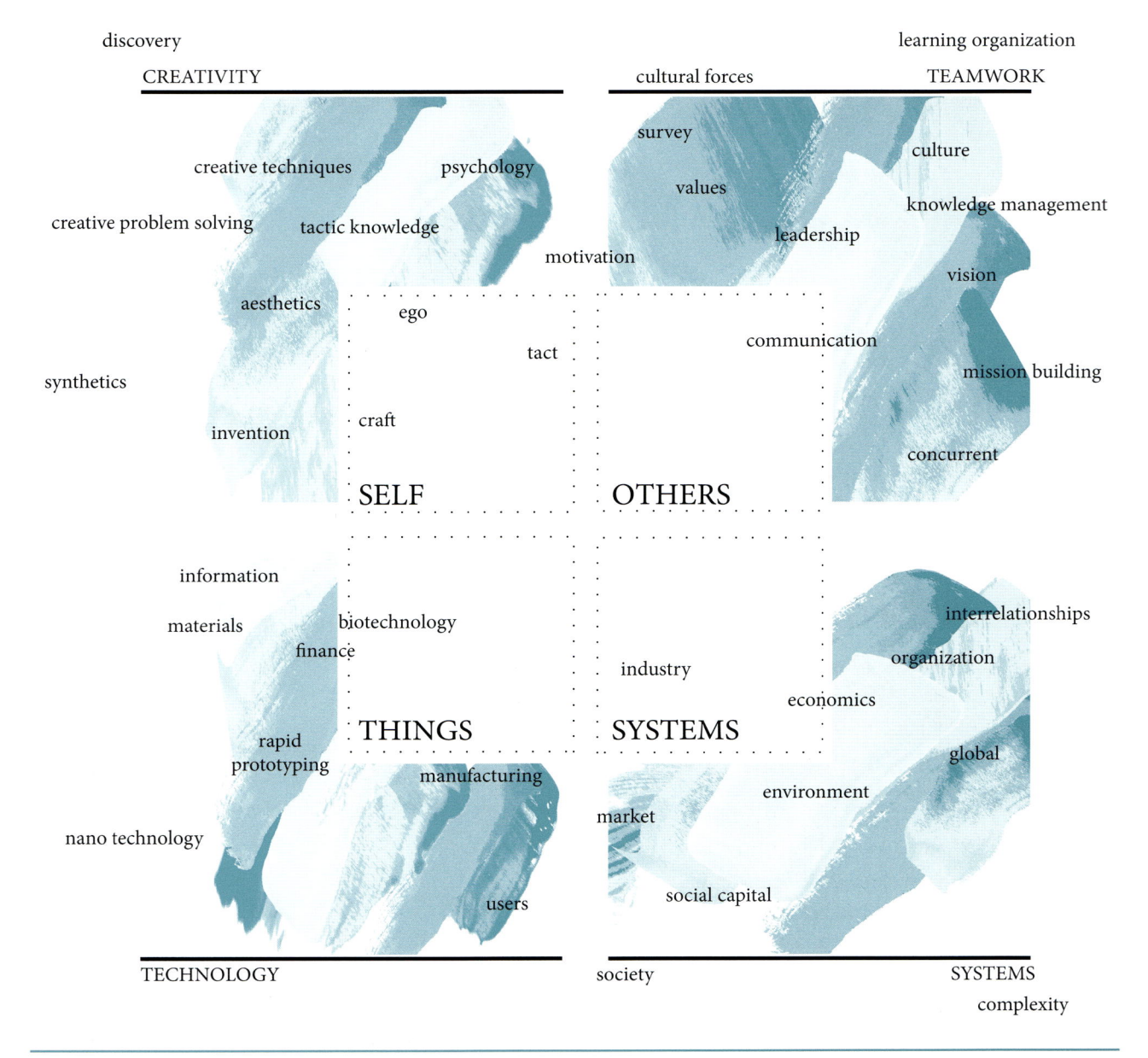

Figure 2.9 The fourfold division into self, others, things and systems
The fourfold division into self, others, things and systems is derived from the work of Boyatzis and Burgoyne on management competencies.

understanding of the willing market will help in the management of creativity and innovation. The supporting context provides an understanding of the individual and organizational competencies and capabilities, as well as of the aspirations and values; whereas the willing market indicates an understanding of the process of the ideas, concepts and products becoming accepted.

Creativity is the power to connect the seemingly unconnected

– William Plomer

Consent means permission to take or make visual images, but also to use images subsequently. In the collaborative mode of working, consent to take and to use images entails the express agreement of the individual(s) concerned. Some researchers might view initial consent to cover both consent for making images and for their use; others might view these as things that have to be negotiated separately. In some cases, when visual data is being obtained for illustrative purposes, or when general, but not specific, consent has been given, a verbal request before photographing or filming may be appropriate.

This might simply entail asking if an individual objects to having their image taken and explaining the purpose of taking the image. In other situations, for example when conducting ethnographic work within a community, written consent (or consent recorded by some other means) after extensive discussion is necessary. This discussion should involve explaining the purposes of the research to participants in detail, the images that it is anticipated will be taken, the process of consent for obtaining and using specific images, and the plans for dissemination. Once detailed consent is obtained, researchers may still choose (with participants' agreement) to take photographs or film without participants' awareness so that 'natural' images might be obtained.

With the increase in ethical regulation, there has been a significant move to the use of signed consent forms for research participants. Signed consent forms are viewed as a means to safeguard researchers, to make issues of consent clear to research participants and to ensure attention to issues of copyright. However, using signed consent forms does not negate the necessity of explaining the research to potential participants and the reasons why their consent is being sought. Equally, signed consent does not give researchers the right to use images in unrestricted ways. Often, it is the case that consent forms are used at various different points during the research process as the need for specific visual data or the significance of particular images emerges.

THINK BOX
Issues of feasibility

Very soon after you get an idea for your research project, you begin to wonder whether or not you can do it. Is it feasible? This section discusses the issues that you will need to consider before starting your research project.

Rigour and practicality

There are several major considerations and many of these involve making compromises somewhere between rigour and practicality. To do a research project well, you may have to control the implementation of your project more carefully than you otherwise might. Or, you may have to ask participants lots of questions that you usually wouldn't if you weren't doing research. If you had unlimited resources and control over the circumstances, you would always be able to do the best quality research. But those ideal circumstances seldom exist, and researchers are almost always forced to look for the best trade-offs they can find in order to operate with the rigour they desire.

Is it feasible?

There are several practical considerations that almost always need to be considered when deciding on the feasibility of a research project. First, you have to think about how long the research will take to accomplish. Second, you have to question whether there are important ethical constraints that need consideration. Third, can you achieve the needed cooperation to take the project to its successful conclusion? Fourthly, how significant are the costs of conducting the research? Failure to consider any of these factors can mean disaster later on in the project.

difficult to accomplish, especially in situations where participants have to be measured at multiple points in time (a pre-post study, for example).

Increasingly, researchers have had to deal with the ethical issue of a person's right to service. Good research practice often requires the use of a no-treatment control group – a group of participants who do not get the attention of the group that is being studied. But when that research may have beneficial effects, persons assigned to the non-attention control may feel that their rights to equal access to services are being curtailed.

ETHICS IN VISUAL RESEARCH

This section outlines the key ethical issues which visual researchers need to consider when undergoing research using photographs, film and video images. Prosser and Loxley (2008) have identified four different types of visual data: 'found data'; 'researcher-created data'; 'respondent-created data'; and 'representations'. Visual data includes photographs, film, video, drawings, advertisements or media images, sketches, graphical representations and models created by a range of creative media. It is because these media produce identifiable images that ethical dilemmas can occur. The issues identified relate to consent for the collection and dissemination of visual material, and to the importance of consent, both to participation and to the ways and forms by which the visual data will be used. Written consent for the use of images that identify individuals is preferable, as it provides an opportunity for study participants to see the visual data collected on them and to reflect on its proposed use.

It is important to consider carefully how research will be disseminated over the internet and researchers need to be cautious in making judgements about the well-being of online research participants. Caution is also advised in relation to covert research which, because of the ethical and legal issues it poses, is deemed as necessary only in 'certain circumstances'. Visual research is subject to a number of legal considerations that relate to both the taking of images (photos or film) and the use to which those images are subsequently put. There is a close relationship between law and ethics, but not everything that is legal is ethical. Frequently, law only sets the minimum acceptable standard. The

aspirations of ethical practice are higher and it can never be appropriate to defend proposed practice solely on the basis that it is legal.

CONSENT ISSUES

Informed consent is a central principle in ethical research. Researchers can easily hide from public view when taking photos; they can use strategies that conceal the subject of the photograph, or devices, such as a telephoto lens, that enable photos to be taken from a distance. Such covert or clandestine photography or film research is considered by many as both unethical and as intellectually limiting, given that it often only provides a very limited understanding of people's views and experiences, which are central to much visual research.

Although many visual researchers may not condone covert research, they might question whether it is always necessary to obtain consent from people who are the subject of photographs. If you are taking images of groups of people in public spaces, or at events, it is not practical, or indeed necessary, to obtain consent. However, when taking images of identifiable individuals (whether in public or private spaces), or of people in private spaces or organizations where people might reasonably expect not to be photographed or filmed, then it is polite and good ethical practice to seek consent, as well as being in the interests of obtaining good data. Visual researchers identify the importance of developing relationships of mutual trust with participants, so that images taken emerge from collaborations between researcher and participant and are jointly co-owned.

Figure 2.5 The fundamentals

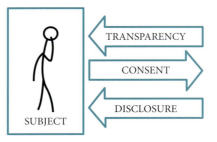

MANAGING THE RESEARCH PROCESS

This is the stage at which you will define your topic through your literature review and decide on which research tools you will use to answer your research question. This part of the book outlines how research tools from other disciplines might be used within the creative industries. The aim of this section is to introduce some of the wide array of tools available to you, and to provide some in-depth examples, by way of the practitioners section, of photo interviewing and action research.

CHAPTER 20
USING THE LITERATURE

We cannot really say what a literature review is, what it is for, where to put it, or whether to have one at all until we have explored the reasons why we might want to refer to what other researchers have said and done. There is also the issue of authority in research. What is it and do we need it? Here then, are three analogies to describe some of the ways in which literature can be used in research. Of course, some will blend into others and you may agree or disagree with them; but bear in mind that they can help to clarify what you might use literature for, what authority is and why we need it.

PHYSICAL ANALOGIES

Literature as a detective

In the earliest stages of research, we are detectives following trails and clues that we may only be partially familiar with. Some of these clues don't lead anywhere; others are so old that they are of no use, although they will help you to understand the context of your research. At this stage, literature can be used to find out where others have been before.

Literature as money

Literature reviews are expected to be up to date and worth something like money, and money has a value. A literature review can be evaluative, weighing up the strengths of previous work. Criticism, analysis and interpretation are all part of this evaluative element.

Literature as a foundation

Traditionally, the literature review has been described as a foundation from which you can start building your own work. This fits with the notion that you may be building on someone else's work and perhaps adding to an existing foundation of knowledge. If your project is not based on a tradition of scientific inquiry and is not based on what has been done before, you will need to ask yourself whether or not it is likely to be valued.

Literature as a framework

Research is expected to not only ask questions but to also address a problem. If certain questions have already been answered to everyone's satisfaction, or if a problem has essentially been solved, then we don't need to do it. We are expected to show what related questions and problems have been addressed, and why our own proposal is different. You may construct the literature review as a narrative of what you have done to date and provide an argument about what has not yet been researched in sufficient depth or what has not yet been dealt with. This will then form a framework for building a theoretical justification of your own project.

VISUAL ANALOGIES

Literature as a reflection

This is similar in some ways to 'literature as a detective' (for finding things out) and 'literature as a framework' (for seeing ourselves in context). If we look at our reflection, we see that both ourselves and the literature can be a way of comparing our ideas with others, and seeing how they are different or the ways in which they are similar. We can ask ourselves what we can learn about our own research project from our reactions to the literature.

Literature as a telescope

A telescope will help you to focus on something and the literature review can help you to focus on a problem, questions or justification for using particular methods. A telescope magnifies objects so that we can see them more clearly and in more detail. If we turn the telescope around, an object can look smaller than it really is – helpful sometimes, when one needs to regain a sense of proportion, and see how our own project fits into the bigger picture.

Literature as an arrow

When we are writing, we cannot describe everything; but by referencing appropriate sources we can guide our readers to find out more detailed information about subjects which are relevant, but perhaps not central, to our argument. It is a bit like following arrows on a road map that show you that the map only covers a certain area, and that there are lots of other interesting places you could explore if you had another map. These 'arrows' can also be useful for indicating where to find a fuller explanation of the arguments that might justify your writing, and so act as a form of shorthand.

Literature as a demonstration

Rather than generate new data by doing primary research, you may wish to present or support a claim by referring to particular examples from the literature to illustrate your point.

PERSONIFICATIONS

Literature as a magician

If you are able to speak knowledgeably of related literature and other people's work you can sometimes add weight to your own argument. Often it is a case of saying (or writing) that the reader should pay attention either because you know what you are talking (or writing) about or because other people have said (or written) about the same thing.

But this can also be a bit like a magician's act, making the audience look for authority in the wrong place by using the magician's assistant to distract you from what is really going on.

Literature as the expert

This is similar to 'literature as a magician', except that it can be positive because you may make a claim which could only realistically be accepted by reference to someone who has done a systematic study in that area (literature as a demonstration).

Literature as a guru

A guru is someone you can refer to throughout your research project and by using their knowledge you can dip into the literature through them. When you are writing up your final project, references to the literature will normally be found throughout the report. Using the literature as a guru or your supervisor as a literature guru may allow you to discover other relevant ideas worth exploring; or you may find inconsistencies in your own work or in that of others and so become aware of what you are or are not doing (literature as a reflection).

Literature as a voice

We don't need to believe that our idea is more important, just because someone who is better known and has more authority has already had the same idea. So why do we need to quote other people's work? Because someone else has said something just the way you would like to say it and they said it first; by attributing the quotation you show respect for the work of others and how it influences your own work.

CHAPTER 21
THE LITERATURE REVIEW

A literature review summarizes, interprets and evaluates existing 'literature' (or published material) in order to establish current knowledge of a subject. The purpose for doing so relates to ongoing research to develop that knowledge: the literature review may resolve a controversy, establish the need for additional research, and/or define a topic of inquiry. This section is intended as a guide which outlines the steps in preparing a literature review and assumes that a library search has been performed or is about to be performed.

WHY DO YOU NEED TO REVIEW THE LITERATURE?

Your review of the literature has the following functions:

- To justify your choice of research question, theoretical or conceptual framework, and method
- To establish the importance of the topic
- To provide background information needed to understand your research project
- To show readers you are familiar with significant and/or up-to-date research relevant to your chosen topic
- To establish your research project as one link in a chain of research that is developing knowledge in your field
- To avoid reinventing the wheel (at the very least this will save time and it can stop you from making the same mistakes as others)
- To identify other people working in the same fields (a researcher network is a valuable resource)
- To increase your breadth of knowledge of your subject area
- To identify seminal works in your area

- To provide the intellectual context for your own work, enabling you to position your project relative to other work
- To identify opposing views
- To put your work into perspective
- To demonstrate that you can access previous work in an area
- To identify information and ideas that may be relevant to your project
- To identify methods that could be relevant to your project

The review traditionally provides a historical overview of the theory and the research literature, with a special emphasis on the literature specific to your research project. It should also support your argument within your research project, using evidence drawn from authorities or experts in your research field.

WHAT SHOULD THE LITERATURE REVIEW INCLUDE?

The literature review can be given its own chapter, be embedded within the discussion chapter or be divided between a series of chapters on several topics.

The review needs to be shaped by a focus on key areas of interest, including research, which provides a background to the topic. It should also be selective, rather than commenting on everything you have read regardless of its relevance to your topic. The review should funnel down, starting wide with the overview and then quickly narrowing into discussing the research that relates to your specific topic. Another way of looking at the process, particularly if you are examining several topics (or variables), is to provide a solid sense of the background; then narrow down to introduce key figures and elements to be examined; then narrow down further to illustrate where the precise focus of your work is pinpointed.

'Literature' can include a range of sources:

- Journal articles
- Monographs
- Computerized databases
- Conference proceedings
- Dissertations
- Empirical studies
- Government reports and reports from other bodies
- Historical records
- Statistical handbooks

WHAT SHOULD THE LITERATURE REVIEW DO?

Your literature review should be used to set up a theoretical framework for your research and show your reader(s) that you have a clear understanding of the key concepts/ideas/studies/models related to your topic. It should also show that you know about the history of your research area and any related controversies, and that you can discuss these ideas in a context appropriate for your own research project. You can use this as an opportunity to evaluate the work of others and clarify important definitions and terminology. It should result in your narrowing the problem down, making the research project feasible.

Asking the following questions will help you to plan and draft your literature review:

- What has been done in my field of research?
- What principles of selection am I going to use?
- How am I going to order my discussion?
- Chronological, thematic, conceptual, methodological or a combination?
- What section headings will I use?
- How do the various studies relate to each other?
- What precise contribution do they make to the field?
- What are their limitations?
- How does my own research fit into what has already been done?
- Can I point out any gaps in the literature?

Points for guidance

Use direct quotations sparingly in your literature review because direct quotes often do not convey their full meaning without context; and quoting context is usually less efficient than paraphrasing the main idea(s) of the author. Frequent quotations may disrupt the flow of the review because of the varying writing styles of the authors. Quotations often bog the reader down in details that are not essential for the purpose of providing a literature overview. Try not to give too many details of the literature being cited, because the research is already published and the reader can obtain copies of any literature about which they wish to learn more details.

DISTINGUISHING SCHOLARLY JOURNALS FROM OTHER PERIODICALS

Journals and magazines are important sources for up-to-date information in all disciplines. You need to distinguish between the various levels of scholarship found in the periodical literature. These can fall into four categories:

- Scholarly
- Substantive news/general interest
- Popular
- Sensational

Scholarly

Scholarly journals generally have a sober, serious look. They often contain many graphs and charts, but few glossy pages or exciting pictures. Scholarly journals always cite their sources in the form of footnotes or bibliographies. Articles are written by a scholar in the field or by someone who has done research in the field. The language of scholarly journals is that of the discipline covered. It assumes some scholarly background on the part of the reader.

The main purpose of a scholarly journal is to report on original research or experimentation in order to make such information available to the rest of the scholarly world. Many scholarly journals, though by no means all, are published by a specific professional organization.

Substantive news or general interest

These periodicals may be quite attractive in appearance, although some are in newspaper format. Articles are often heavily illustrated, generally with photographs. News and general interest periodicals sometimes cite sources, though more often do not. Articles may be written by a member of the editorial staff, a scholar or a freelance writer.

The language of these publications is geared to any educated audience. There is no speciality assumed, only interest and a certain level of intelligence. They are generally published by commercial enterprises or individuals, although some emanate from specific professional organizations. The main purpose of periodicals in this category is to provide information, in a general manner, to a broad audience of concerned citizens.

Popular

Popular periodicals come in many formats, although they are often somewhat slick and attractive in appearance. They contain lots of graphics (photographs, drawings and so on). These publications rarely, if ever, cite sources. Information published in such journals is often second or third hand and the original source is sometimes obscure. Articles are usually very short, are written in simple language and are designed to meet a minimal educational level. There is generally little depth to the content of these articles. The main purpose of popular periodicals is to entertain the reader, to sell products (their own or their advertisers'), and/or to promote a viewpoint.

Sensational

Sensational periodicals come in a variety of styles, but often use a newspaper format. Their language is elementary and occasionally inflammatory or sensational. They assume a certain gullibility in their audience. The main purpose of sensational magazines seems to be to arouse curiosity and to cater to popular superstitions.

Comment

Using scholarly journals will give your research project more credibility and will demonstrate your ability to criticize and use high-quality work. Although other types of trade journals and popular periodicals may give an up-to-date and relevant flavour to your research project, try to limit their use and aim to include some references from scholarly journals.

CONTENT ANALYSIS

Having made an initial appraisal, you should now examine the body of the source. Read the abstract to determine the author's intentions. For books, scan the table of contents and the index to get a broad overview of the material it covers. Note whether bibliographic references are included (if they are not, then it is not a scholarly publication). Read book chapters that specifically address your topic. Scanning the table of contents of a journal or magazine issue is also useful. As with books, the presence and quality of a bibliography at the end of the article may reflect the care with which the authors have prepared their work.

THINK BOX
Interrogate the literature

Here are some questions you should ask of what you are reading.

Intended audience

What type of audience is the author addressing? Is the publication aimed at a specialized or a general audience? Is this source too elementary, too technical, too advanced or just right for your needs?

Objective reasoning

Is the information covered factual, opinion-based or plain old propaganda? It is not always easy to separate fact from opinion. Facts can usually be verified; opinions, though they may be based on factual information, evolve from the interpretation of facts. Skilled writers can actually make you think that their interpretations are factual.

- Does the information appear to be valid and well researched, or is it questionable and unsupported by evidence? Assumptions should be reasonable. Note errors or omissions.

- Are the ideas and arguments advanced more or less in line with other works that you have read on the same topic? The more radically an author departs from the views of others in the same field, the more carefully and critically you should scrutinize his or her ideas.
- Is the author's point of view objective and impartial? Is the language free of emotion-arousing words and bias?

Coverage

- Does the work update other sources, substantiate other materials you have read, or add new information? Does it extensively or marginally cover your topic? You should explore enough sources to obtain a variety of viewpoints.
- Is the material primary or secondary in nature? Primary sources are the raw material of the research process. Secondary sources are based on primary sources. Choose both primary and secondary sources when you have the opportunity.

CHAPTER 22
THE PROCESS OF ANALYSIS

The results of a literature review should not be a report, but an analysis of the issues or research topic you have chosen, complete with justification of your conclusions. This section aims to explain a few highly structured techniques for analysis.

RELATIONSHIP DIAGRAMS

Relationship diagrams are drawn to show all the different relationships between factors, areas or processes. They are useful because they make it easy

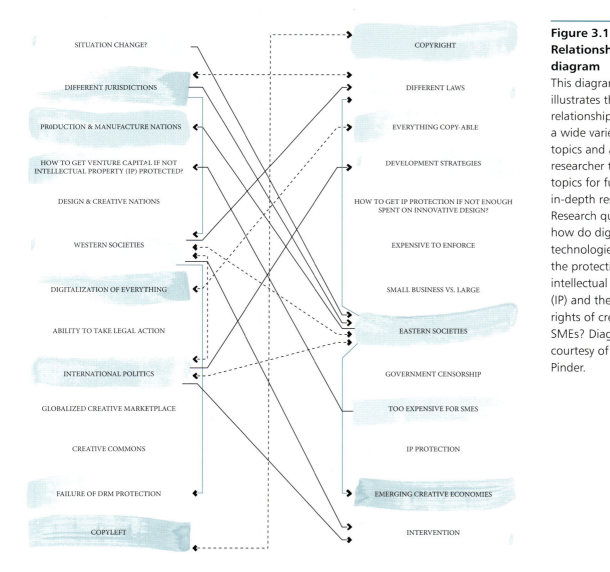

Figure 3.1 Relationship diagram
This diagram illustrates the relationship between a wide variety of topics and allows the researcher to 'cluster' topics for further in-depth research. Research question: how do digital technologies affect the protection of intellectual property (IP) and the design rights of creative SMEs? Diagram courtesy of Mike Pinder.

to pick out the factors in a situation which are drivers of other factors. For example, a relations diagram that explores how digital technologies affect the protection of intellectual property might start out something like the example shown on the facing page.

Instead of one item following another in a logical sequence, each item is connected to many other pieces, showing that they have an impact on each one. Once all the relevant connections between items have been drawn, the connections are counted. Those with the most connections will usually be the most important factors to focus on. In a fairly tangled situation, this is a powerful means of forcing a group to map out the interactions between factors, and usually helps bring the most important issues into focus.

To create a relationship diagram, do the following:

- Agree on the issue or question.
- Add a symbol to the diagram for every element involved in the issue.
- Compare each element to all others. Use an 'influence' arrow to connect related elements.

- The arrows should be drawn from the element that influences to the one being influenced.
- If two elements influence each other, the arrow should be drawn to reflect the stronger influence – count the arrows; the elements with the most outgoing arrows will be root causes or drivers.
- The ones with the most incoming arrows will be key outcomes or results.

AFFINITY DIAGRAMS

Affinity diagramming is designed to sort a raw list, using 'gut feel' to begin to categorize the raw ideas. It is a next step beyond your initial literature search in which you found a vast collection of ideas, results and opinions. The affinity diagram, or KJ method (after its author, Kawakita Jiro), was developed to discover meaningful groups of ideas within a raw list.

In doing so, it is important to let the groupings emerge naturally using the right side of the brain, rather than according to pre-ordained categories. Usually, an

TABLE 3.1

AFFINITY DIAGRAM

International politics	Macro environment	Legal	Situational	Financial
International politics	Situation change	IP protection	Everything copy-able	How to get IP protection if not enough spent on innovative design
Design & creative nations	Develop strategies	Ability to take legal action	Creative commons	Expensive to enforce
Eastern societies	Emerging creative economies	Intervention	Failure of DRM protection	Small business vs. large
Western societies	Digitalization of everything	Jurisdiction different	Copyleft	Too expensive for SMEs
Government censorship	Globalized creative market	Different laws	Copyright	How to get venture capital if not IP protected?
Emerging creative economies			Globalized creative marketplace	
Production & manufacture nations				
Globalized creative market				

This is a sorting device that shows how the research question can be grouped into sets of sub-topics. Research question: How do digital technologies affect the protection of IP and design rights of creative SMEs?

affinity diagram is used to refine an initial literature review into something that makes sense and can be dealt with more easily.

In *The 7 New QC Tools*, Kaoru Ishikawa recommends using the affinity diagram when facts or thoughts are uncertain and need to be organized, when pre-existing ideas or paradigms need to be overcome, and when ideas need to be clarified.

A sample affinity diagram is shown on the facing page. In the first column is a list of ideas, which are then grouped into affinity sets. In this case, the sorting is in an advanced state, and affinity sets have already been given titles. It's important, however, not to add titles too early in the sorting process.

To create an affinity diagram

- Rapidly, group ideas that seem to belong together
- It isn't important to define why they belong together
- Clarify any ambiguous ideas
- Copy an idea into more than one affinity set if appropriate
- Look for small sets. Should they belong in a larger group?
- Do large sets need to be broken down more precisely?
- When most of the ideas have been sorted, you can start to enter titles for each affinity set.

CAUSE-AND-EFFECT DIAGRAM

The cause-and-effect diagram is another brainchild of Kaoru Ishikawa, who pioneered quality management processes in the Kawasaki shipyards and in the process became one of the founding fathers of modern management.

The cause-and-effect diagram is used to explore all the potential or real causes (or inputs) that result in a single effect (or output). Causes are arranged according to their level of importance or detail, resulting in a depiction of relationships and a hierarchy of events. This can help you to search for root causes, to identify areas where there may be problems, and to compare the relative importance of different causes.

Causes in a cause-and-effect diagram are frequently arranged into four major categories. These categories can define anything. The categories you use should suit your needs. You can often create the branches of the cause-and-effect tree from the titles of the affinity sets in a preceding affinity diagram. The cause-and-effect diagram is also known as the fishbone diagram because it was drawn to resemble the skeleton of a fish, with the main causal categories drawn as 'bones' attached to the spine of the fish, as shown on page 125.

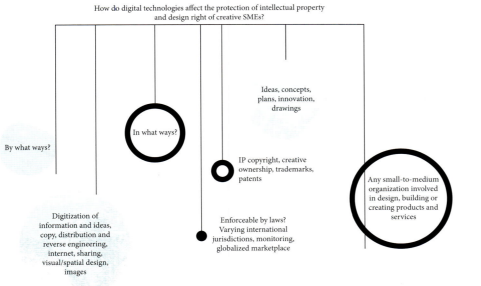

How do digital technologies affect the protection of intellectual property and design right of creative SMEs?

By what ways?

In what ways?

Ideas, concepts, plans, innovation, drawings

IP copyright, creative ownership, trademarks, patents

Any small-to-medium organization involved in design, building or creating products and services

Digitization of information and ideas, copy, distribution and reverse engineering, internet, sharing, visual/spatial design, images

Enforceable by laws? Varying international jurisdictions, monitoring, globalized marketplace

Figure 3.2 Cause-and-effect 'tree' diagram
This diagram shows how the research question can be deconstructed into more manageable chunks to allow the researcher to focus on interconnecting aspects of the problem.

Cause-and-effect diagrams can also be drawn as tree diagrams, resembling a tree turned on its side. From a single outcome or trunk, branches extend to represent major categories of inputs or causes that create that single outcome. These large branches then lead to smaller and smaller branches of causes all the way down to twigs at the ends.

To create a cause-and-effect diagram, do the following:

- Be sure that everyone agrees on the effect or problem statement before beginning – be succinct; for each node, think about what its causes could be and add them to the tree
- Pursue each line of causality back to its root cause
- Consider grafting relatively empty branches on to others
- Consider splitting up overcrowded branches
- Consider which root causes are most likely to merit further investigation

The tree structure

The tree structure has an advantage over the fishbone-style diagram. As a fishbone diagram becomes more and more complex, it becomes difficult to find and compare items that are the same distance from the effect because they are dispersed over the diagram. With the tree structure, all items on the same causal level are aligned vertically.

To create a tree diagram:

- Be sure everyone agrees on the main goal before beginning
- Be succinct
- Think of the main tasks involved in accomplishing the goal and add them to the tree
- For each task node, think of the sub-tasks that will be required, and add them to the tree
- Ask yourselves if there is anything that has been forgotten
- As you work through the project towards the goal, change the colours of nodes that are finished, so that you can see an indication of progress.

Figure 3.3 Cause-and-effect or 'fishbone' diagram
This diagram illustrates potential or real causes that have resulted in a single output. Research question: How do digital technologies affect the protection of IP and design rights of creative SMEs?

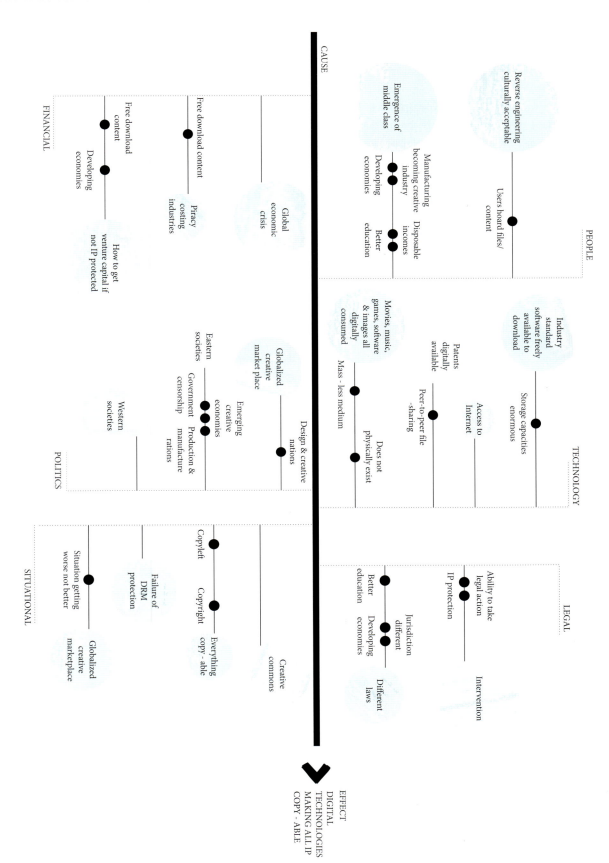

CHAPTER 23
USING SECONDARY DATA

Secondary research involves using information that other people have gathered through primary research. Secondary data is data that is neither collected directly by the user nor specifically for the user; and is often collected under conditions not known to the user. Tertiary research involves using other people's secondary research. It is generally a good idea to avoid tertiary research. This section discusses the purpose of using secondary data.

THE NEED FOR SECONDARY RESEARCH

The natural question you may ask is, 'Why do I need to perform secondary research?'

Secondary information has already been collected for some other purposes. It may be available from internal sources, or it may have been collected and published by another organization. Secondary data is cheaper and more quickly available than primary data, but it is likely to need processing before it is useful.

For example, secondary sources of market penetration of an organization represent data collected already for accountancy and operational purposes. Total product sales may already have been collected and published by some external body such as the government, or by a trade association as a secondary source of information.

There are various advantages and disadvantages of using secondary data-collection techniques in research. The major advantage is that secondary data collection provides easy access to knowledge. Secondly, the costs involved in acquiring this data are low. Secondary data collection might also help to clarify the research question. Secondary data is often used to help align the focus of primary research on a larger scale and it can also help to identify the answer.

On the other hand, a major disadvantage of secondary data is that it is largely self-governed and must therefore be scrutinized closely. Most of the time, secondary data is not presented in a form that you as the researcher will need. Secondary data may also fail to give the full version of data. Furthermore, there can be time issues with this data, because data collected five years ago may not match the data collected now. You should be clear at what stage of the project and for what reason secondary research is being undertaken. Outlined below are some reasons for using secondary research.

Defining the detailed project specification is arguably one of the most difficult phases of the research project. It is at this point that secondary research is most valuable to you; it will help you to define areas of possible investigation that could be interesting and valuable. At this stage, you should ask the question, 'What have other people done previously within my domain of interest?' By finding out what has previously been carried out via, for example, other research projects and other reliable sources of secondary research, you can identify possible gaps in previous work or identify possible logical extensions or analysis of existing work which has been completed. In this way, you should identify possible areas of investigation for your own research project.

Secondary research can also help you to rule out potentially irrelevant project proposals. The proposed work may have already been carried out to completion, or trends in technology might have moved on, making the proposal irrelevant.

Once your research project is underway, this form of secondary research will always be useful in identifying resources which are already available for your use.

The value of secondary research lies in what it can bring to you as a researcher as a basis for your own work and individual contribution. Merely copying or summarizing resources identified by secondary research has no value as far as a research project is concerned. Secondary research is of value when, for example, reports are compared and analysed or set within a particular context, or when you perform a critical review of existing work.

TYPES OF SECONDARY DATA

Secondary data is the subsequent publication of primary literature that has already been collected and analysed by someone else for some other purpose. Secondary data can be generated by governments, business, consumer research organizations, academies and independent researchers. These types of data are rapid and far reaching, and are a very popular type of data for most research projects. They might even form the main data to answer your question. There are a number of types of secondary data. They can be divided into three categories: documentary, survey and multi-source.

Documentary

Documentary sources can be written or unwritten. Examples of written documentary sources include journals, books, newspapers and commercial sources, including databases, diaries/memoirs and communications such as emails, letters, memos, websites, reports and meeting minutes. Interview transcripts would be included in this group. Examples of unwritten documentary sources include TV and radio, voice and video recordings, and images.

Journals can be divided into three categories. Revered academic journals have a theoretical basis and therefore carry high academic credibility. They are vital literature for a major project and because they are published regularly, they are easily accessible. They can carry a personal or professional bias but are well indexed via tertiary data. Professional journals contain a mix of news stories and articles. They tend to have a commercial interest bias. Trade journals are industry specialized and cover new products, services and news. Trade journals carry a commercial interest bias.

Books are a very useful secondary source. They cover a huge range of topics and approaches, including academic theory and professional practice. They are a useful introductory source and can help you to clarify your research question, objectives and methods. However, books should be treated with caution as they become outdated quickly when compared to digital and media channels. Newspapers are useful sources of topical events and statistical information and many are kept on record as far back as the early 1990s – even earlier on microfilm. Newspapers can, however, carry a political, geographical, commercial or personal bias.

Survey

Surveys are useful for setting findings into context. They tend to be carried out in the form of questionnaires or interviews and contain specifically determined content in an attempt to define response parameters. To evaluate the findings of a survey, you will need to sample the original data, and analyse the definitions for collection and indexing methods. For comparative analysis across societies or nations, the design of surveys is crucial for the building of cumulative empirical knowledge over space and time. Types of survey include census, regular and ad hoc or one-off.

Multi-source

Multi-source research can be carried out using a combination of methods. It is created by extracting and combining comparable variables. It can be longitudinal (time-based) or geographical (area-based) data. Time-based research can be collected quickly, through data such as statistics and company documents; but it is important to remember that environmental and political influences at the time of fieldwork may differ significantly from today/your research.

ADVANTAGES OF SECONDARY DATA

Secondary data is useful for the literature review and for formulating research questions. It is quick and accessible – it allows for analyses of processes in otherwise inaccessible settings and it leaves you more time to analyse more data and theory. Secondary research allows for data of a higher quality than you could collect yourself quickly. It is also unobtrusive and is feasible to carry out. Research of this nature supplies comparative and contextual data between regions and nations in which to situate and triangulate your own findings. It also allows for new discoveries and is always available. Digital resources also save re-inputting data.

DISADVANTAGES OF SECONDARY DATA

In order for secondary research to be credible, it may be necessary to combine it with primary data, and careful evaluation is crucial. Commercial data can be costly but the ready access to so much secondary research can mean that there is too much information to choose from and focus can be lost. Secondary data can carry personal, political or commercial bias and its permanence means that it can become outdated quickly.

EVALUATING SECONDARY DATA

The purpose of conducting secondary data analysis is to develop an improved understanding of your subject. It must enable you to answer your question and meet your learning objectives. View secondary data with the same caution as primary data and evaluate as you collect. This will save false assumptions and should mean that you won't waste time rejecting masses of data later. Ensure that you use the correct type of data. It must provide information to answer your question – irrelevant information will invalidate your answer. Assess the purpose and methods of the original data collection – sampling techniques, response rates and errors, intended audience and coverage of data. Check the credentials of the source(s) and author(s) – validate their authority, reliability and trustworthiness. To avoid personal bias, always cross-check the verification required in order to triangulate findings with independent sources.

GETTING STARTED

Using secondary research – begin your research by creating an outline of what the final research project will look like: clearly define the goals of your research and the type of design that you anticipate using. Establish what kind of data you plan on using for your research. In order to use secondary data, three steps must be completed:

- Locate the data
- Evaluate the data
- Verify the data.

Figure 3.4 A classification of secondary data
This diagram illustrates the different classifications of secondary data.

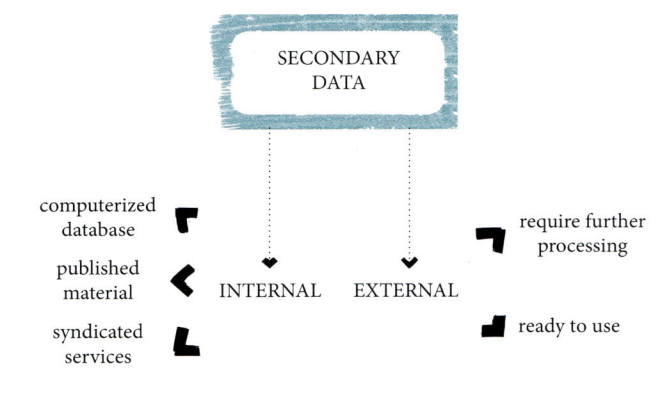

CHAPTER 24
USING PRIMARY DATA

In primary data collection, you collect the data yourself using methods such as interviews and questionnaires. The key point here is that the data you collect is unique to you and your research and, until you publish, no one else has access to it.

THE NEED FOR PRIMARY RESEARCH

By the time you have written your project proposal and undertaken your background reading, you will have realized the extent to which the research problem can be answered by secondary research. It is at this point that you will be designing a pilot study to try and find answers to the as yet unsolved problem area. You need to evaluate primary research tools and ascertain their suitability to both fit in with your research philosophy and to answer the problem in a way that is both rigorous and valid. Primary research is undertaken to answer the parts of your research problem that you either cannot answer by secondary research or by checking out, confirming or refuting published secondary data. Undertaking primary research divides off what has been done by others in secondary research and what you have done by yourself or within a research team to answer your problem area.

THE VALUE OF PRIMARY RESEARCH

The value of primary research within your project is that you have designed and undertaken research specifically to answer the problem you have defined. Therefore, your research should be pertinent to the topic. The data collected should be up to date and should come from trustworthy sources. You will have also checked and confirmed data you have collected by using additional primary research tools to confirm what you have found. Therefore, when you write up the research project and explain the importance of your work, your narrative will be trustworthy and believable.

TYPES OF PRIMARY DATA

There are a number of types of primary data and the following section lists the types with their advantages and disadvantages. However, the main focus of this section is to describe the primary data-collection tools which are particularly relevant to the creative industries, as well as to describe those primary research tools that are more commonly used in other fields but which can be adapted to the creative industries. For these reasons, the following tools will be discussed in detail in the focus sections: questionnaires, interviews, observation, focus group interviews, elicitation techniques, visual research, photography and narrative. The primary data generated by these methods may be qualitative in nature (usually in the form of words) or quantitative (usually in the form of numbers, or where you can make word counts).

Focus group interviews

A focus group is an interview conducted by a trained moderator in a non-structured and natural manner with a small group of respondents. The moderator leads the discussion. The main purpose of a focus group is to gain insight by listening to a group of people from the appropriate target market talk about specific issues of interest.

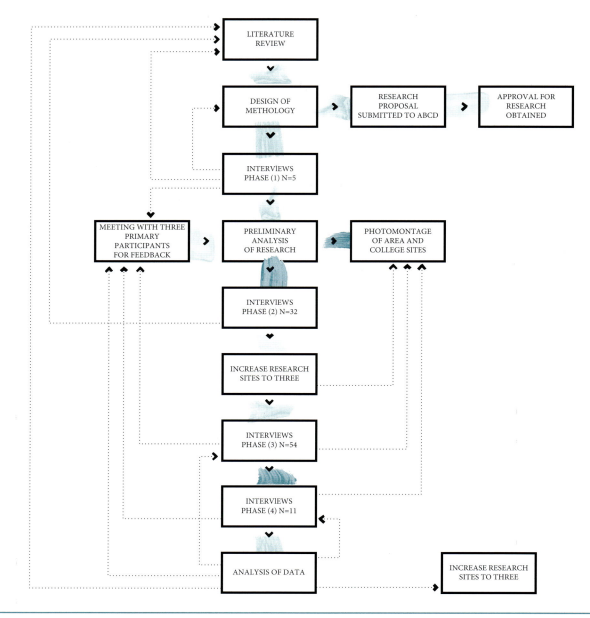

Figure 3.5 Research process: the role of primary research
A diagram of the research process, which illustrates the role of primary research in a research project.

Case studies

The term 'case study' usually refers to a fairly intensive examination of a single unit such as a person, a small group of people or a single company. Case studies involve measuring what is present and how it got there. In this sense, it is historical. It can enable the researcher to explore, unravel and understand problems, issues and relationships. It cannot, however, allow the researcher to generalize (argue that the results, findings or theory from one case study apply to other similar case studies).

The case looked at may be unique and therefore not representative of other instances. It is, of course, possible to look at several case studies to represent certain features of management that we are interested in studying. The case study approach is often used to make practical improvements. Contributions to general knowledge are incidental.

The case study method has four steps:

- Determine the present situation.
- Gather background information about the past and key variables.
- Test hypotheses. The background information collected will have been analysed for possible hypotheses. In this step, specific evidence about each hypothesis can be gathered. This step aims to eliminate possibilities that conflict with the evidence collected and to gain confidence for the important hypotheses. The culmination of this step might be the development of an experimental design to test out more rigorously the hypotheses developed, or it might be to take action to remedy the problem.
- Take remedial action. The aim is to check that the hypotheses tested actually work out in practice. Some action, correction or improvement is made and a further check carried out on the situation to see what effect the change has brought about.

The case study enables rich information to be gathered, from which potentially useful hypotheses can then be generated. It can be a time-consuming process. It is also inefficient in researching situations that are already well structured and where the important variables have been identified. They lack utility when attempting to reach rigorous conclusions or determining precise relationships between variables.

Diaries

A diary is a way of gathering information about the way in which individuals spend their time on professional activities. They are not about records of engagement or personal journals of thought! Diaries can record either quantitative or qualitative data, and in management research can provide information about work patterns and activities.

Diaries can be useful for collecting information from employees and can be used as a preliminary basis for intensive interviewing. Different writers can be compared and contrasted simultaneously and the researcher does not need to be involved personally. This also allows the researcher to move freely from one organization to another. They are a useful source

when resources are limited or if an alternative to direct observation is required.

However, subjects need to be clear about what they are being asked to do, why and what you plan to do with the data. Diarists need to be of a certain educational level and some structure is necessary to give the diarist focus, for example, a list of headings. Encouragement and reassurance are needed as completing a diary is time-consuming and can be irritating after a while. Progress needs checking from time to time and confidentiality is required as content may be critical.

Critical incidents

The critical incident technique is an attempt to identify the more 'noteworthy' aspects of job behaviour and is based on the assumption that jobs are composed of critical and non-critical tasks. For example, a critical task might be defined as one that makes the difference between success and failure in carrying out important parts of the job. The idea is to collect reports about what in particular contributes to good performance. The incidents are scaled in order of difficulty, frequency and importance to the job as a whole. The technique scores more highly over the use of diaries as it is centred on specific happenings and on what is judged as effective behaviour. However, it is laborious and does not lend itself to objective quantification.

Portfolios

A measure of a creative's ability may be expressed in terms of the number and duration of 'issues' or problems being tackled at any one time. The compilation of problem portfolios allows information about how each problem arose, the methods used to solve it and the difficulties encountered to be recorded. This analysis also raises questions about the person's use of time. What proportion of time is occupied in checking; in handling problems given by others; on self-generated problems; on 'top-priority' problems; on minor issues and so forth? The main problem with this method and the use of diaries is getting people to agree to record everything in sufficient detail for you to analyse.

CHAPTER 25
QUESTIONNAIRES

Questionnaires are a popular means of collecting data, but are difficult to design and often require many rewrites before an acceptable questionnaire is produced.

WHY USE QUESTIONNAIRES?

Questionnaires can be used as a method in their own right or as a basis for interviewing or a telephone survey. They can be posted, emailed or faxed and therefore can cover a large number of people or organizations. They are relatively cheap and no prior arrangement is needed, thus ensuring anonymity and avoiding any embarrassment on the part of the respondent. Questionnaires allow plenty of time for the respondent to formulate their responses and also avoid any interviewer bias. However, questionnaires also have their disadvantages. Questions must be relatively simple and they assume no literacy problems. The researcher has no control over who completes the questionnaire and it is not possible to give assistance if required. There can be large time delays waiting for responses to be returned and reminders may need to be sent. Responses may not be complete and may not be entirely spontaneous or independent of other respondents' replies. The question of how to design a postal questionnaire is covered in the following sections.

Theme and covering letter

The general theme of the questionnaire should be made explicit in a covering letter. State who you are and why the data is required, and give, if necessary, an assurance of confidentiality and/or anonymity, along with a contact address or telephone number. This ensures that the respondents know what they are committing themselves to, and also that they understand the context of their replies. If possible, you should offer an estimate of the completion time. Instructions for return should be included with the return date made obvious.

Instructions for completion

Provide clear and unambiguous instructions for completion. Within most questionnaires, these are both general and more specific instructions for particular question structures. It is usually best to separate these, supplying the general instructions as a preamble to the questionnaire, but leaving the specific instructions until the questions to which they apply. The response method should be indicated (circle, tick, cross and so forth). Wherever possible, and certainly if a slightly unfamiliar response system is employed, you should give an example.

Appearance

Appearance is usually the first feature of the questionnaire to which the recipient reacts. A neat and professional appearance will encourage further consideration of your request, increasing your response rate. In addition, careful thought to layout should help your analysis. The following simple rules can help to improve questionnaire appearance:

- Liberal spacing makes the reading easier
- Photo reduction can produce more space without reducing content
- Consistent positioning of response boxes, usually to the right, speeds up completion and also avoids inadvertent omission of responses
- Choose the font style to maximize legibility
- Differentiate between instructions and questions; either lower case and capitals can be used, or responses can be boxed

Length

There may be a strong temptation to include any vaguely interesting questions, but you should resist this at all costs. Excessive size can only reduce response rates. If a long questionnaire is necessary, then you must give even more thought to appearance. It is best to leave pages unnumbered; it can be very disconcerting for respondents to flick to the end and see 'page 17'!

Order

Probably the most crucial stage in the questionnaire is the introduction. Once the respondents have started to complete the questions they will normally finish the task, unless it is very long or difficult. Consequently, you need to select the opening questions with care. Usually, the best approach is to ask for biographical details first, as the respondents should know all the answers without much thought. Another benefit is that an easy start provides practice in answering questions.

Once the introduction has been achieved, the subsequent order will depend on many considerations. You should be aware of the varying importance of different questions. Essential information should appear early, just in case the questionnaire is not completed. For the same reasons, relatively unimportant questions can be placed towards the end. If questions are likely to provoke the respondent and remain unanswered, these too are best left until the end, in the hope of obtaining answers to everything else.

Coding

If analysis of the results is to be carried out using a statistical package or spreadsheet, it is advisable to code non-numerical responses when designing the questionnaire, rather than trying to code the responses when they are returned. An example of coding follows:

Designer   [ ]   Manager   [ ]
       1   2

The coded responses (1 or 2) are used for the analysis.

Thank you

Respondents to questionnaires rarely benefit personally from their efforts and the least the researcher can do is to thank them. Even though the covering letter will express appreciation for the help given, it is also a nice gesture to finish the questionnaire with a further thank you.

Questions

When compiling questions, keep them short, simple and to the point; avoid unnecessary words. Use words and phrases that are unambiguous and familiar to the respondent. For example, 'dinner' has a number of different interpretations; use an alternative expression such as 'evening meal'. Only ask questions that the respondent can answer. Hypothetical questions should be avoided. Avoid calculations and questions that require a lot of memory work; for example, 'how many people stayed in your hotel last year?' Avoid loaded or leading questions that imply a certain answer; for example, by mentioning one particular item in the question: 'Do you agree that Colgate toothpaste is the best toothpaste?'

Vacuous words or phrases should be avoided. 'Generally', 'usually' or 'normally' are imprecise terms with various meanings. They should be replaced with quantitative statements, for example, 'at least once a week'. Questions should only address a single issue. For example, questions like 'do you take annual holidays to Spain?' should be broken down into two discrete stages, first to find out if the respondent takes an annual holiday, and then secondly to find out if they go to Spain. Do not ask two questions in one by using 'and'; for example, 'did you watch television last night and read a newspaper?' Avoid double negatives. For example, 'is it not true that you did not read a newspaper yesterday?' Respondents may tackle a double negative by switching both negatives and then assuming that the same answer applies. This is not necessarily valid. State the units required, but do not aim for too high a degree of accuracy. For instance, use an interval rather than an exact figure:

> 'How much did you earn last year?'
> Less than £10,000 [ ]
> More than £10,000 but less than £20,000 [ ]

Avoid emotive or embarrassing words – usually connected with race, religion, politics, sex or money.

Closed questions

These involve a question being asked and then a number of possible answers being provided for the respondent. The respondent selects the answer that is appropriate. Closed questions are particularly useful in obtaining factual information:

> Sex: Male [ ] Female [ ]
>
> Did you watch television last night? Yes [ ] No [ ]

Some 'Yes/No' questions have a third category: 'Do not know'. Experience shows that as long as this alternative is not mentioned, people will make a choice. Also, the phrase 'do not know' is ambiguous:

> Do you agree with the introduction of the ticket queuing machine?
> Yes [ ] No [ ] Do not know [ ]
>
> What was your main way of travelling to the venue? Tick one box only.
> Car [ ] Coach [ ] Motorbike [ ] Train [ ]
> Other (please specify) [ ]

With such lists you should always include an 'other' category, because not all possible responses might have been included in the list of answers. Sometimes the respondent can select more than one from the list. However, this makes analysis difficult:

> Why have you visited the art gallery? Tick the relevant answer(s). You may tick as many as you like.
>
> I enjoy visiting art galleries [ ]
> The weather was bad and I could not enjoy outdoor activities [ ]
> I have visited the art gallery before and wished to return [ ]
> Other reason (please specify) [ ]

Attitude questions

Frequently, questions are asked to find out the respondents' opinions or attitudes to a given situation. A Likert scale provides a battery of attitude statements. The respondent then says how much they agree or disagree with each one:

Read the following statements and then indicate by a tick whether you strongly agree, agree, disagree or strongly disagree with the statement:

> My visit has been good value for money
> Strongly agree [ ]
> Agree [ ]
> Disagree [ ]
> Strongly disagree [ ]

There are many variations on this type of question. One variation is to have a 'middle statement'; for example, 'neither agree nor disagree'. However, many respondents take this as the easy option. Only having four statements, as above, forces the respondent into making a positive or negative choice. Another variation is to rank the various attitude statements. However, this can cause analysis problems:

> Which of these characteristics do you like about your job? Indicate the best three in order, with the best being number 1.
> Varied work [ ]
> Good salary [ ]
> Opportunities for promotion [ ]
> Good working conditions [ ]
> High amount of responsibility [ ]
> Friendly colleagues [ ]

A semantic differential scale attempts to show how strongly an attitude is held by the respondent. With these scales, double-ended terms are given to the respondents who are asked to indicate where their attitude lies on the scale between the terms. The response can be indicated by putting a cross in a particular position or circling a number:

Work is (circle the appropriate number):		
Difficult	1 2 3 4 5 6 7	Easy
Useless	1 2 3 4 5 6 7	Useful
Interesting	1 2 3 4 5 6 7	Boring

For summary and analysis purposes, a 'score' of one to seven may be allocated to the seven points of the scale, thus quantifying the various degrees of opinion expressed. This procedure has some disadvantages. It is implicitly assumed that two people with the same strength of feeling will mark the same point on the scale. This almost certainly will not be the case. When faced with a semantic differential scale, some people will never, as a matter of principle, use the two end indicators of one and seven. Effectively, therefore, they are using a five-point scale. Also, scoring the scale from between one to seven assumes that they represent equidistant points on the continuous spectrum of opinion. This again is probably not true. Nevertheless, within its limitations, the semantic differential can provide a useful way of measuring and summarizing subjective opinions. Other types of questions to determine peoples' opinions or attitudes are as follows: Which one/two words best describes? Which of the following statements best describes? How much do you agree with the following statement?

Open questions

An open question such as 'what are the essential skills a manager should possess?' should be used as an adjunct to the main theme of the questionnaire and may allow the respondent to elaborate upon an earlier, more specific question. Open questions figured at the end of major sections, or at the end of the questionnaire, can act as safety valves, and may possibly offer additional information. However, they should not be used to introduce a section, since there is a high risk of influencing later responses. The main problem of open questions is that many different answers have to be summarized and possibly coded.

Testing – pilot survey

Questionnaire design is fraught with difficulties and problems. A number of rewrites will be necessary, together with refinement and rethinks on a regular basis. Do not assume that you will design the questionnaire accurately and perfectly at the first attempt. If poorly designed, you will collect inappropriate or inaccurate data and good analysis cannot then rectify the situation.

To refine the questionnaire, you need to conduct a pilot survey. This is a small-scale trial prior to the main survey that tests all your question planning. Amendments to questions can be made. After making some amendments, the new version is then re-tested. If this produces more changes, another pilot can be undertaken and so on. For example, perhaps responses to open-ended questions become closed; questions which are all answered in the same way can be omitted; difficult words replaced, and so forth.

It is usual to pilot the questionnaires personally so that the respondent can be observed and questioned if necessary. By timing each question, you can identify any questions that appear too difficult, and you can also obtain a reliable estimate of the anticipated completion time for inclusion in the covering letter. The result can also be used to test the coding and analytical procedures to be performed later.

Distribution and return

The questionnaire should be checked for completeness to ensure that all pages are present and that none is blank or illegible. It is usual to supply a pre-paid addressed envelope for the return of the questionnaire. You need to explain this in the covering letter and reinforce it at the end of the questionnaire, after the 'thank you'. Finally, many organizations are approached continually for information. Many, as a matter of course, will not respond in a positive way.

CHAPTER 26
OBSERVATIONS

This section describes how to undertake observations. Observation involves recording the behavioural patterns of people, objects and events in a systematic manner. Explained below are some of the forms that observational methods can take.

STRUCTURED OR UNSTRUCTURED

In structured observation, the researcher specifies in detail what is to be observed and how the measurements are to be recorded. It is appropriate when the problem is clearly defined and the information needed is specified. In unstructured observation, the researcher monitors all aspects of the phenomenon that seem relevant. It is appropriate when the problem has yet to be formulated precisely and flexibility is needed in observation to identify key components of the problem and to develop hypotheses. The potential for bias is high. Observation findings should be treated as hypotheses to be tested, rather than as conclusive findings.

DISGUISED OR UNDISGUISED

In disguised observation, respondents are unaware that they are being observed and thus behave naturally. Disguise is achieved, for example, by hiding, using concealed equipment or people disguised as shoppers. In undisguised observation, respondents are aware that they are being observed. There is a danger of people behaving differently when being observed.

NATURAL OR CONTRIVED

Natural observation involves observing behaviour as it takes place in the environment, such as working in a design studio, for example. In contrived observation, the respondent's behaviour is observed in an artificial environment; for example, designing in a controlled environment.

PERSONAL

In personal observation, a researcher observes actual behaviour as it occurs. The observer may or may not normally attempt to control or manipulate the phenomenon being observed. The observer merely records what takes place.

MECHANICAL

Mechanical devices (video, closed-circuit television) record what is being observed. These devices may or may not require the respondent's direct participation. They are used for continuously recording ongoing behaviour.

NON-PARTICIPANT

The observer does not normally question or communicate with the people being observed. He or she does not participate.

PARTICIPANT

In participant observation, the researcher becomes part of the group that is being investigated. Participant observation has its roots in ethnographic studies, whereby researchers would typically live in indigenous villages, seeking to understand the customs and practices of the local culture. It has a very extensive literature, particularly in sociology (development, nature and laws of human society) and anthropology (the study of cultural and social practices within small-scale societies or units). Organizations can be similarly viewed as 'tribes' with their own customs and practices. The role of the participant observer is not simple. Different ways of classifying the role are explained further in the following paragraphs.

Researcher as employee

The researcher works within the organization alongside other employees, effectively as one of them. The role of the researcher may or may not be explicit and this will have implications for the extent to which he or she will be able to move around and gather information and perspectives from other sources. This role is appropriate when the researcher needs to become totally immersed and experience the work or situation at first-hand. There are a number of dilemmas. Do you tell management and the unions? Friendships may compromise the research. What are the ethics of the process? Can anonymity be maintained? Skill and competence to undertake the work may be required. The research may take place over a long period of time, thus making it tricky to sustain anonymity.

Researcher as an explicit role

The researcher is present every day over a period of time, but entry is negotiated in advance with management and preferably with employees as well. The individual quite clearly takes the role of a researcher and can move around, observe, interview and participate in the work as appropriate. This type of role is the most favoured, as it provides many of the insights that the complete observer would gain, while offering much greater flexibility without the ethical problems that deception entails.

In an interrupted involvement role, the researcher is present sporadically over a period of time; for example, moving in and out of the organization to deal with other work or to conduct interviews with, or observations of, different people across a number of different organizations. It rarely involves much participation in the context. A purely observational role is often disliked by participants, since it appears as a sort of 'eavesdropping'. The inevitable detachment it involves prevents a degree of trust and friendship forming between the researcher and respondent, which is an important component in other methods.

Choice of roles

The role adopted depends on the following considerations:

- Purpose of the research: does the research require continued longitudinal involvement (will it take place over a long period of time?); or will in-depth interviews, for example, be conducted over time given the type of insights required?
- Cost of the research: to what extent can the researcher afford to be committed for extended periods of time? Are there additional costs?
- The extent to which access can be gained: gaining access where the role of the researcher is either explicit or covert can be difficult, and may take time.
- The extent to which the researcher would be comfortable in the role: if the researcher intends to keep his identity concealed, will he or she also feel able to develop the type of trusting relationships that are important? What are the ethical issues involved?
- The amount of time the researcher has at their disposal: some methods involve a considerable amount of time. If time proves to be a problem, alternative approaches will need to be sought.

CHAPTER 27
INTERVIEWS

Interviewing is a technique that is primarily used to gain an understanding of the underlying reasons and motivations for people's attitudes, preferences or behaviour. Interviews can be undertaken on a personal one-to-one basis or in a group. They can be conducted at work, at home, in the street or in a shopping centre, or in some other agreed location.

WHY USE PERSONAL INTERVIEWS?

Personal interviews have many advantages. They offer a serious approach to data collection, resulting in accurate information from the respondent. The response rate is good and data will be complete and immediate – there is also an opportunity for the respondent to go into more detail. The interviewer remains in control throughout the interview and can offer help if a problem arises. Personal interviews also enable the interviewer to investigate motives and feelings, and provide them with the ability to identify certain respondent characteristics (tone of voice, facial expression or hesitation, for example). Props and recording equipment can be used; and if only one interviewer is employed, the approach will be uniform throughout.

Unfortunately, however, interviews need to be set up. This can be time-consuming and expensive and can impose geographical limitations. With personal interviews, there is often a respondent bias – there may be a tendency to please or impress, to create a false personal image, or end the interview quickly. If questions are of a personal nature, the respondent may also become embarrassed.

TYPES OF INTERVIEW

There are three main types of interview, which are outlined in the following sections.

Structured

Structured interviews are based on a carefully worded interview schedule. They frequently require short answers which are then ticked off, and are useful when there are a lot of questions which are not particularly contentious or thought-provoking. The respondent may become irritated at having to give over-simplified answers.

Semi-structured

The interview is focused by asking certain questions but with scope for the respondent to express himself or herself at length.

Unstructured

This is also called an in-depth interview. The interviewer begins by asking a general question and then encourages the respondent to talk freely. The interviewer uses an unstructured format, the subsequent direction of the interview being determined by the respondent's initial reply. The interviewer then probes for elaboration – 'why do you say that?', 'that's interesting, tell me more' or, 'would you like to add anything else?' being typical probes.

TABLE 3.2

COMPARISON OF POSTAL, TELEPHONE AND PERSONAL INTERVIEW SURVEYS

	Postal survey	Telephone survey	Personal interview
Cost (assuming a good response rate)	Often lowest	Usually in between	Usually highest
Ability to probe	No personal contact or observation	Some chance for gathering additional data through elaboration on questions, but no personal questions	Greatest opportunity for observation, building rapport and additional probing
Respondent ability to complete at own convenience	Yes	Perhaps, but usually no	Perhaps, if interview time is prearranged with respondent
Interview bias	No chance	Some, perhaps due to voice inflection	Greatest chance
Ability to decide who actually responds to the questions	Least	Some	Greatest
Impersonality	Greatest	Some due to lack of face-to-face contact	Least
Complex questions	Least suitable	Somewhat suitable	More suitable
Visual aids	Little opportunity	No opportunity	Greatest opportunity
Potential negative respondent reaction	'Junk mail'	'Junk calls'	Invasion of privacy
Interviewer control over interview environment	Least	Some in selection of time to call	Greatest
Time lag between soliciting and receiving response	Greatest	Least	May be considerable if a large area is involved
Suitable types of questions	Simple, mostly dich-otomous (yes/no) and multiple choice	Some opportunity for open-ended questions, especially if interview is recorded	Greatest opportunity for open-ended questions
Requirement for technical skills in conducting interview	Least	Medium	Greatest
Response rate	Low	Usually high	High

THINK BOX
Conducting an interview

The following section is a step-by-step guide to conducting an interview. You should remember that all situations are different and therefore you may need to make refinements to this approach.

Planning an interview

- List the areas in which you require information
- Decide on type of interview
- Transform areas into actual questions
- Try them out on a friend or relative
- Make an appointment with respondent(s)
- Discuss details of why and how long
- Try and fix a venue and time when you will not be disturbed

Tips for carrying out an interview

- Be personable: arrive on time, dress smartly, smile, employ good manners and strike a balance between friendliness and objectivity.
- Introduce yourself: re-confirming the purpose of the interview assures confidentiality.
- If relevant, specify what will happen to the data.
- Ask the questions: speak slowly in a soft, yet audible tone of voice and control your body language. Know the questions and topic. Ask all the questions.
- Record responses: writing these up verbatim as you go is both slow and time-consuming, so summarize instead and tape answers – having agreed this beforehand. Use an alternative method if not acceptable, and consider the effect of recording on respondents' answers. Ensure proper equipment is in good working order, that you have sufficient tapes and batteries, and that there is a minimum of background noise.
- Finally: ask if the respondent would like to give further details about anything or if they have any questions about the research; then thank them for their time.

Telephone interview

A telephone interview is an alternative to the personal, face-to-face interview. It is relatively cheap and quick and can cover reasonably large numbers of people, organizations and geographic areas. Telephone interviews carry a high response rate and time is saved by not having to wait for a response. As with personal interviews, the interviewer can help out with responses and the data can be recorded.

Despite this, telephone interviews are often connected with selling, so they can cause irritation. A good telephone manner and straightforward questions are required. The respondent also has little time to formulate a response and visual aids cannot be used. Time will also be wasted finding respondents who will actually take part. It takes on average two and a half phone calls to find someone who will participate in a telephone interview.

Conducting a telephone interview

Locate the respondent: repeat calls may be necessary, especially if you are trying to contact people in organizations where you may have to go through a switchboard. You may not know an individual's name or title, so there is also the possibility of interviewing the wrong person. You can send an advance letter informing the respondent that you will be telephoning. This can explain the purpose of your research.

Getting respondents to take part

You need to state concisely the purpose of the call – scripted and similar to the introductory letter of a postal questionnaire. Respondents will normally listen to this introduction before they decide whether to cooperate or not. When contact is made, respondents may have questions or raise objections about why they could not participate. You should be prepared for these.

Ensuring quality

To ensure the quality of the questionnaire, follow the principles of questionnaire design. However, the questionnaire must be easy to move through, as you cannot have long silences on the telephone. Follow the principles of face-to-face interviewing.

Smooth implementation

Each interview schedule should have a cover page with the respondent's number, name and address. The cover sheet should make provisions for you to record which call it is, the date and time, the interviewer and the outcome of the call, along with space to note down specific times at which a call-back has been arranged. Space should be provided to record the final outcome of the call. Was an interview refused, contact never made or the number disconnected? A system for call-backs needs to be implemented. Interview schedules should be sorted according to their status: weekday call-back, evening call-back, weekend call-back or specific time call-back.

CHAPTER 28
VISUAL RESEARCH

The creative industries can use visual research in two forms: visual records produced by the researcher, and visual documents produced by those under research. In recent years, however, this dichotomy between researcher and the researched has begun to collapse and a third kind of visual record or representation has emerged: the collaborative representation. Visual research proceeds methodologically by making visual representations, which includes studying artefacts and contexts by producing images and by collaborating with social actors in the production of visual representations.

WHAT IS VISUAL RESEARCH?

Visual research can be broadly divided into four categories and these are: researcher created (video, photographs or drawings); researcher discovered (taken from comics or magazines); participant generated visual data; and representation and visual research.

Respondent-generated visual data is a flexible approach adopting a wide range of tools that are modelled on different questions and are individually suited to participants' own preferences: for example, time-lines; self-portraits; draw and write; diaries (paper, electronic, photographic, video); shooting back; and participants' photographs (video/walkabout, shadowing).

Photo/object elicitation is an example of respondent-generated visual data. Photographs, film, video, drawings or objects are introduced as part of an interview. The aim is to explore the significance or meaning of the images or objects with the participant. These can be useful as icebreakers and they break down the power distance between researcher and participant. These images or objects act as a neutral or third party.

Respondents can use their own cultural artefacts; for example, their favourite clothes, cell phones, icons, symbols or spaces they frequent, to help them explain an issue or context. Equally, respondents can use their own artwork; for example, drawings, doodles, sketches, posters, photographs or videos they have created.

ISSUES OF REPRESENTATION

Researchers within the creative industries can adopt a dual perspective on visual media. On the one hand, they are concerned with the content of a particular visual representation. What is the meaning of this particular design motif on an art object? Who is the person in the photograph? On the other hand, they are concerned with the context of a given visual representation. Who produced the art object, and for whom? Why was a photograph taken of this particular person, and then kept by that other person?

However, when the visual representations in question are produced by the researcher themselves, there is a danger of the content taking priority over the context. Within documentary film, the direct cinema movement in the 1960s sought to correct this imbalance by ensuring that the conditions of film-making were revealed to the viewer. Typically, this involved the deliberate inclusion of the film-makers' kit in the image (lights, microphones, and so forth), or even the film-makers themselves. Such ideas were absorbed into ethnographic film practice at the same time as the introduction of new techniques thought to bring the human subjects of the film closer to the viewer (principally, the use of subtitles to render speech in foreign languages more 'neutrally' than as with inevitably inflected voice-over translations).

With still photography, more sensitive or reflexive representations are perhaps slightly harder to accomplish. In many cases, social investigators choose to create some marriage of text and image, where each provides a commentary on the other. It is important to remember, however, that all visual representations are not only produced but are also consumed in a social context, one which invokes a family resemblance to similar representations – such as television and cinema in the case of film and video. Members of an audience will bring to the screening certain expectations of narrative form, plot development, 'good' and 'bad' composition and so forth, however unconscious or inchoate their understandings. Nor can a single reading of a film necessarily be presumed.

ISSUES OF COLLABORATION

Perhaps the least collaborative visual project is the semi-mythical project of setting up a (possibly concealed) film or video camera in a social context, for no other reason than to document whatever passes before it; and that involves leaving a camera running, or using a stills camera to record a specific aspect of social behaviour, where the actors are either unaware of being recorded or are encouraged to ignore the camera's presence.

It is, however, a premise of the ethnographic method that the investigator is to some extent involved in the cultural and social projects of those under investigation, if only to the extent that asking questions often forces those questioned to formalize social knowledge or representations that may have only a semi-propositional status.

As a result, visual anthropologists and visual sociologists often directly collaborate with their informants or subjects in the production of visual texts of various kinds. This may be done for purely documentary purposes; for example, asking a designer to pause in the process of ideas generation at various stages, in order to photograph the process.

It may be done for some projects that are of more interest to the investigator than to the subjects themselves. Interestingly, it may involve working together on a project that simultaneously provides information for the investigator while fulfilling a goal for the subjects. A wide range of projects have been accomplished using collaborative representation, and these range from encouraging the subjects to discuss their family photographs through photo elicitation, learning more about themselves through helping people to document incidents within their own lives, to full-blown attempts to empower people through visual media.

CHAPTER 29
PHOTOGRAPHY

Photography has been increasingly used in research and particularly within the creative industries to improve conventional ethnographic narratives. As a result, photographs are neither perceived to be, nor used as, mere illustrations of written text anymore. Not only can they be contextualized in relation to text, but they can also be presented as self-sufficient photo essays depicting certain events, behaviours, people, cultures or social forms. The use of photographic images for ethnographic representation involves three fundamental components: description, analysis and interpretation. Each stage makes it possible for photographs to produce knowledge by providing a more thorough understanding of human social phenomena.

HOW PHOTOGRAPHY CAN BE USED IN RESEARCH

The advantage of photography over text stems from the fact that it depicts the visual characteristics of objects. Phenomenologically speaking, photography is a visual system of representation. We can look at the relationship between what is physically depicted and what that represents. Photographs do not simply capture reality. Spatial dimensions are reduced to a surface, meaning that the angles we take the photograph from and the lens we use on the camera both have an effect on how images are created and perceived. Photographs are not objective and do not present the objective views of the person taking them; they rather depict a way to see or understand an object or context. Our interpretation of photographs is also influenced by our culture.

In contrast to language, where meanings are more or less clearly defined, visual photography offers multilayered meanings. Photographs are polysemic, which means that recipients may see and understand them in different ways. Even if we each interpret photographs differently, this does not mean that attributing a meaning to a photograph happens arbitrarily and completely subjectively.

Rather, a related but subjectively divided understanding of a photograph is possible if producers and recipients share common sociocultural practices. Against this background of common sociocultural practices, photographs do not create visual copies of objects, but are rather perceived images of them.

Image analysis in the context of discourse analysis

If you are using photographs for discourse analysis, three levels of analysing images must be taken into consideration. Not only will you analyse the composition of photographs, their content and design, but also the context within which they were produced and published, their historic timeline, how they are presented and how they will be used. Although there is no established method of discourse analysis for photography, we will now explore a practical methodological approach which is generally useful for research in the creative industries.

The aim of this method is to understand the communicative intentions and, ultimately, the ideologies and cultural meanings embedded in images. There are three stages to this process. In the first stage, which could be termed a pre-iconographic description, all details of the image are systematically described. In the second stage, which could be termed the iconographic analysis, the meaning of the image is established by using knowledge from beyond the image, along with knowledge coming from other, comparable images and information about the image's production and use. Although the focus rests on analysing the image itself, both the narrow and broader contexts of the image are taken into consideration in its interpretation. Finally, in the third stage, which could be termed the iconologic interpretation, the unintended meanings of the image can be reconstructed by considering its historic, political, social and cultural context. A fourth stage can be created, during which the iconographic interpretation is added and the photographer's intentions are ascertained.

Another method which can be employed is structural-hermeneutical symbol analysis, which, apart from describing topical and aesthetic elements, analyses textual aspects and systematically takes the image–text relationship into consideration, from which a view of the publication context of images can be understood. In addition to these methods, photographs can be used as interview stimuli to ask participants about the meanings they connect to images. In the context of an ethnographic approach, situations can be observed during various public events, in the course of which actors take up images by themselves, use them, refer to them, comment on them and so contribute to the discourse.

TYPES OF PHOTOGRAPHIC RESEARCH

Some photographic methods which can be useful for the creative industries are outlined below.

Photo interviewing

While some limitations exist with this method, including ethical, privacy, sampling and validity issues, photo interviewing in its various forms can be a particularly powerful tool for the researcher. It can challenge participants, provide nuances, trigger memories, lead to new perspectives and explanations, and help to avoid researcher misinterpretation. The technique can be used at any stage of research and provide a means of 'getting inside' a programme and its context. Photo interviewing can also bridge psychological and physical realities, can allow for a combination of visual and verbal language, and assist with building trust and rapport.

Although it might produce unpredictable infor- mation, it can also promote longer, more detailed interviews in comparison with verbal interviews, can

provide a component of multi-methods triangulation to improve rigour and can form a core technique to enhance collaborative/participatory research and needs assessments.

Photo novella

Photo novella refers to the creation of 'picture stories'. Photos are used to encourage participants to talk about daily routines and events, and cameras are not entrusted to researchers or professional photographers but are given to children, the elderly or other marginalized groups to use. A key component of the photo novella process is dialogue. This grounding of the images in real experience makes the photos more valuable than a set of images created by outsiders. A photo novella is designed to be a tool of empowerment, enabling those with little money, power or status to communicate to policymakers about where change should occur.

Photo elicitation

Many elicitation techniques grew from early cognitive anthropology. Their general purpose is to elicit participants' subjective understanding of some given domain or body of cultural knowledge. They can be used to develop models or ethnographic descriptions. The use of photographs to provoke a response became known as photo elicitation. These picture interviews can be flooded with encyclopaedic community information, whereas in exclusively verbal interviews, communication difficulties and memory blocks can inhibit the flow of information. Participants respond to photographs without hesitation. By providing informants with a task similar to viewing a family album, tensions arising from the interview situation can be averted.

Auto-driving

In the field of marketing, photo interviewing has been used to enhance informant involvement and to elicit information about consumer behaviour. However, instead of being presented with photos to comment upon, photos are taken by interviewees themselves. This was termed auto-driving, to indicate that interviews are 'driven' by informants who witness their own behaviour.

CHAPTER 30
NARRATIVE

Social contexts can be understood as socially constructed verbal systems: stories, discourses and texts. Each actor within the social context has a voice in the narrative. These voices can be loud, articulate and powerful or silent or unheard. The differences and possibilities are exposed when we visualize a social context as comprising simultaneously occurring dialogues, with each actor's voice being the centre of their own social context. In order to undertake research that identifies and allows each of these voices to be heard, a storytelling approach can be used.

SOCIAL CONTEXT STORIES

Social context stories can be defined as an exchange between two or more actors during which a past or anticipated experience is referred to, recounted, interpreted or challenged. Narratives are a practical source of information from which you can base an inquiry into social events or interactions. Using stories is convenient because they are easy to collect and they reduce complexity; rather than discussing attitudes and beliefs directly with actors, stories are said to represent them. Stories get to the heart of actors' meaning by explaining the nature of an individual's own reality. As well as revealing individual meaning, storytelling is a symbolic form by which actors construct the shared meanings of a social context. Stories are a narrative sense-making structure that link a sequence of events. Using stories as a source of research data allows you to conveniently access the interpretations, meaning and order that individuals and groups place on their organizational lives.

More important than the convenience of using stories to gain access to individual and shared contextual meanings, storytelling is a research technique with a pluralistic and diverse approach to social contextual analysis. Rather than assuming that there is a single reality expressed by one authoritative voice, stories taken from a variety of sources can provide an opportunity to see the inbuilt differences in how actors make sense of their social experience.

Stories can bring subjectivity back to a platform from where it can be observed and allow for a presentation of the interactions of social life based on the different personal experiences and sense-making assumptions of actors.

THE RESEARCH PROCESS

The first step in undertaking research of this nature is to collect stories from actors who have been involved in events relating to your research question. This puts the onus on you as the researcher to decide and select whose stories to listen to. Using storytelling as a research technique aims to give a voice to stories that are not heard in the traditional research framework. In particular, stories of disagreement and resistance need to be heard alongside the legitimized stories of power holders. The value of this approach is that it creates opportunities for reflective discussion and comparison of diverse story meanings and themes. These themes can also be contrasted to theoretically abstract models in the literature to see if the common sense understandings of actors match up to the prescribed preferences. Stories are available from a number of sources. They are told face to face on a daily basis as people at work interact with one another; and in writing, through electronic media such as email and blogs.

Stories which are available to each actor as they carry out their work or social interactions may not, however, be equally available to you as a researcher. Nevertheless, it is possible to gather stories for the specific purposes of research, providing that the researcher can gain access to the storytellers. Researching using storytelling can then be done by asking individuals to recount events they perceive in social contexts. These stories can be used to research how actors make sense of their situations and to highlight differences between individuals in this process. Studies of this nature are equally applicable to inquiry into multiple perspectives within a social context or to inquire into social contexts across different settings.

The process of gathering this type of data is first to select storytellers from diverse perspectives. The researcher then needs to use story-listening skills to be able to receive the stories effectively. These skills are similar to active listening and involve suspending judgements based on stereotypes, empathizing with the storyteller and providing reflective responses to encourage storytellers to tell their stories to the end, then giving feedback to the storyteller to ensure that the story has been accurately received.

REPRESENTATION OF RESEARCH DATA

You need to pay attention to the issue of representation. Concerns have been raised about how researchers construct accounts of their fieldwork using epic and heroic narratives that prioritize the author's voice-over that of the actors. This monological format of the representation of data curbs the empowerment of diverse and indigenous voices and does not allow for ambiguity, heterogeneity and discord. This difficult issue relates to how we can resolve a conflict between interpretation and representation. In an attempt to resolve this issue, we can use an analogy of the researcher as less of a 'lone interpreter' and as more of a 'ghostwriter'.

Research can be represented in the form of text (stories) told by the organizational storytellers, where the initial role of the researcher is merely to write up the story. Research findings can be represented as they were discovered and the stories told in the first person. Following the recounting of these stories, the researcher

can write up his or her own story relating to how the stories were gathered and his or her own interpretations of those stories. The researcher is now not 'the lone interpreter' who got to the heart of a particular culture assisted by powerful theoretical understanding, but rather just another voice in the orchestra of social life.

SIDES OF THE STORY

One popular metaphor for storytelling is to look at the 'sides' of a story. This metaphor is unsuitably related to the material world. To see stories in this way draws a parallel between social reality as a physical geometric object with many sides. Each actor has a 'side' of his or her own and the role of the researcher is to reveal each of the sides in order to expose the totality of the social situation. But in a social world, any series of events has as many sides as there are individuals to interpret it. The representation of these interpretations again has as many sides as there are further interpretations. We therefore cannot see the object as a whole, as it has become too complex. It is an object with innumerable sides, each side itself having innumerable sides, and so it goes on. There will be no definite social reality.

One approach to researching within social contexts is based on the assumption that social groups are characterized by this indefinite difference and diversity among their members. Based on this diversity, different actors construct different 'realities' about their situations. If you research using this tool, you will not be seeking to develop a consensus about the criteria as legitimate or representing the whole, but rather to expose a part of the multiplicity of perspectives available in the given setting. In doing this, particular attention is placed on those perspectives or 'voices' that are suppressed by the process of becoming legitimate and the unprincipled tendencies of performance and efficiency. Researching in this way uses a storytelling technique through which the researcher seeks to gather stories from a range of organizational actors, with a focus on diverse and oppositional accounts. Stories are represented as first-person narratives, with the implicit recognition that the writer has only one voice.

PROBLEMS WITH STORIES

As discussed earlier, stories used as accounts of actors' experience can be seen to be the embodiment of their beliefs, which get to the heart of an individual's reality and represent actors' symbolically constructed and shared meanings. But do they restore subjectivity to the platform from which they can be observed? Storytelling is a seductive approach that can lead us to believe that we are doing research that is pluralistic, multi-vocal, non-discriminatory and non-privileging. But is asserting that this statement of stories is unproblematic an illusion that is equally as idealistic and unsound as the search for quantitatively represented empirical social truths?

There is no way we can actually place a real-life actor and their experiences between the pages. Stories are not real life; they are reconstructed representations of an actor's experience. They are always subject to further and different undocumented reconstructions by the storyteller and deconstruction by whoever reads or hears them. They can always be seen in potential contrast to the undocumented stories of other people who experienced the events in the story. If we assume that there is no theoretically neutral language of observation that can describe the supposedly fixed properties of the physical world, then stories cannot provide any factual accuracy, but can only highlight the problems of representation.

This can be partially addressed by suggesting the presentation of stories as first-person narratives, which would then allow for the presence of multiple voices. It seems that problems of representation cannot be ultimately resolved in research, but can only be recognized. Acknowledging this is a step away from the misleading assumptions and conclusions that can only result from a purely denotative view of language. This perspective sees interpretation and representation as being problematic. It calls for a more self-reflective approach that pays attention to how stories are produced and read. The story should be more open and should reflect ambiguities in the social world and in language. It must be recognized that the product of the research is not knowledge, but the written text itself. The production of this text is merely a means by which social actors define and reflect on their environments. By looking at research from multiple perspectives and producing a narrative that contains diverse voices, we attempt to write in a way that does not determine reality, but which rather imagines different possibilities.

TYPES AND FORMS OF STORIES

Writer David M. Boje defines a story as any 'oral or written performance involving two or more people interpreting past or anticipated experience'. He further asserts that stories are 'the preferred sense-making currency of human relationships among internal and external stakeholders in organizations'. We can say that design itself is an act of storytelling and that designers are storytellers. Here are a few of the main types of stories:

- Hero stories feature characters who show skill and achieve great things.
- Survivor stories talk about how things go wrong but are put right. It is the opposite of the hero story, which often sends a message that the organization and its leaders are incompetent, but that 'we found a way around them'.
- 'Steam valve' stories reduce stress and build friendship and loyalty, often in a humorous, dramatic and irreverent manner.
- 'Learn from mistakes' stories tell of pending or present threats that we should change to avoid; or of lessons we learned because of past threats gone unheeded.
- 'Trust' stories build affinity, heal conflict and facilitate change.

Apart from written and oral narratives that we hear every day, stories can come in other, often abstract, forms such as

- Rites (events), which re-enact important narratives in cultures. Examples include rites of passage, which denote promotion or progression; political rites, in which people or practices are validated or invalidated; calendar rites, which call on us to remember; rites of exchange, which accompany important transactions; rites of communion, which solidify alliances and partnerships; and rites of affliction, which commemorate loss.

- Physical objects, in the form of logos, symbols, art objects, buildings, and so on, are abstract stories that express the underlying character, ideology or values of an organization.
- People, particularly leaders, are stories when they embody and live out a narrative that inspires admiration and imitation or warns against a way of being.
- Games, in the form of simulations, role plays and exercises are also abstract stories that teach lessons and allow experimentation with actual or alternative realities.

It is important to note that any story form can carry any particular story type.

CHAPTER 31
CASE STUDY

This section examines how you can start to combine theory using a case study approach. Five analytic (and not strictly sequential) phases of theory building can be used with case studies and these are: research design, data collection, data ordering, data analysis and literature comparison. The tables that appear over the following pages detail nine possible steps that you can follow in order to achieve these stages. Both the phases and steps can be evaluated against four research quality criteria: construct validity, internal validity, external validity and reliability.

RESEARCH QUALITY CRITERIA

Construct validity can be enhanced by establishing clearly specified operational procedures. Internal validity can be enhanced by establishing causal relationships when certain conditions are shown to lead to other conditions, as distinguished from false relationships.

In this sense, internal validity addresses the credibility or truth value of the project's findings. External validity means that you need to find out where and in what context the project's findings can be generalized. The focus here is on analytic and not statistical generalization, and will require generalizing some broader theory and not the broader population. To establish reliability, you should demonstrate that the operations of a project – such as data-collection procedures – can be repeated with the same results. The figure on page 151 provides an overview of the phases, steps and tests that can be used as a template for subsequent discussion that moves from a normative or prescriptive account of recommended activities to a descriptive account of how these prescriptions will be applied in your project.

RESEARCH DESIGN PHASE

Research design is defined by Easterby-Smith et al. (1990, p. 21) as 'the overall configuration of a piece of research: what kind of evidence is gathered from where, and how such evidence is interpreted in order to provide good answers to the basic research question[s]'.

The first step is to define your basic research questions. These should be defined narrowly enough so that your research is focused, and broad enough to allow for flexibility. A good source of research questions is the technical literature (such as reports of research studies, and theoretical and philosophical papers characteristic of professional and disciplinary writing) on the general problem area. Once you have generated your basic research questions, your research is focused. The next aspect of research design and the second step is to select your first case. Here you can use theoretical sampling, but unlike the sampling done in quantitative investigations, theoretical sampling cannot be planned before embarking on an inductive approach.

Specific sampling decisions evolve during the research process itself. During initial data collection, when the main categories are emerging, a full 'deep' coverage of the data is necessary. Subsequently, theoretical sampling requires you to only collect data on categories, for the development of properties and propositions. The criterion for judging when to stop theoretical sampling is the category's 'theoretical saturation'. This occurs when you cannot find any additional data. As you see similar instances over and over again, you will become confident that a category is saturated. When one category is saturated, nothing remains but to go on to new groups for data on other categories, and attempt to saturate these categories also.

Remember, not all categories will be equally relevant, and accordingly the depth of inquiry into each one should not be the same. Core categories, those with the greatest explanatory power, should be saturated as completely as possible. A theory is saturated when it remains constant in the face of new data and rich in detail. You will select an initial case and on the basis of the data analysis relating to that case and the emerging theory you will select additional cases.

You can use the literature as a source of secondary data. Research publications often include quoted materials from interviews and field notes, and these quotations can be used as secondary sources of data for your own purposes. The publications may also include descriptive materials concerning events, actions, settings and actors' perspectives that can be used as data using the methods described.

You can start by analysing a ('literature') case, which may lead on to the generation of the initial theoretical framework. Then you can select additional ('empirical') cases one at a time, to test and extend your framework. If you are using theoretical sampling, each additional case should serve specific purposes within the overall scope of enquiry. Three options are identified by Yin (1989):

1. choose a case to fill theoretical categories, to extend the emerging theory; and/or
2. choose a case to replicate previous case(s) to test the emerging theory; or
3. choose a case that is a polar opposite to extend the emerging theory.

This implies that each additional case must be carefully selected so that it produces similar results (a literal replication – options (a) and (b)); or so that it produces contrary results, but for predictable reasons (a theoretical replication – option (c)). By the time three or four sets of data have been analysed, you will have discovered the majority of useful concepts.

DATA-COLLECTION PHASE

In theoretical sampling, there is no 'correct' choice of data or technique for data collection. Different kinds of data will give you different views or vantage points from which you can understand a category and from which to develop its properties. These different views are called slices of data. While you may focus on one

technique of data collection by sampling for saturation of a category, you will have a multifaceted investigation where there are no limits to the techniques of data collection, the way they are used, or the types of data acquired.

Case study research can involve qualitative data only, quantitative only or both. Moreover, the combination of data types can be highly synergistic. The synergy (or 'data triangulation') can happen in this way: quantitative data can indicate directly observable relationships and corroborate the findings from qualitative data. Qualitative data can help you to understand the rationale of the theory and underlying relationships. The use of multiple data sources can enhance construct validity and reliability.

Validity and reliability can be further enhanced through the preparation of a case study database, which is a formal assembly of evidence distinct from the case study report. This database will allow other investigators to review the evidence directly and not be limited to the written reports. This way, the database will increase the reliability of your entire case study.

The third step will be to develop data-collection protocol by employing multiple data-collection methods using both qualitative and quantitative data and systematically establishing a case study database.

One example could be archival material, in the form of reports in newspapers, trade journals, business journals, government publications, broker reviews, annual company documents and press releases. These data can be extracted in computerized form. Case study databases can be constructed within qualitative data-analysis software packages.

The fourth step will be to ensure that you collect data and analyse it simultaneously and flexibly and that this is maintained. This overlap will allow you to make adjustments to the data-collection process in light of the emerging findings.

DATA ORDERING PHASE

The fifth step will be data ordering. Data can be ordered chronologically. By arranging the events into a chronology, it will enable you to determine causal events over time. However, unlike the more general time-series approaches, the chronology is likely to cover many different types of variables and not be limited to a single independent or dependent variable.

DATA ANALYSIS PHASE

Once your data is ordered, the sixth step will be to analyse the data. Data analysis is central to theory building research. For an inductive project, data collection, data ordering and data analysis will be interrelated as depicted in Figure 3.6 (the attached numbers indicate the activity's analytic sequence).

Within this general framework, data analysis for each case will involve you generating concepts through the process of coding, which represents the operations by which data are deconstructed, conceptualized and put back together in new ways. It is the central process from which you can build theories from data.

There are three types of coding: open coding, axial coding and selective coding. These are analytic types and it does not necessarily follow that you will move from open through axial to selective coding in a strict, consecutive manner.

Open coding refers to that part of the analysis that deals with the labelling and categorizing of phenomena as indicated by the data. The products of labelling and categorizing are concepts – the basic building blocks in inductive theory construction.

Open coding requires application of what is referred to as 'the comparative method', that is, the asking of questions and the making of comparisons. Data are initially broken down by asking simple questions such as what, where, how, when, how much, and so forth. Subsequently, data are compared and similar incidents are grouped together and given the same conceptual label. The process of grouping concepts at a higher, more abstract level is termed categorizing.

Whereas open coding fractures the data into concepts and categories, axial coding puts those data back together in new ways by making connections between a category and its sub-categories (that is, not between discrete categories, which is done in selective coding). Therefore, axial coding refers to the process of developing main categories and their sub-categories.

Selective coding involves the integration of the categories that have been developed to form the initial theoretical framework.

A storyline is either generated or made explicit. A story is simply a descriptive narrative about the central phenomenon of the project and the storyline is the conceptualization of this story (abstracting). When analysed, the storyline becomes the core category.

Subsidiary categories are related to the core category according to the paradigm model. The basic purpose of this is to enable you to think systematically about data and to relate them in complex ways. The basic idea is to propose linkages and look to the data for validation (move between asking questions, generating propositions and making comparisons). The core category (that is, the central idea, event or happening) is defined as the phenomenon. Other categories are then related to this core category according to the schema.

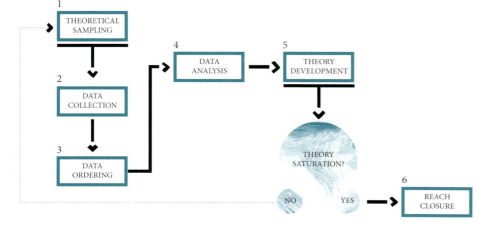

Figure 3.6 The interrelated processes of data collection, data ordering, and data analysis to build theory
Once you have collected your data, you will need to order it and analyse it so that you can build your theory.

Causal conditions are the events that lead to the development of the phenomenon. Context refers to the particular set of conditions and intervening conditions, the broader set of conditions, in which the phenomenon is situated. Action/interaction strategies refer to the actions and responses that occur as the result of the phenomenon. The outcomes – both intended and unintended – of these actions and responses are referred to as 'consequences'.

An important activity during coding is the writing of memos. Writing theoretical memos is an integral part of doing qualitative inductive work. You cannot readily keep track of all the categories, properties, hypotheses and generative questions that evolve from the analytical process, so you need a system for doing this. Using memos is one such system. Memos are not simply 'ideas'. They are involved in the formulation and revision of theory during the research process.

At least three types of memo may be distinguished: code memos, theoretical memos and operational memos. Code memos relate to open coding and thus focus on conceptual labelling. Theoretical memos relate to axial and selective coding and thus focus on paradigm features and indications of process. Finally, operational memos contain directions relating to the evolving research design.

In the past, the tools used to aid the type of data analysis elucidated above were simply scissors, a copier and piles of blank paper. Now you can also choose to analyse your data using qualitative data-analysis software packages, which can also facilitate the construction of case study databases. The principal advantage of using a programme is that it simplifies and speeds the mechanical aspects of data analysis without sacrificing flexibility, thereby freeing you up to concentrate to a greater extent on the more creative aspects of theory building. The thinking, judging, deciding, interpreting and so forth will still be done by you. The computer does not make conceptual decisions, such as which words or themes are important to focus on, or which analytical step to take next. These analytical tasks are still left entirely to you.

Once a theoretical framework relating to the first case has been generated, the next and seventh step in theory building case research is to test and develop this framework by selecting additional cases according to the principle of theoretical sampling; that is, with the aim to extend and/or sharpen the emerging theory by filling in categories that may need further refinement and/or development.

LITERATURE COMPARISON PHASE

The eighth step, reaching closure, is taken according to the principle of theoretical saturation, that is, when the marginal value of the new data is minimal. The ninth and final step is to compare the emerged theory with the extant literature and examine what is similar, what is different and why. Tying the emergent theory to existing literature enhances your projects' internal validity, generalizability and theoretical level of the theory building from case study research, because your findings often rest on a very limited number of cases. You can then compare the emergent theory of your case study with the extant theories in the broader field of study in order to find similarities and differences.

CHAPTER 32
EMERGING TOOLS

This section gives a brief description of some research tools that are emerging in the creative industries, and situations they can be used in.

CULTURAL PROBES

Cultural probes (also known as diary studies) provide a way of gathering information about people and their activities. Unlike direct observation (like usability testing or traditional field studies), the technique allows users to self-report. Information gathered from cultural probes is particularly useful early in the design process.

When can I use cultural probes?

Cultural probes are appropriate when you need to gather information from users with minimal influence on their actions, or when the process or event you're exploring takes place intermittently or over a long period. For example, you could use cultural probes to explore how designers manage their work.

How can I conduct a cultural probe?

Your selected participants are given the materials you want them to use, for example, diary, camera or voice recorder and then briefed about the method of recording or noting specific events, feelings or interactions over a specified period. It is worth giving thought to how you present your kit, as participants respond positively when it is attractive and contains all they need to use. You can then have a later meeting with your participants to follow up on their progress after the briefing session. This helps you to ensure that participants are actively engaged, and are collecting the required information. At the end of the specified period, the materials are collected and analysed. A debriefing session is also typically conducted, in order to supplement, validate and otherwise explore the information gathered by the participants. Information gathered is then analysed and documented.

Recruiting participants

Who you recruit as a participant is particularly important with cultural probes, as these rely on a large investment of time. Participants in cultural probes are expected to devote at least several hours to the activity. They usually cannot be monitored closely, so problems may not be picked up at the time. Therefore, you need to monitor and support them as much as possible throughout the process.

How can I obtain the right data?

You can help participants to gather the right information by briefing them carefully, and by providing kits that prompt them for the types of information that you want. Take care not to unduly restrict the information that they gather, in case you miss out on important insights, and make sure that they can get in touch with you if they need to get advice. You can use affinity diagrams to analyse the data (see Table 3.1 on page 122).

SCENARIOS

A scenario is a description of a person's interaction with a system. Scenarios help focus design efforts on the user's requirements, which are distinct from technical or business requirements. They may be related to 'use cases', which describe interactions at a technical level. Unlike use cases, however, scenarios can be understood by people who do not have any technical background. They are therefore suitable for use during participatory design activities.

When can I use scenarios?

Scenarios are appropriate whenever you need to describe a system interaction from the user's perspective. They are particularly useful when you need to remove focus from the technology in order to open up design possibilities; or to ensure that technical or budgetary constraints do not override usability constraints without due consideration. Scenarios can help confine complexity to the technology layer (where it belongs), and prevent it from becoming manifest within the user interface.

How can I write scenarios?

To write a scenario, you need a basic understanding of the tasks to be supported by the system. You also need to have an understanding of the users and the context of use. Scenarios can be derived from data gathered during contextual inquiry activities. If you do not have access to such data, you can write scenarios based on prior knowledge or even 'your best guess', provided they will be subject to review by users prior to being used as a basis for making design decisions.

To write a scenario, describe in simple language the interaction that needs to take place. It is important to avoid references to technology, except where the technology represents a design constraint that must be acknowledged. Include references to all relevant aspects of the interaction, even where they are outside the current scope of the technology. Such references may include cultural and attitudinal issues. For example, the fact that Mike is continually interrupted by telephone calls may be just as relevant as the design software he uses. After you have written a scenario, review it and remove any unwarranted references to systems or technologies. You should also have the scenario reviewed by users to ensure that it is representative of the real world.

How can I use scenarios?

Use scenarios during design to ensure that all participants understand and agree to the design parameters, and to specify exactly what interactions the system must support. Translate scenarios into tasks for conducting walk-through activities and usability tests. Be prepared to review scenarios based on feedback from users. In particular, be prepared to modify or even abandon any unrealistic or unrepresentative scenarios.

DESIGN ETHNOGRAPHY – UNDERSTANDING HUMAN BEHAVIOUR AND CULTURES

Design ethnography is based on ethnography, which is a branch of anthropology that uses various techniques and ways of thinking to understand modern human behaviours and cultures. Design ethnography, however, is a fast and effective method for developing innovative products and services, because frameworks emerge from the data you collect and these can be used to facilitate decisions.

Design ethnography combines human-centred design methods with ethnographic techniques to take you on a guided tour of your users' world, for the purposes of designing new products and/or experiences. The method is qualitative, and research is focused and capable of revealing a deep, contextual understanding of what users do and why.

When can I use design ethnography?

Design ethnography research can be used to reveal the spoken and unspoken needs and wants of product users. It will assist you in understanding the needs and challenges of the users and help you to identify problems and issues that need solving. It can also be used to design more efficient workflows in products and services.

CHAPTER 33
THE PRACTICE: AN EXAMPLE OF ELICITATION TECHNIQUES

The following section is an extract from the methodology section of a research project (which formed part of the author's PhD). The aim of the project was to find out how participants identified with physical artefacts in the work environment. The aim of using this technique was to elicit 'experience near' phenomena. These are phenomena that are so close to us emotionally that it is difficult for us to express. Once this information was obtained a 'ladder' was created. Laddering originated from Kelly (1955) and his personal construct theory.

PROCESS OF LADDERING

Laddering can be conducted in different directions: downwards to seek explanation and upwards to elicit goals and values, or sideways to provide further examples at the same level. I decided to concentrate on single direction upward laddering. The average interview took about forty-five minutes during which I took handwritten notes, rather than tape recording in the majority of cases. Although the research of Reynolds and Gutman (1998) tended to elicit short responses (in this case perhaps because the focus was on identity meaning and values), the responses were wordy; so whenever it was possible to record the responses, it was helpful to be able to listen to them after the interview to search for meaning and explanation.

DATA-COLLECTION PROCEDURES AND PROCESSING

Means-end theory was designed to explain the relationship between goods and consumers. In this case,

it was used to explain the relationship between physical artefacts in the organizational built environment and the organizational actors. In the original definition a good is defined by a series of attributes which yield consequences when the good is used.

The importance of these consequences is based on their ability to satisfy personally motivating values and goals of people. So in means-end theory, the relationship between attributes and values is also indirect but the consequences can be quite broad. It can encompass everyday activities but also consequences that are more functional or psychosocial in nature.

In addition, means-end is more 'bottom up' in its approach in the sense that the meaning an artefact has for the individual is investigated from the point of the individual. The attributes, consequences and values that are relevant are determined in the first place by the organizational actor and not the interviewer. A means-end is a model that provides a way for relating the choice of an artefact to its contribution to the realization of objectives and values. In the original context, means are goods that people consume and activities that they carry out. Ends are positively evaluated (end) situations such as privacy and freedom. The most important linkages between value and objectives influence choice processes.

Secondly, it is assumed that people can keep track of the enormous diversity of goods by grouping them in sets or classes so as to reduce complexities of choice. This means that we not only classify goods in product fields (furniture, equipment) but also create functional classifications such as 'preserving my image' or 'showing my status in the organization' and these classifications may contain the objects used for this such as a cell office or a leather chair. Thirdly, it is assumed that our behaviour has consequences and that these are not the same for everyone. Finally, there is the assumption that we learn to associate particular consequences with particular behaviours.

Laddering interviews

The key phase in measuring the means-end chain is the laddering interview. This involves a tailored interview format, using a series of probes asking 'why is this important to you?' (Easterby-Smith, Thorpe and Holman, 1996). This has a goal of establishing the link between the essential elements of a means-end chain: attributes – consequences – values. If a participant said that glazed walling was important in assessing his or her position in the organization (identity), then they would be asked 'why do you find glazed walling important to your assessment of yourself/group/organization?' The 'why' question is then repeated as a reaction to the answer of the respondent. This process stops when the participant can no longer answer why.

By allowing participants to begin at the concrete level of the attributes and then continuously asking 'why?' enables the underlying consequences and values of a certain choice to be brought into the open. In this way, a means-end chain can be determined for each participant and each attribute level is called the ladder. A ladder shows the previously unvocalized reasons for choosing the attribute and may reveal the underlying values of the individual in relation to the object. Fourteen laddering interviews were undertaken. During the interviews, participants often gave forked answers (Grunet and Grunet, 1995). This means that several consequences are linked to only one attribute. This can occur with participants who have thought thoroughly about a certain preference or decision and consequently have an extensive meaning structure in the area concerned.

Means-end to ladder

In the next phase, the means-end chains were determined on the basis of the interviews. The data from the laddering interviews was transcribed and then a content analysis was carried out. This resulted in a set of ladders for each respondent. This information was subsequently grouped into 'incidents'. Subsequently, the elements of these means-end chains were coded, dividing them according to topic and level in the hierarchy (attribute, consequence, value).

The original and simplest means-end model has three levels: product – attributes (A) – consequences (C) – values (V). A simple example of a means-end chain model related to the organizational built environment would be: glazed office walling (attribute) – more light (consequence) – less claustrophobic (value). An example of laddering is illustrated below.

The summary ladder for (2) FACULTY AREA is

- (V) STATUS REDUCED
- (C) WORK ETHIC
- (C) DIRECTORS' STRATEGY
- (C) MESS
- (C) CHECKING ON STAFF
- (A) CLOCKS

CHAPTER 34

THE PRACTITIONERS: BETTINA KOLB ON PARTICIPATORY PHOTO-INTERVIEW

Bettina Kolb has been working for many years with the visual method of participatory photo-interviews and has developed the method as a sociological tool for interdisciplinary and transdisciplinary research. She is a lecturer in the Department of Sociology at the University of Vienna and a practising social scientist at the Vienna Institute for Urban Sustainability, Austria. Research fields: visual sociology, participatory photo-interview, social sustainability, social aspects of public space. This interview is based on written contact with and the writings of Bettina Kolb. The photo-interview has proven particularly useful for sustainability and environmental studies, in which eliciting community points of view is crucial to the research effort. Based on experiences in several countries, Bettina Kolb describes and analyses the photo-interview process and its three key phases – involving, sharing and analysing – and explores potential influences on data quality.

WHAT ARE THE PHASES INVOLVED IN THE PHOTO-INTERVIEW METHOD?

In the first phase, researchers use the photo-interview method to involve participants in the research process. In the second phase, the photo-interview method encourages participants to share insights and to partner in developing a common understanding. In the third phase, the photo-interview method allows researchers to analyse visual and textual data as a representation of a local societal context. In decoding images, researchers

ground the analysis in subjective perspectives, using participants' visual codes to further analyse the context, in relation to the wider societal context in which the study is embedded.

WHAT IS THE PARTICIPATORY PHOTO-INTERVIEW?

The photo-interview method invites participants to answer a research question by taking photos and explaining them to the researcher. Once the photo-interview is completed, the photos and interview text are available as data for further research and sociological interpretation using different methods of scientific analysis.

HOW DOES THIS METHOD RELATE TO OTHER PHOTO-INTERVIEW METHODS?

Researchers have used photos to elicit information in research settings for more than fifty years. For several decades, however, photos used were always taken by professional photographers or the researchers themselves. The participatory aspect of the photo-interview process, in which participants take the photos, distinguishes the photo-interview method from other research approaches using photos. The photo-interview allows the research discussion to start with real places and experiences, and to envision possible, desired futures. As participants 'audience' their images for each other and for researchers, they begin a cognitive process of developing and expressing their ideas, feelings and concerns.

WHAT ARE THE PHASES OF THE PHOTO-INTERVIEW?

Based on practical experience using the method in different cultural settings, a common structure for an effective photo-interview process with four phases has emerged.

In the first phase, researchers invite respondents to consider a general research question and how to take photos that reflect their viewpoint on the influence or meaningfulness of the scientific question for their own concepts and life experiences. In the second or active photo-shooting phase, participants take photos of specific subjects in their social and material surroundings; for example, places, buildings, people, social networks or local activities and businesses that relate to the research question and are meaningful to them.

In the third (decoding) phase, participants consider their photos and verbalize their thinking in an interview with a researcher and, when desired or culturally appropriate, in collaboration with other participants also. The final or analytical scientific interpretation phase involves researchers analysing the data – photos, interview transcripts and observations – generated by the first three phases.

WHAT IS THE EXTENT OF PARTICIPANT ENGAGEMENT?

During the active photo-shooting phase, respondents continue to reflect on the research question. Participants' tacit knowledge about an issue emerges as they go through a process of visualizing the issue and producing images; respondents often find this phase empowering as they gain new insights into their lives through the camera lens. They become researchers of their own culture, lives, homes and neighbourhoods as they take photos.

The process appears to encourage participant ownership of the problem or question at hand and initiate a process of role transformation – from resident to advocate. During the interview, when participants discuss their photos, their photo-taking strategies are often an important part of their narration and may reflect participants' sense of engagement and empowerment in the research process. The photo-interview thus encourages people to become more active in their social environment.

DO YOU INVOLVE DISADVANTAGED GROUPS?

The photo-interview method improves communication with participants from disadvantaged groups, particularly the elderly, children and those who are illiterate or have little education. Mutual engagement by social scientists and local residents as they discuss participant photographs results in a levelling of the power imbalance between them.

WHO DECODES VISUAL INFORMATION?

Members of societies learn through cultural socialization to interpret visual information. This understanding enables participants in transdisciplinary studies using the photo-interview method to decode images, just as they do already with images from the media, and to feel that they are members in a common societal communication process. Respondents in cultural settings as diverse as Vienna, Damascus, Cairo and China have used their cultural knowledge to code (in taking photos) and decode (narratively in the interview) visual images during the photo-interview.

HOW DO YOU START THE DIALOGUE?

After the participatory phase of taking the photo, the phase of decoding the visual information begins. Participants take on an expert role here, as they describe their photos and initiate dialogue between respondent and researcher. The photo provides the impulse to speak: for the setting of the photo-interview, photos motivate respondents to participate in the interview.

The decoding phase thus opens up a new level of engagement between respondents and researcher.

Participants describe their photos in their own words in non-scientific language and the researcher encourages them to speak about their personal values. This phase establishes dialogue and trust, and the researcher encourages participants to argue their viewpoint. Ideally, the photo-interview promotes mutual learning by both scientists and residents in a conversation between equals. During this phase, respondents introduce the researcher to their world through their photos and give their verbal explanations of the images. Thus, the photo-interview is an important moment of interpretation and understanding, when the respondent explains and makes explicit his or her intention in capturing the image and recounts their first interpretation of it.

WHAT IS THE STANDPOINT OF THE PHOTOGRAPHER?

Experience shows that participants are very engaged in the research process while taking the photos. In the active photo-shooting phase, participants act freely on their own and are not observed by the researcher. They act within their own social environment with its particular rules and normative behaviours, outside the purview of the researcher. The scientist perceives social activity through the photographer's perspective, which in turn illuminates the action before the camera.

HOW ARE PARTICIPANTS INVOLVED IN IMAGE PRODUCTION?

In analysing the photo-interview, visual and interview data has two distinct aspects: the process of image production and the photo and text material. In the photo-production process, participants contribute to the overall research question and present their individual subjective viewpoint, visible in the photo content and also in the image's technical aspects. The photographer's point of view tells a story about them, within the broader context of the participatory photo-interview process involving several respondents taking photos for the study. Thus, researchers may have a great number of photos to analyse. A useful, even necessary first step in the analysis involves classifying photos from participants into 'specific' groups, categories or themes, irrespective of the photographer. Participants' photos can be seen as respondent answers to the research questions; categories for codifying the visual material should therefore emerge from this empirical data.

HOW IS INFORMATION SHARED?

The data – photo and text – generated by the photo-interview process has a dense, holistic character and is produced with a logical, emotional motivation to communicate a specific topic to the researcher. This motivation is explained in the interview situation, when participants give a narrative of the photos a certain way of 'reading' and decoding the image. Within the photo-interview, the respondent and photographer describe what the image represents and what the photographer intended to show. The delicate question of the objective content of the photo is postponed. The respondent organizes what to think about the photo and expresses a subjective reading of the image within the context of the photo-interview.

Generally, the photo is considered as valuable material for research, embedded in a research process centred on a question that matters both to the researchers and to the participants. The narration becomes a first interpretation by the participant as he or she explains the motivation for taking the photo. The first interpretation can be seen as a kind of 'participant's reading', and becomes a foundation for common knowledge between researcher and participant. Ideally, the interview produces an autonomous reading of the photo that supports the respondent's conception of the world. In a further step, this reading by the respondent can be augmented by an additional reading by the researcher.

AND THE RESEARCHER'S ROLE?

Focusing on the image itself, its subjects and motifs is an essential aspect of exploring patterns and social constructions within a sociological analysis. The researcher's reading or 'audiencing' of the image also provides a valuable resource for understanding the cultural content of the photo expressed in visual codes. A photo is meaningful for the photographer in a way that is not always explicit to other audiences. Thus, the first essential step in the scientist's interpretation is to communicate the 'content' of an image for a scientific audience. One task is to list the main contents of the image; this 'fixing' of the photo identifies the visual content that the researcher is able to read and understand, and becomes the basis for further interpretation.

This interview has explained the origin of the photo-interview method and its development within sociological studies, and has showed how the participatory photo-interview was successfully used in the interdisciplinary and transdisciplinary research setting of sustainability and environmental research.

MANAGING THE RESEARCH

This part of the book focuses on the management of the research process, analysis of data and drawing conclusions.

There is also a section on semiotics and its influence on design research. There are sections that focus on specific types of data analysis and give examples of their uses in the creative industries. In the 'Practice' section, the use of theory building using case studies is discussed, and practical examples of research involving organizations are highlighted.

THINK BOX
Ideology

The meaning of ideology

Ideology is all about considering two important features of human beings. First, it recognizes that different individuals, groups, organizations and societies have *distinctive worldviews* that meaningfully shape our thoughts and behaviour. In order to understand, explain or predict what these people or collections of people say, think and do, we need to identify and then understand these worldviews. Ideology reflects an awareness that we cannot only study the role of our own individual ideas in isolation but rather need to understand these in the context within which they are situated. By understanding and analysing ideology we can then explain why individuals will accept certain ideas and how and why these ideas may affect their behaviour in certain ways, and in consequence appreciate how those ideas work within a broader *system of ideas*.

CHAPTER 35
IDEOLOGY IN DESIGN

In the context of design, ideology relates to those beliefs we and perhaps groups we belong to have, for example the role of design or the purpose of design. Victor Papanek and Allan Chochinov strongly make a case that design is 'dangerous' and that the entire ecosystem needs to be considered within when embarking upon a design project. In this context sustainability should always be considered. This is in contrast to a view that design is just an aesthetical consideration concerned with the appearance of objects. You may agree with either of these statements or hold another view. Perhaps you believe a designer should create solutions with maximum positive impact to society. Alternatively, you may believe that sustainability is a responsibility of us all and not only the design team.

ANALYSIS IN IDEOLOGY

There are many definitions of ideology so it is important to clarify what you mean by 'ideology' and that different definitions need to be justified according to how functionally useful they are for your research.

This functional usefulness should be assessed with reference to three main considerations:

a. essential features about the way ideology has been used in research and what is an example of ideology within the context of the creative industries
b. the functional usefulness of the conception for your *specific research project*

c. the functional usefulness of the conception for *broader academic understanding across projects and disciplines*

Since (b) and (c) can pull us in opposite directions, striking a balance between them is necessary.

No one can engage in some kind of perfectly rational disembodied reflection about design that simply 'sees the world as it is' not influenced by prior thinking. Instead every individual's thinking about design occurs via networks of values, meanings, narratives, theories, assumptions, concepts, expectations, exemplars, past experiences, images, stereotypes, and beliefs about matters of fact already existing in their mind (Geertz, 1964; Berger and Luckmann, 1967; Wittgenstein, 2001). These networks of ideas vary, at least somewhat, from person to person, group to group and society to society, which is what makes them important objects of study. And individuals' ideologies are, in turn, shaped by the discourse of themselves and others – as new ideas are encountered in communication, engaged with, and rejected or internalized. Many ideologies are also represented socially in discourse, picking up social meanings and connotations, and they may inhabit social movements and become embedded in social institutions and groups through discourses and practices. Analysis of ideology is therefore concerned with not just how people think, but also how they talk and act.

CHAPTER 36

HOW CAN SEMIOTICS AND SYMBOLS BE USED IN DESIGN RESEARCH?

HOW IS MEANING ATTRIBUTED TO OR CONSTRUCTED FROM SYMBOLS AND ARTEFACTS?

We often only act upon meanings created from appearance (Blumer, 1969) so physical symbols are important tools, not only in appearance management (in relation to our surroundings) but also as a tool of social control (McVeigh, 2000). Symbols allow the user to publicly and concretely affirm or display their affiliation with, or affection for, a product or service. Association with a group is visibly marked and proclaimed through using or displaying a symbol. Visible symbols are in fact powerful statements of affiliation and identity perhaps because they are physical. Accumulating objects (and clothing) can be seen as 'extending the self' (Belk, 1988). Displayed objects in our homes or work environment can reveal a great deal about personal meaning and personal and social identity. Designs including product, architectural and graphic can instantly affirm claims of identity. By displaying symbols of that group, a chair of a designated quality, a brand of headphones, they do not need to say a word but the symbol is interpreted as belonging to that group. The object speaks for itself and is more likely to be believed than words alone. Research has shown that we are more likely to ascribe affiliation to people displaying such symbols (McVeigh, 2000). Given the potentially powerful communication impact of symbols it is worthwhile to research the relationship between symbols and design and how this may influence the design concept.

DENOTIVE/PHYSICAL PROPERTIES OF SYMBOLS

There is a two-way relationship between identification with a product or brand and attraction to its symbols. Higher levels of identification with the product and brand lead to higher levels of identification to the product and brands symbols. The idea of corporate identity design implicitly assumes that stakeholders can be drawn to organizations with the help of design (Schrubbe-Potts, 2000). There are two ways in which symbols vary from one another. One is the structure of the symbol (denotation) and the other is the content of the symbol (connotation). The structural aspects (denotation) are the physical properties that describe the product, for example colour, shape and construction. This refers to the symbol's most explicit, obvious and straight forward characteristics (Leed-Hurwitz, 1993). For example is the desk circular, oblong or square?

Henderson and Cotes (1998) studied denotative aspects of symbols and found that several physical aspects of a symbol (in this case the work was specifically on logos) naturalness, harmony, elaborateness, its proportional relationship all have an effect on whether the symbol is recognized and how much shared meaning arises from that recognition. They also tested other variables such as 'roundness', 'organic' and 'symmetric'. Research by Feucht (1989) suggests that men prefer diamond shapes and women prefer heart shapes and that the combined preference of two genders is an 's' shape. Perhaps shapes that relate specifically to a products use or its industry lead to higher instances of shared meaning. This highlights the fuzzy nature of the difference between denotative and connotative meaning in symbols. Perhaps the specific meaning of a shape cannot be captured in a denotative measurement of 'symmetry'. Uher (1991) suggests that both zigzag lines (which resemble bared teeth) and shapes which look like eyes elicit physiological avoidance behaviour, so specific features of symbolic products may generate special biological or physiological responses.

DENOTATIVE / CONNOTATIVE PROPERTIES

The symbolic content or connotative content of products will influence its liking and attractiveness and the level of identification with the product in a way which is different from the products' physical properties. The denotative aspect of the product looks at how the symbol depicts meaning, and the connotative aspect looks at what it depicts (Mollerup, 1997).

Research in semiotics has categorized the sign in three ways: an icon, an index and a symbol. An icon is a sign that visually depicts what it represents and is linked to the things they represent through a similarity between the signifier and the signified. A building can be represented as an icon with a picture of the building and can vary from being highly realistic, as in a photograph, to highly abstract. Icons can vary from being simplistic to complex and from specific to universal (McCloud, 1994). The building photograph can represent the building and Mollerup (1997) calls icons at this realistic end of the spectrum 'images'. The more abstract he labels 'diagrams' and these McCloud (1994) labels as the border between iconic and linguistic representation. 'Diagrams' are schematic signs that depict the simplest structure and most recognizable aspects of an object. McCloud (1994) defines abstraction as lying near the border between icon and language and this is telling because it points to its object. Therefore a door can be an indexical sign for a building. Because of the physical linking and pointing aspects of indexical signs meanings these meanings are dependent upon their physical placement (Mollerup, 1997).

For example, a wine glass on a carton implies that the goods are fragile but a wine glass in an airport probably means a bar. This would suggest that context places an important role on meaning. In the case of both the icon and the index, the signifier uses an explicit cue to suggest the signified.

Symbols are the third type of sign and they are signs whose meaning has been arrived at by convention. Their meanings have been socially constructed. Symbolic meanings change over time and are not necessarily universal at any given moment in time. There are also metaphoric icons, which share the conceptual qualities with the objects they represent. For example, outstretched hands can be the protective qualities of insurance.

Symbols are, in the case of language, wrapped up with their social histories so we are unable to recognize and understand the meanings of symbols unless we have been taught or have socially constructed these meanings over time and through our own personal, group or organizational experience. Most human language is made up of the symbol type of sign. Ultimately, language choices are arbitrary. For example, in one culture white flowers stand for purity, in others, death. Without explanation the viewer will not be able to ascertain the meaning of the symbol. It is an arbitrary symbol or an ideograph. In general, representations of familiar and loved things will also result in positive feelings towards the symbol and the product that incorporates them. If a symbolic product contains a representation of something that we have a positive attitude towards then we can reasonably expect that these positive attitudes will transfer, at least in part, to the symbol containing that depiction or representation.

A symbol does not exist unless it can be invented, revealed, expressed or indicated. Therefore the product is symbolic when it is understood and has meaning for someone in the environment. Symbols and signs help people to find direction in their hectic world. As we try to fit more and more into each day we increasingly need to compress the information that is thrown at us into something more digestible. Symbols can accomplish this allowing us to assimilate the barrage of details with which we are assailed each day.

Therefore it is important to design, and research with creativity and design, to understand the meaning symbols and signs can have for us and to be able to find out what this is, what it means and how this information can be used in the process of design.

CHAPTER 37
THE PILOT STUDY

A pilot study is a pre-study of your major project. You may think of it as a miniature version of your project. You may limit it by using fewer subjects than you plan to include in the full research project, or you may limit it because your scope is smaller in some other way; for example, the range of types of subjects may be more limited (e.g. you use only undergraduates in the pilot when you plan to use a broader range of the general population in the full research project) or the procedures may be more limited (e.g. you ask people about their perception of advertising images of one product when in the full research project you plan to ask people about their perception of a range of products). A pilot study can help you work out the best procedure for undertaking the research even though you know it is not likely to add anything new or important to your main research project. Some more reasons to consider a pilot study are explored further in the sections that follow.

REASONS FOR A PILOT STUDY

- It permits preliminary investigation of a research question or testing of your proposition that leads to testing, more precise investigation or testing in the main research project. It may lead to changing some questions or propositions, deleting some, or developing new questions or propositions.
- A pilot study can often provide you with ideas, approaches, and clues you may not have foreseen before conducting the pilot study. These ideas and clues increase the chances of getting clearer findings in the main research project.
- It allows you to undertake a thorough check of your planned analysis procedures, giving you a chance to evaluate their usefulness for the data. You may

then need to make alterations to the data-collecting methods so as to analyse data in the main research more efficiently.

- It can significantly reduce the number of unanticipated problems because you have an opportunity to redesign parts of your research framework to overcome difficulties that the pilot study may reveal.
- It may save you a lot of time. Unfortunately, many research ideas that seem to show great promise are unproductive when you actually carry them out. The pilot study almost always provides enough data for you to decide whether to go ahead with the main study.
- In the pilot study, you can try out a number of alternative measures and then select those that produce the clearest results for the main study.

Pilot studies can be based on quantitative and/or qualitative methods and large-scale commercial or academic pieces of research might use a number of pilot studies before the main data collection is conducted. Researchers may start with qualitative data collection and analysis on a relatively broad or previously unexplored topic and then use the results to design a subsequent quantitative phase of the study to test what your pilot study has revealed. The first phase of a pilot might involve using in-depth interviews or focus groups to establish the issues to be addressed in a large-scale questionnaire survey. Next the questionnaire: for example the wording and the order of the questions, or the range of answers on multiple-choice questions, might be piloted. A final pilot could be conducted to test the research process, for example the different ways of distributing and collecting the questionnaires.

Pilot studies may also try to identify potential practical problems in following the research procedure.

For example, it may mean that the proposed means of distributing the questionnaires would not be adhered to. Other problems such as poor recording and response rates can also be identified and precautionary procedures or safety nets can be devised. Pilot studies can also uncover local politics or problems that may affect the research process.

PILOT STUDY PROCEDURES TO IMPROVE THE INTERNAL VALIDITY OF A QUESTIONNAIRE

Administer the questionnaire to pilot subjects in exactly the same way as it will be administered in the main study. Ask the subjects for feedback to identify ambiguities and difficult questions. Remember to record the time taken to complete the questionnaire and decide whether it is reasonable to discard all unnecessary, difficult or ambiguous questions. Assess whether each question gives an adequate range of responses and establish that the replies can be interpreted in terms of the information that is required. Take time to check that all the questions are answered. If necessary reword or re-scale any questions that are not answered as you would have expected. If necessary, revise and, if possible, pilot again.

PROBLEMS WITH PILOT STUDIES

You may encounter some problems with your pilot study. These include the possibility of making inaccurate predictions or assumptions on the basis of pilot data or problems arising from contamination. These issues are now discussed in turn.

Completing a pilot study successfully is not a guarantee of the success of the full-scale research project. Although pilot study findings may offer some indication of the likely size of the response rate in the main survey, they cannot guarantee this because they do not have a statistical foundation and are nearly always based on small numbers. Furthermore, other problems may not become obvious until the larger-scale study is

conducted. A further concern is that of contamination. This may arise where data from the pilot study are included in the main results and where pilot participants are included in the main study, but new data are collected from these people.

If your research pilot is predominantly quantitative it is important that the pilot study data are not used to test a proposition or included with data from the actual study when the results are presented. The obvious concern is that if there were problems with the research tool and modifications had to be made in the light of the findings from the pilot study, data could be flawed or inaccurate. However, where an established and validated tool is being used and the pilot study is determining other methodological aspects such as recruitment rates of designers in high technology industries, for example, it could be argued that such data may be of value.

A more common problem is deciding whether to include pilot study participants or site(s) in the main study. Here the concern is that they have already been exposed to an intervention and, therefore, may respond differently from those who have not previously experienced it. This may be positive; for example, the participants may become more adept at using a new tool or procedure. However, it may also be negative with participants showing a decline in following a protocol because it is no longer new and fresh. Changes in behaviour have been recognized for a long time, and a run-in period, where an intervention is introduced prior to a study, is often used for these reasons.

The concern about including participants from the pilot study in the main study arises because only those involved in the pilot, and not the whole group, will have had the experience. In some cases, however, it is simply not possible to exclude these pilot study participants because to do so would mean you might have too small a sample in the main study. This problem occurs in particular where the samples are clusters, for example, companies. In these cases you could conduct a sensitivity analysis (or sub-group analysis) to assess to what extent the process of piloting influences the size of the intervention effect. Sensitivity analysis is the study of how the uncertainty in the output of a mathematical model or system (numerical or otherwise) can be apportioned to different sources of uncertainty in its inputs.

Contamination is less of a concern in qualitative research, where researchers often use some or all of their pilot data as part of the main study. Qualitative data collection and analysis is often progressive, in that a second or subsequent interview in a series should be 'better' than the previous one as the interviewer may have gained insights from previous interviews which are used to improve interview schedules and specific questions.

It can be argued that in qualitative approaches separate pilot studies are not necessary. For example, a qualitative interviewer conducting five focus group interviews will listen to the recordings or read through the transcripts of the first three or four in order to improve the questions, the way of introducing the issues into the group interview or even to add new topics. Therefore, although there is no specific pilot study, analysis of the earlier focus groups may help improve the later ones. Piloting can provide a qualitative researcher with a clear focus for the research project, which in turn helps the researcher to concentrate data collection on a narrow range of projected analytical topics. A pilot of an interview can be particularly helpful when using interview techniques.

Some of these processes and outcomes from both successful and failed pilot studies might be very useful to others who are starting projects using similar methods and instruments. This is particularly important because pilot studies can be time-consuming and frustrating. It is better to deal with them before investing a great deal of time and effort in the full study. Well-designed and well-conducted pilot studies can inform us about the best research process and occasionally about likely outcomes.

Research is to see what everybody else has seen and to think what nobody else has thought.

— Albert Szent-Gyorgyi

CHAPTER 38
ANALYSING QUALITATIVE DATA

Qualitative analysis is the process of interpreting data collected during the course of qualitative research. It is important not only to interpret the data but to describe and justify the choice of the process you have used. The analysis of the data depends on its type.

ISSUES OF ANALYSIS

In qualitative research data you need to establish trustworthiness and to do this it must be auditable through checking that the interpretations are credible, transferable, dependable and confirmable. Credibility is improved through long engagement with the respondents or by triangulation in data collection (internal validity). Transferability can be achieved through a thick description of the research process to allow the person reading it to see if the results can be transferred to a different setting (external validity). Dependability can be examined through the audit trail (reliability). An example of this is member checking. A member check, which is also known as informant feedback or respondent validation, is a technique used by researchers to help improve the accuracy, credibility, validity and transferability.

A member check can take many forms including narrative accuracy checks, interpretive validity, descriptive validity, theoretical validity and evaluative validity. The interpretation and report (or a portion of it) is given to members of the sample (informants) in order to check the authenticity of the work. Their comments serve as a check on the viability of the interpretation.

Confirmability is obtained by the audit trail categories used, for example raw data included, data analysis and reduction processes described, data reconstruction and synthesis including structuring of categories and themes, process notes included, instrument development information included.

TECHNIQUES OF ANALYSIS

In the following sections further techniques of analyses that you can use as part of the research process are explored.

Context

The first step to understanding data is to understand the context within which it is set. To understand a context you have to gain access to the way people attribute meaning to what goes on around them, and find out how they react to action or lack of action, the events that have or have not occurred and the people or the absence of people involved. One way of gaining access to people's understanding is to capture their talk. This can literally

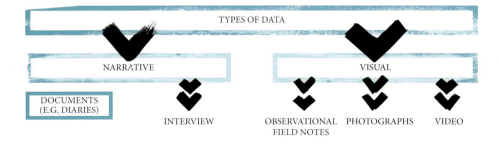

Figure 4.1 Qualitative data

This diagram illustrates the techniques available to researchers conducting qualitative analysis.

mean their spoken words turned into text, or it may mean the words written down by them for themselves (e.g. diaries) or for others to read (e.g. letters).

Prefiguring the field

Analysis of qualitative data begins before it is collected. This may sound a little strange, but the data-collection field is framed by actually posing a research question or problem and being aware of the theoretical positions available on the topic.

Rigour

Prefiguring the field runs the risk of the researcher only finding out what they want to find by exclusively looking for a specific phenomena, or by being blind to other issues that arise. By employing checks and balances built into qualitative research you can make sure it is believable, trustworthy and credible, thereby instilling rigour into your project.

Reflexivity

By being aware of the pitfalls of prefiguring the field, you can maintain an openness to the situation you are investigating. You can be attentive to issues that are not expected or do not conform to existing accounts or theories of society. This idea of being aware of your own values, ideas and pre-judgements as a researcher is known as 'reflexivity'.

Iteration

Iteration means moving back and forth. In qualitative research it is difficult to cleanly separate out data collection or generation from data analysis because there is movement back and forth between generation and analysis. This moving back and forth allows you to go back into published data to clarify what your next steps will be.

Analytical memos

Researchers usually generate data at a specified point in time and also write analytical notes about that data. These notes are then processed into memos or guiding notes to inform the next stage of data collection. The sort of information included in memos is the identification of patterns running through data.

Memos can also include your thoughts on the limitations, exceptions and variations present in whatever is being investigated. You can, in addition, generate tentative explanations for the patterns and see if they are present or absent in other settings or situations. You can then move on to working explanations into a theoretical model and finally confirming or modifying your theoretical model.

This information is presented as if it is an inevitable process that follows a straight line and does not deviate. However, these stages are an ideal type and are presented in this way to help you understand the process. What makes qualitative data analysis dynamic, exciting and intellectually challenging is the iteration between generation and analysis, and within the different types of analytical work, and this is often the way it works out in practice.

Triangulation of analysis

It is very rare for qualitative data to be collected all in one go, then processed and analysed. If this happened we might criticize the project for not being true to the context in which it was generalized, which would make it a weak piece of work. One way of producing believable, credible and trustworthy work is to use triangulation. This means including more than one perspective on a situation, for example clients, designers and stakeholders or comparing primary data-collection to secondary data-collection findings.

Fluency

To analyse texts for their meaning, researchers have to be fluent in the language used by the research participants. This is not just the formal language, but also the colloquialisms used in everyday conversation. The richness of everyday language bears little resemblance to standard English. Check your interpretation of a phrase or word with that of someone else involved in the research project. An inability to understand what is meant will restrict your ability in gaining an understanding of participants' motives, meanings and behaviour.

Capturing conversation

The act of capturing talk may shape what is said and in turn influence how it is analysed. Recording conversation means that researchers may attend to the interviewee without having to focus on writing down their talk verbatim. However, the recording will have to be clear to allow an accurate transcription so attention to equipment and environment will have a direct effect on the quality of the analysis.

Processing texts and archiving

The most common way of processing texts is to transcribe taped talk into word-processed documents. These may then be read and re-read to identify meaning, patterns and models.

Analytical notes and memos will be made, and all of these need to be stored carefully, to protect the integrity of the original document, to allow the various components of the current analysis to be identified and to locate the source of the comments made. There are software programs that provide an orderly and rigorous framework for data archival and administrative tasks. Each programme has built-in assumptions about data and how it should be handled. Researchers need to choose with care a programme that is similar to their own perspective and to the characteristics of their data.

Ensuring the voice of the participants is heard

The way in which qualitative research is presented to us as readers is crucial for us to have confidence in the rigour of the work. A good way to show that theories come from the understanding of the research participants is to allow their voices to be heard. This means including representative quotations from the participants to illustrate specific points. These can be called 'data vignettes'. This is where qualitative data analysis software programs come to be used because they allow researchers to tag segments of text, apply descriptive labels to the segments, and build up categories and themes of analysis. When it comes to writing the definitive research document these segments can then be found easily in the archive, and directly inserted into the text.

Bits and pieces

Research is rarely neatly packaged up into tidy bundles. There are always extra bits and pieces such as themes which peter out or are inconsistent with one another. The temptation in qualitative research is to ignore the odd categories that do not fit neatly into the emerging theory. All qualitative research projects will have odd bits of data that defy characterization, but these still need to be acknowledged as part of the whole.

THINK BOX
Evaluating your research project

This section is designed to assist you in evaluating your own work. It is a fantastic feeling to finish your research project, but before you submit it, plan in the time to evaluate it yourself using the following checklist.

Introduction

Have you clearly outlined the purpose of the project ? Are research questions or propositions clear? Is there a value or use in the project? Is the origin of the research project clear? Is the focus and context made explicit?

Literature review

Does your literature thoroughly underpin the theory relating to your project? Have you funnelled down to the specific from the general using a range of sources? Have you acknowledged the work of others accurately? Have you related and synthesized the literature with your objectives? Are your quotations pertinent and relevant?

Research methodology

Have you justified your choice of possible methodologies through a critical review of your options? Have you demonstrated a convincing rationale for the style and approach you have used?

Have you discussed possible techniques for data collection?

Have you discussed the population and sample?

Have you demonstrated your consideration of issues of reliability and validity?

Data collection and analysis

Have you shown that the data was collected systematically and logically using appropriate methods? Have you interpreted the data convincingly? Are the analysis techniques used relevant and effective?

Conclusions and recommendations

Do your conclusions follow on logically from the data presented? Have you maintained a clear link with the objectives of your research? Are your conclusions a fair assessment of your results? Are your recommendations convincing and practical?

Structure and presentation

Are your chapters and sections well-structured and balanced? Have you checked grammar, spelling and punctuation? Are your references accurate and consistent?

General considerations

Is your project coherent? Has your project made a contribution to understanding, knowledge or practice?

CHAPTER 39
ANALYSING QUANTITATIVE DATA

Design and creativity have always had an element of quantitative data. Designers have discussed width, height, dimensions and quantities. However, as the creative industries take on strategic challenges there is an increasing application of quantitative user research. This section introduces some of the more frequently used techniques for quantitative analysis and their application in research projects for the creative industries.

Recent rapid globalization and digitalization has meant that design and creative solutions are being adopted by an increasingly diverse audience. Faced with new cultures and rising market fragmentation, designers have found that they sometimes require different methods other than the traditional use of ethnography and focus groups to inform their designs with an understanding of the specific end-user, and for justifying their designs to a newly engaged business world, accustomed to the recommendations of strategists and consultants.

ETHNOGRAPHY

Ethnography, a technique drawn from anthropology and the social sciences as a way of formalizing the study of behaviour, has long been a part of the design process. Ethnography offers rich generative insights for designers by encouraging the researcher to suspend their value systems and observe, as transparently as possible, the context in which proposed designs will operate.

However, although it is a powerful technique, it is not always enough when we require depth and breadth of knowledge and the application to a more generalizable context. While ethnography facilitates the generation of ideas in relation to specific users and use scenarios, it doesn't inform us about which of these will satisfy

a wider audience. For this, we need complementary methods that scale and validate the research project and for this we need quantitative research.

The idea of embedding an empirical quantitative approach to design research is not new. Companies like IDEO, Smart Design and Ziba have labelled themselves strategic design firms, promising clients a bridge between 'innovation, research, management and design' by making design decisions 'on the basis of facts rather than aesthetics or intuition'.

QUANTITATIVE ANALYSIS – WHAT IS IT?

Once you have selected the topic of the research and have gone through the process of literature survey, established your own focus of research, selected the research paradigm and methodology, prepared your own research plan and have collected the data, the next step before finally writing the research report is analysis of the data collected.

Data analysis is an ongoing activity, which not only answers your question but also gives you the directions for future data collection. Data analysis procedures (DAP) help you to arrive at the data analysis. Such procedures put your research project into perspective and assist you in testing the hypotheses with which you have started your quantitative research. Hence with the use of DAP, you can convert data into information and knowledge, and explore the relationship between variables.

The literature review which you carried out guides you through the various data analysis methods that have been used in similar studies. Depending upon your research paradigm, methodology and the type of data collection, this also assists you in data analysis.

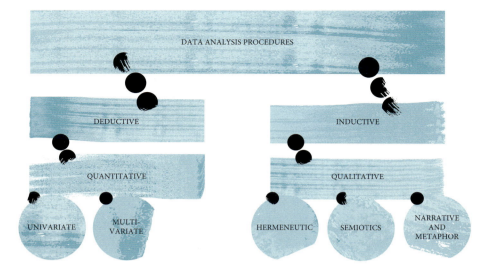

Figure 4.2 Data analysis procedures
Data analysis procedures enable you to arrive at the data analysis, to put your research project into perspective and assist you in testing your hypotheses.

Once you know which particular procedure is relevant to your research project, you can find out what kinds of data analysis tools have been used for similar research projects and what DAP you should use. There are a number of DAP and a few of these are illustrated in Figure 4.2. There are a number of software packages available that facilitate data analysis. These include statistical packages like SPSS, SAS and Microsoft Excel and so forth. Similarly, tools such as spreadsheets and word-processing software are multipurpose and very useful for data analysis.

PLANNING YOUR ANALYSIS

Your choice of analysis should be based on the question you want answered. So when planning your analysis, start at the end and work backwards.

- What conclusion are you trying to reach?
- What type of analysis do you need to perform in order to demonstrate that conclusion?
- What type of data do you need to perform that analysis?

When looking for data, you need to consider what variables you need, what time periods you need the data to cover, and how the data was collected. Particularly with analysis of economic and financial data, time is an important factor. There are two basic types of time-dependent analyses: cross-section time-series and panel study.

- Cross-sectional data means that different people, companies or other entities were sampled over the different time periods. For example, a survey using a different random sample of the population each year.
- Panel data means that the same people, companies or entities were sampled repeatedly.

Here we will examine two common types of analysis that are relevant to research in the creative industries, factor analysis and multiple regression.

FACTOR ANALYSIS

Factor analysis can be used to sort through a list of product criteria, suggesting which are related to each other in the user's mind (size and weight, for example) and which represent independent ideas (perhaps appliance size versus perceived value). Factor analysis is a statistical method used to describe variability among observed variables in terms of fewer unobserved variables called 'factors'. The observed variables are modelled as linear combinations of the factors, plus 'error' terms. The information gained about the interdependencies can be used later to reduce the set of variables in a data-set. Factor analysis originated in psychometrics, and is used in behavioural sciences, social sciences, marketing, product management, operations research and other applied sciences that deal with large quantities of data.

Remember, factor analysis requires that you have data in the form of correlations, so all of the assumptions that apply to correlations are relevant. There are two main types of factor analysis. Principal component analysis is a method that provides a unique solution, so that original data can be reconstructed from the results. It looks at the total variance among the variables, so the solution generated will include as many factors as there are variables, although it is unlikely that they will all meet the criteria for retention. There is only one method for completing a principal components analysis; this is not true of any other multidimensional methods.

Common factor analysis is what people generally mean when they say 'factor analysis'. This family of techniques uses an estimate of common variance among the original variables to generate the factor solution. Because of this, the number of factors will always be lower than the number of original variables. So, choosing the number of factors to keep for further analysis is more problematic using common factor analysis than in principal components.

How is it used?

Factor analysis is a frequently used statistical approach that can be used to analyse interrelationships among a large number of variables and to explain these variables in terms of their common underlying dimensions (factors). The statistical approach involves finding a way of condensing the information contained in a number of original variables into a smaller set of dimensions (factors) with a minimum loss of information.

Factor analysis could be used to verify your conceptualization of a construct of interest. For example, the construct of 'design strategy' can be composed of 'task skills' and 'people skills'. Imagine, for example, you are developing a new questionnaire about design strategy and you create twenty items. You think ten will reflect 'task' elements and ten 'people' elements, but since your items are new, you will want to test your conceptualization.

Before you use the questionnaire on your sample, you decide to pre-test it on a group of people who are similar to those who will be completing your survey. When you analyse your data, you do a factor analysis to see if there are really two factors, and if those factors represent the dimensions of task and people skills. If they do, you will be able to create two separate scales, by summing up the items on each dimension. If they don't, you will need to try another method of analysis.

How do you do factor analysis?

There are four basic factor analysis steps:

- Data collection and generation of the correlation matrix
- Extraction of initial factor solution
- Rotation and interpretation
- Construction of scales or factor scores to use in further analyses

It is possible to do several things with factor analysis results, but the most common are to use factor scores, or to make summated scales based on the factor structure. The results of a factor analysis can be strongly influenced by the presence of error in the original data.

You can use factor scores if the scales used to collect the original data are well-constructed, valid and reliable instruments. If the scales are untested and exploratory, with little or no evidence of reliability or validity, summarized scores should be constructed. An added benefit of summarized scores is that if they are to be used in further analysis, they preserve the variation in the data.

REGRESSION ANALYSIS

Regression analysis can explain how strongly each of your chosen factors will impact on, for example, a consumer's purchasing decision, helping to prioritize design considerations in a cost- or time-limited project. By exploring and quantifying the chain of considerations that influence a complex consumer decision, you can gain insight into how each step impacts the next, yielding breakthroughs from formerly intractable problems.

In statistics, regression analysis includes any techniques for modelling and analysing several variables, when the focus is on the relationship between a dependent variable and one or more independent variables.

How is it used?

Regression analysis is a very useful statistical process for forecasting. Its purpose is to take a series of independent variables and work out whether a particular dependent variable is related to the independent variables. Historical analysis is used to devise a trend line for future values. Regression analysis creates forecasts that do not rely on time. Dependent variables can rely on many different independent variables. Regression analysis is widely used for prediction (including forecasting of time-series data). Regression analysis is also used to understand which among the independent variables are related to the dependent variable, and to explore the forms of these relationships. In some circumstances, regression analysis can be used to infer causal relationships between the independent and dependent variables.

> You can use all the quantitative data you can get, but you still have to distrust it and use your own intelligence and judgement.
>
> — Alvin Toffler

How do you undertake a regression analysis?

The performance of regression analysis methods in practice depends on the form of the data-generating process, and how it relates to the regression approach being used. Since the true form of the data-generating process is not known, regression analysis depends to some extent on making assumptions about this process.

These assumptions are sometimes (but not always) testable if a large amount of data is available.

Can regression models be used for prediction?

Regression models for prediction are often useful even when the assumptions are moderately violated, although they may not perform optimally. However, when carrying out inference using regression models, especially involving small effects or questions of causality based on observational data, regression methods must be used cautiously as they can easily give misleading results.

Can I combine qualitative and quantitative methods?

Whether you choose qualitative or quantitative analysis will depend on several things:

- Your preferred philosophical approach (realist, phenomenologist or constructionist)
- Your skills and abilities with methods of data collection (if needed) and analysis
- The topic or issue you are interested in
- How you frame your research question

How do I know if I have chosen the right method?

Research will never replace inspiration, creative thinking and hard work. Rather, it is a means for us to better understand the world and better inform our designs or creations. Methodology is not a fixed track to a fixed destination, but a conversation about everything that could be possible.

CHAPTER 40
SAMPLING

Collecting data is time-consuming and expensive, even for relatively small amounts of data. Hence, it is highly unlikely that a complete population will be investigated. Because of the time and cost implications, the amount of data you collect will be limited and the number of people or organizations you contact will be small in number. You will, therefore, have to take a sample – and usually a small sample.

SAMPLING THEORY

Sampling theory says a correctly taken sample of an appropriate size will yield results that can be applied to the population as a whole. There is a lot in this statement but the two fundamental questions to ensure generalization are

- How is a sample taken correctly?
- How big should the sample be?

The answer to the second question is 'as large as possible given the circumstances'. This is a little ambiguous and it all depends on the circumstances. While you are not expected to generalize your results and take a large sample, you will be expected to follow a recognized sampling procedure, such that if the sample was increased generalization would be possible.

The theory of sampling is based on random samples – where all items in the population have the same chance of being selected as sample units. Random samples can be drawn in a number of ways but are usually based on having some information about population members. This information is usually in the form of an alphabetical list – called the sampling frame. You need to choose a sample type, but it is important to explain and justify the reasons for this choice.

CHAPTER 41

FROM CRITICAL READING TO CRITICAL WRITING

This section aims to demonstrate how critical writing depends on critical reading. Your research project will involve reflection on written texts from books, journals or online sources. This represents the thinking and research that has already been done on your subject. When you decide to write your own analysis of this subject, you will need to carefully read written sources and to use them critically to make your own argument. The judgements and interpretations you make of the texts you read are the first steps towards formulating your own approach.

CRITICALITY

Throughout your studies you will have been asked to adopt a critical approach to theory and practice. Developing your skill in critical analysis takes time and constant practice. It is not always easy to appreciate when you are being critical and when not. One way that you can approach this is to use a checklist of when you are being descriptive in your writing and approach, and when you are taking a critical viewpoint. In Table 4.1 you will see four key areas taken from Cottrell (2011).

TABLE 4.1

EMPLOYING A CRITICAL APPROACH

Activity	Critical approach	Uncritical approach
Critical reading	Recognizing underlying assumptions and implicit arguments.	Accepting assumptions, arguments and claims unquestioningly.
Finding and evaluating sources of evidence	Recognizing the difference between primary and secondary sources; Understand concepts such as authenticity, validity, relevance and bias.	Using research evidence without questioning: the source; potential bias; who collected it and why; whether it was primary or secondary data.
Evaluating a body of evidence	Identifying and evaluating the most reputable sources; evaluating the most reliable sources.	Using a number of different sources of evidence without questioning how reputable or reliable they are.
Using theory	Evaluating different theories and why they may be useful for your research. Showing the capability to adapt the theory or stop using it altogether if it no longer serves its intended purpose. This also includes explaining within your project why you changed tack and what it means for your project.	Adopting a theory that appeals to you and using it as a framework without evaluating other theories. It also means that you will persist in using theory even though it may not be working well in relation to your research.

Each of these areas applies to an element that will probably be in your project brief and explains what we mean by taking a critical approach and approaching an activity uncritically.

WHAT IS CRITICAL THINKING?

Critical thinking is about analytical evaluation. If you are applying critical thinking you are expected to evaluate the information, concepts, frameworks and ideas that are being presented to you in your course, rather than accept them automatically, uncritically and without reflection on their potential value and relevance to you in your professional practice or as a student. Try to always test them against different perspectives to see if you find them convincing.

Therefore critical thinking means

- selecting appropriate theoretical concepts and frameworks to apply to case studies or current events in industries or firms;
- using theoretical concepts and frameworks critically and being aware of their shortcomings;
- identifying relevant academic debates in the field of literature you have chosen;
- considering contradictory or opposing viewpoints and paradoxes;
- assessing all material to take account of potential weaknesses.

CRITICAL OR NEGATIVE?

Being critical is not the same as being negative. To think critically is to examine ideas, evaluate them against what you already know and make decisions about their merit. In academic terms, being critical should not be understood as being negative. It means that you recognize that information produced by people, however, it is derived, will contain their biases, whether conscious or unconscious. From a critical perspective, there is no such thing as bias-free knowledge: knowledge is always subjective.

Perceiving knowledge as biased or subjective does not mean that it is devalued. Instead, it means that we recognize and accept that knowledge is a human construct. Therefore, knowing about the author of a particular text and what they do professionally may

lead us to question why a particular idea or approach is being suggested. Critical thinking is about selecting, rearranging and recombining ideas from multiple sources to inform your view.

You should also be aware that your own thinking is equally subjective. You can claim that a decision you have made is free from bias by saying you have made an objective decision. By calling it an objective decision, you are claiming that your personal feelings have been removed from your decision making and that other people with access to the same information would have made the same decision. Yet our decisions are always influenced by our feelings, by self-interest, by the desire for power, by our aspirations and by the context. This goes to the heart of your working life as a creative since we do not leave such feelings at home when we go to work or university. Therefore, critical thinking means reflecting on the interplay between the professional and the personal.

> **We can ask the following questions:**
> Why has 'this' problem been raised?
> Why has 'this' decision been made (or put off)?
> What factors are promoting or suppressing particular information?
> What is shaping the agendas of discussions or meetings?

Often these issues are not addressed directly in organizations but they do, nevertheless, have deep impact on what happens in organizations, including decision making and practice.

WHAT IS CRITICAL READING?

Critical reading means making judgements about how a text is argued. This is a highly reflective skill, which means you need to gain some distance from the text you are reading. You will probably need to read a text through once to get a basic understanding of the content before you start an intensive critical reading. Look for ways of thinking about the subject matter rather than looking only for information. When you are reading, highlighting or taking notes, avoid extracting and compiling lists of evidence, facts and examples. Ask yourself how the text works, how it is argued and how it reaches its conclusions, rather than looking purely for information.

How can I read critically?

First, determine the central claims or purpose of the text. When critically reading you are attempting to assess how these central claims are developed or argued. Then you can start to make some judgements about context by asking yourself what type of audience the text was written for and who the dialogue is with. This will probably be other scholars or authors with differing viewpoints. You also need to take into account the historical context within which the text was written. All these matters of context can contribute to your assessment of what is going on in a text.

Secondly, distinguish the kinds of reasoning the text uses by understanding the concepts and how they are defined and used. Ask yourself if the text relates to a theory or theories and whether a specific methodology is laid out. If there is a direct link to a particular concept, theory or method, how is that concept, theory or method then used to organize and interpret the data? You might also examine how the text is organized and how the author has analysed and broken down the material. You may be reading material from different disciplines (i.e. history, sociology, philosophy) and these will have different ways of arguing.

Examine the evidence (the supporting facts, examples and so forth) the text uses because supporting evidence is indispensable to an argument. You should now be able to understand how the evidence is used to develop the argument and its controlling claims and concepts. Consider the kinds of evidence used and what counts as evidence in this argument as well as the sources from which the evidence is taken and whether they are primary or secondary.

A critical reading may also involve evaluation because you may make a series of judgements about how a text is argued. You may need to consider the strengths and weaknesses of an argument and whether or not it could be differently supported. Determine whether or not there are gaps, leaps or inconsistencies in the argument or whether the method of analysis is problematic. Are there different ways of interpreting the evidence and are the conclusions warranted by the evidence presented? What might an opposing argument be?

Advice

You can read critically after some preliminary processes of reading. Begin by skimming research materials, especially introductions and conclusions, in order to strategically choose where to focus your critical efforts. When highlighting a text or taking notes from it, extract the argument: those places in a text where an author explains their analytical moves, the concepts they use, how they are used, how they arrive at conclusions. Look for the patterns that give purpose, order and meaning to those examples.

When you begin to think about how you might use a portion of a text in the argument that you are defining in your own research project, remain aware of how this portion fits into the whole argument from which it is taken, as its original context is fundamental. When you quote directly from a source, use the quotation critically. This means that you should not substitute the quotation for your own articulation of a point. Rather, introduce the quotation by laying out the judgements you are making about it, and the reasons why you are using it. Often a quotation is followed by further analysis.

WHAT IS CRITICAL WRITING?

Most research projects will require you to adopt a critical approach, to explain, compare, analyse, evaluate or in some other way to develop an argument. To do this it may be helpful to distinguish between weak and strong critical approaches.

Weak critical writing may involve evaluating alternative points of view, especially for the soundness of their reasoning and the legitimacy of their conclusions. It may well also involve developing your own arguments and advancing your own conclusions; and may sometimes involve making personal value judgements, for example about what government policy you would support on a given issue.

How can I develop an argument?

Demonstrating the ability to analyse, evaluate or in some other way to develop an argument, is very important.

In many cases, an argument can be constructed and evaluated using a traditional model of critical reasoning.

DEFINITIONS

Arguments are reasons given in support of a conclusion. Reasons include evidence, principles and assumptions which are normally written and logical, for example inferences and causal connections. Conclusions include facts, judgements and recommendations.

The traditional view of critical reasoning is more closely aligned with weak, than with strong, critical approaches to argument and writing. It is based on an unproblematized view of knowledge – where the evaluation of arguments can be undertaken using primarily objective criteria. In particular, this approach depends upon the following assumptions:

- It is ultimately possible to evaluate most arguments in terms of their proximity to a singular and definitive 'truth' – which account is 'right' and which ones are flawed.
- Soundness of reasoning and sufficiency of evidence may be relevant to the evaluation of an argument's persuasiveness, but not the communicative devices through which the argument is advanced – for example, the language and the rhetoric.
- Experts can normally be relied upon to provide truthful accounts. Their interests and allegiances are less important than their privileged access to the truth.
- Critical reasoning can be undertaken objectively by users, who have no personal interest other than the relevance of an argument to their own work and no other personal qualities that might intervene between the soundness of the argument and their evaluation of it.

A strongly critical approach would question each of these premises. For example, it suggests that you should be critically aware of your own values, assumptions and interests and that you should try to make these explicit, rather than ignoring and concealing them.

It also suggests that you should take a sceptical view of the claims advanced by experts and anticipate that experts who identify with different knowledge communities will tend to base their arguments on different underlying values and assumptions.

THINK BOX
Critical writing techniques

Make it relevant

Material that is not directly relevant to the title should normally be kept to a minimum. This is all the more important if your word limit is tightly constrained.

On the one hand, you will want to include sufficient evidence, conceptual and theoretical underpinning, explanatory detail and illustrative material, to support the case you are making.

On the other hand, there may be a body of broadly uncontested ground that can be assumed to be shared knowledge, between writer and reader – and which can be left unsaid; this may include low-level facts, widely understood concepts or even the theoretical positions of authors whose work is relevant to your research. The question of what can be left unsaid is clearly one which requires careful judgement.

Make it authoritative

You should use bibliographic citation to lend authoritative support to your arguments. This will generally be provided by academic books and articles. However, there are circumstances where non-academic sources (e.g. newspaper articles or television broadcasts) will be relevant.

Strong critical approaches to writing will take account of the potential plurality of expert views, and will look to identify their underlying allegiances, values and assumptions – so try not to just cite them uncritically.

However, there may be circumstances in which you will also wish to acknowledge layman perspectives, particularly in relation to publicly disputed issues, where they call into question the authority of expert opinion.

Bibliographic citation may be helpful where aspects of the case you are making have been left unsaid, but judgements are again required. For example, widely held and undisputed knowledge does not normally require authoritative support.

Signpost, sequence, structure, summarize and synthesize

Look for advantageous ways of signposting, sequencing, structuring, summarizing and synthesizing your arguments. Paragraphing is often the most effective way of creating a structure. You can use one paragraph for each argument, or for each step in the overall argument you want to make. If you are considering arguments and counter-arguments before reaching an overall judgement, you may also want to present and examine these opposing viewpoints in separate paragraphs.

For each paragraph, the opening statement may be used to signpost the direction and substance of your case in the form of a key sentence, which filters out the essence of the point which is to be developed in the remainder of that paragraph. Here you would introduce evidence, conceptual and theoretical underpinning, explanatory detail and illustrative material.

CHAPTER 42

GUIDELINES FOR DRAWING CONCLUSIONS AND MAKING RECOMMENDATIONS

The aim of this section is to explain the most important parts of your research project – the conclusion and recommendations. The conclusions you come to are really the main goal of writing your research project. For your reader, the conclusion section is often the focal point of the reading of your research because it enables them to understand the meaning of the whole research report.

CONCLUSIONS

Your conclusion needs to be based on the evidence you present in the body of your report. When writing your conclusion, consider these points:

- Keep it relatively short in proportion to the rest of your work.
- Keep the level of technicality relatively low.
- Emphasize what the report means by focusing on the main results and what they mean. Pull the analyses of your results together and interpret the overall meaning of your results by explaining the inferences you want readers to draw from your report.
- Add no new details.
- Do not merely summarize the report.
- Give an overall interpretation of the report by emphasizing the relevance of the work and the main idea/s you want your reader to remember and understand.

What should be in a conclusion?

It may not always be necessary or desirable to include all these elements. However, you will probably want to use some of these in some combination, in order to conclude your work:

- A summary of the main part of the text
- A deduction made on the basis of the main body
- Your personal opinion on what has been discussed
- A statement about the limitations of the work
- A comment about the future based on what has been discussed
- The implications of the work for future research

Advice

Decide what the strongest and most important statement that you can make from your work is and if you met the reader six months from now, what would you want them to remember? Refer back to the problem posed, and describe the conclusions that you reached from carrying out this investigation, summarize new observations, new interpretations and new insights that have resulted from the present work. Include the broader implications of your results but do not repeat word for word the abstract, introduction or discussion.

Make sure that the conclusion is based on what you have said before – it is often tempting to go off at a tangent and to say things that are completely unrelated to the topic. You can give your opinion in the conclusion but try to do so subtly; usually your viewpoint will be obvious from your discussion. Be careful with tenses, you will usually want to use the present perfect (e.g. 'The aim of this project has been to …') followed by the simple past (e.g. 'Chapter 1 provided an overview of').

Conclusions are very important in a dissertation or project, purely because of the length of the work. As well as having an overall conclusion to your dissertation or project, each chapter should also have a conclusion. The reason for this is that it is important to 'remind' the reader of what you have done and why you have done it, before you move on to the next stage. The conclusion of a dissertation or project is not just there to make recommendations or give opinions. You must also draw out key aspects of the literature you have studied and say how they are justified or contradicted by your research.

It is a good idea in a chapter conclusion to remind the reader what happened in the chapter (e.g. 'In this chapter, the literature relating to the perception of designed artefacts was considered.'). After this, you need to build a platform linking this chapter with the next one. For example: 'This will be further discussed in the next chapter.' In a dissertation or project, there is likely to be a longer section on the limitations of your research. Although it is important to recognize your limits you do need to be able to justify your research in the conclusion, so it is best not to be too negative or over-critical about your achievements at this point. The key point is the need to emphasize the contribution that your dissertation or project makes.

In a dissertation or thesis, it is more likely that you will have a section on the need for future research. In an MA or MSc dissertation or project you may like to suggest something that could be developed from your work as a PhD thesis, or a more general need for future research.

RECOMMENDATIONS

If your report leads to recommendations then you should include this in a section. Sometimes, recommendations appear in the conclusion section; other times the recommendations form a separate section. You need to consider what you want to emphasize. In a recommendation chapter you should explain what you want the reader to do and what action(s) should be taken.

WHAT SHOULD BE IN THE RECOMMENDATIONS?

You could break the chapter down into a number of subsections, as detailed in the following paragraphs.

Introduction

Here you will introduce the chapter to the readers and explain that this chapter will review and summarize the dissertation research, identify the main methods used and discuss their implications in the study.

Problem statement and methodology

In this part you will be presenting the problem statement as you have introduced it in the first chapter (i.e. outlining the problem and what you intended to achieve). Then, you should review the methodology, in detail, but without repeating anything that you have already said. Although you should get right to the point, you will still need to review the methodology so that it provides enough information for the reader and they don't have to go and read the first chapter again.

> Omit needless words. Vigorous writing is concise. A sentence should contain no unnecessary words, a paragraph no unnecessary sentences, for the same reason that a drawing should have no unnecessary lines and a machine no unnecessary parts.
>
> — William Strunk, Jr.

Results of summary

You should keep this section brief and identify the result with a general statement paragraph followed by another paragraph that supports the evidence collected. You should avoid interpretation here and be objective.

Discussion of results

You should discuss the meaning of the results here, in brief, and highlight any important areas that you have identified. You should also look at what your research actually means and how this relates to the overall understanding of your dissertation.

Recommendations

These could be either to your employer or to the academic community. You will want to keep this section brief, maybe to one or two paragraphs. Explain what, from the research that has been conducted, will be your recommendations to the relevant organizations or, if you are presenting to academia, what further research should be conducted in the future.

As you can see, if this section is broken up in this way it isn't too hard to establish the different parts of this chapter to round off your research report.

Advice

To make your recommendations believable they should be based on your conclusions. They need to be simple and if you have two or more recommendations you could use a list for emphasis. The tone you use is important because dissertations do not make decisions, people do – so use 'should', 'recommend', or similar terms. These recommendations may or may not form an additional chapter depending on whether you are completing the dissertation while still with an employer or in an internship, as they will want to know that you have some recommendations for their organization.

However, if you are like the majority of students writing a dissertation you will be writing a concluding chapter of your research report and making recommendations to the academic community for further research to be conducted on the matter.

When you are concluding the different parts of your dissertation project, you should understand that the reader will be reading a snapshot of the different aspects that are contained in your research project and the key findings that were realized and identified. You should also be reviewing these different parts to make sure you are covering them. However, this chapter of your work should be clean and crisp and should also quickly get to the point.

CHAPTER 43

THE PRACTICE: A VISUAL RESEARCH APPROACH – PHOTOGRAPHIC ETHNOGRAPHY

THE RESEARCH QUESTION

For this study, researchers went back and forth between industry and consumers to see whether design is a dominating factor over competition. In order to explore this more fully, the researchers obtained a number of photographs of individuals using their MP3 players in their typical environments and asked them to hold up their devices so that the players could be identified individually.

AN EMERGING DESIGN CLASS?

Before conducting the research, a few assumptions were made:

- That the majority of people use Apple iPod devices to listen to MP3 music files.
- That companies who adopt a highly design-oriented approach to business will be more successful.

Is an emerging design class taking over the reins of business? Organizations that put design at the forefront of their business operations are more likely to be successful. Companies such as Apple use uncompromising design standards in everything they do and as a result, a new emerging design standard is now dominating the portable MP3 player marker, like never before.

WHY PHOTO ETHNOGRAPHY?

Photo ethnography is primarily used as a tool to understand underlying structures of culture and people from within. In this context, photo ethnography is used in a slightly different manner, in order to investigate a broad and non-culturally specific research question.

THE PHOTO ANALYSIS

What is the setting of the photograph? What is the likely time of year and day? What is the subject of the photograph? Does it include people, animals, buildings and/or scenery? What is the main activity of the photograph? Does there seem to be a theme to the set of photographs?

Specimen 1

- Photo taken outside looking towards the sea or a lake, of a young white female listening to a music-playing device next to a table with no chairs.
- By the angle of the shadows, it appears to be early summer with green vegetation in the background.
- The subject is a female listening to an unknown music device, while smiling up at the sky.
- The scenery appears to be calm and picturesque with a small mountain in the distance. The female is suntanned and is wearing a casual top and jeans.
- The main activity is the central female contentedly listening to music.

Specimen 2

- Photo taken inside at a desk in the corner of the room of an individual young white male sitting, holding a personal music player.
- It is daytime with bright sunshine entering the room, likely to be in spring or summer.
- The subject appears to be the person holding the music-playing device (Apple iPod) in central frame with a computer screen and keyboard in the background.
- The scenery appears to be an informal working environment at an office or home with close proximity to trees or grass outside.
- The main activity appears to be someone happily listening to music while working at a computer.

Specimen 3

- Photo taken from a low angle of a young black male holding an Apple iPhone.
- The photo appears to have been taken inside a modern room with a yellow painted door.
- It is hard to tell the time of year, but it appears to be daytime.
- The lighting appears mainly artificial.
- The main subject of the photograph is holding an Apple iPhone in central frame while biting the cable with a happy, playful expression on his face.
- The subject is wearing an informal sports t-shirt, suggesting leisure time.
- The photo appears to be taken using the iPhone's camera feature.

Specimen 4

- The setting is a white wall with electrical switches in the background.
- It is hard to tell the time of year but it appears to be taken in daylight.
- The subject of the photo is a young Arabic male in a casual polo shirt, listening to a personal music player with large earphones.
- The main activity seems to be holding and listening to a portable electronic device with the subject's eyes closed as if concentrating on what is being listened to.
- There are no other people or objects.

Specimen 5

- The setting is a red sofa in a white room, suggesting a familiar location such as home.
- There appears to be natural light entering the room, suggesting daytime. The time of year is hard to tell, but the subject's clothes and sunglasses suggest that it is summer.
- The subject is a young, white female.
- The main activity of the photo is listening to an Apple iPod device with large headphones. The subject is smiling and looks contented, relaxed and informal.

Specimen 6

- The setting appears to be indoors between several rooms in white doorways.
- There is daylight hitting the back white door, suggesting daytime, and the subject's sports t-shirt suggests a mild climate: spring, summer or autumn.
- The subject of the photograph is a relaxed, young white male holding an Apple iPod with large earphones and black cables.
- The main activity is listening to music. Both hands are involved in operating the device, suggesting full attention to its operation.

RESEARCH FINDINGS AND ANALYSIS

The set of photographs depicts young individual, adults of various ethnic backgrounds, listening to a variety of electronic music-playing devices, in a number of different locations during daytime. The majority of music-playing devices appear to be Apple iPod products, thus implying that design is one of the crucial factors in consumer purchasing choice.

HOW WELL DID THE TECHNIQUE WORK?

This tool needs to be used in conjunction with other research techniques. Research also needs to be done on a larger scale with many more photographs in order to obtain wider results for a more detailed interpretation. There is also a risk that the researcher will see and interpret what they want to see, rather than what is actually there.

The researcher's background plays a large role in the interpretation of the data so the researcher needs to be neutral and aware of potential biases. On a larger scale, this tool would be very useful in answering the hypothesis, if used in conjunction with other methods such as interviews and focus groups.

RESULTS

This research tool did allow statistical, cultural and demographic data to be collected from individuals in an objective manner (i.e. without the individual being aware of what was being researched). The data gathered from the photographs confirmed the initial research question. However, used on its own, it is not wholly sufficient and the research question would need to be further investigated using other research methods.

CHAPTER 44
THE PRACTITIONERS: SAPSED ET AL. ON THE ECONOMIC VALUE OF RESEARCH

It is important that your research project is up to date. If you are planning to use your research project as evidence of the value of your work to impress a future employer or perhaps move into doctoral studies, it is of particular importance. The value of the creative industries to national economies is now undisputed. Therefore, your research project could have an economic value for you; but in addition, professional and academic research proposals are now receiving international funding. The following is an example of a current research project funded by the Advanced Institute of Management in conjunction with the Economic and Social Research Council (ESRC), the UK's leading research and training agency addressing economic and social concerns.

BUSINESS ENGAGEMENT IN THE CREATIVE INDUSTRIES

The project team of Dr Jonathan Sapsed, Juan Mateos-Garcia, Dr Richard Adams and Professor Andy Neely have highlighted the following six themes that have emerged as management priorities in the UK's creative industries:

- The impact of digital tools and distribution
- Collaboration and outsourcing relationships
- Understanding how innovation changes business models and markets
- The creative process
- Management capabilities and skills
- Small firms and growth

THE IMPACT OF DIGITAL TOOLS AND DISTRIBUTION

Several factors have contrived to radically change the value chain and division of labour in the creative industries, including new tools and technologies, digital distribution and opportunities for outsourcing creative services.

- What is the impact of digital technologies and tools on industrial organization?
- How should integrators best exploit the potential for more collaborative working enabled by new tools?
- What are the effects of digital distribution on the digital content value chain?
- How should creative content developers exploit the internet for promotion, distribution and sales?

COLLABORATION AND OUTSOURCING RELATIONSHIPS

In the current turbulent environment, firms need to find focus: this could be a niche offering entailing alliances and collaborative work. Collaborating firms need to understand enough about their partners' activities to choose the right ones and to manage the collaboration effectively.

- How should collaborative work be managed?
- How should firms decide whether to outsource creative activities to the growing numbers of specialized creative service providers?

- How should creative firms decide whether to outsource technological activities to the growing numbers of new specialized providers of middleware?
- How should the pieces be integrated?

UNDERSTANDING HOW INNOVATION CHANGES BUSINESS MODELS AND MARKETS

New technologies present opportunities for innovation, yet they also present difficulties in conceiving and implementing responses for established organizations. Experimentation and lateral thinking is required to understand and apprehend technologies; and innovation that may potentially disrupt the usual patterns of 'sustaining' innovation. Creative industries are increasingly selling user 'experience' as much as products and services, while user communities are developing innovation themselves and challenging traditional business models.

- How should established firms respond to disruptive innovation? – How should firms search for new business models and innovations?
- What management tactics and strategies may overcome closed mindsets in established organizations?
- How should user 'experience' be designed, delivered and sold?
- How should firms respond or relate to growing user communities that modify and adapt their products and services?
- How should policy makers respond or relate to growing user communities that modify and adapt products and services?

THE CREATIVE PROCESS

The extent to which the creative process can be managed is a perennial research question. Old tensions between creativity and business efficiency continue to be important, as new developments in management practice emerge.

- To what extent can the creative process be managed?
- How do UK creative firms' management practices compare to those in other countries?
- How do new digital technologies affect the creative process?
- How can they best be exploited?
- How should digital creatives be incorporated into the existing mix of disciplines in industries such as advertising?
- What are the implications of creative recombination of existing IP with new content for business models?
- What is the extent of the diffusion of design consulting?
- How does design thinking and consulting add value?

MANAGEMENT CAPABILITIES AND SKILLS

There is a perception, backed up by several industry and government reports over recent years, that UK firms are strong on creativity, but less strong on the practice of management. Reportedly, management tends to be reactive at the expense of maintaining a strategic perspective. Identifying and developing new opportunities, and in particular experimenting and negotiating new business models, are activities that tend to be neglected.

- What is the level of professionalism, experience and skills of managers in the UK's creative industries?
- What is the typical career path of a manager in a creative business?
- How effective are the current training courses and infrastructure for meeting the needs of creative industry?
- How are people managed in the creative industries with regard to working conditions and pay, as compared with other industries?
- To what extent do creative practices and skills diffuse throughout the economy?
- How do managers identify opportunities to apply their skills in other industries?
- What are the barriers to exploiting these opportunities?

SMALL FIRMS AND GROWTH

Most firms in the UK's creative industries are small, frequently self-employed, sole-traders, who operate on a project basis. 'Scaling up' remains a significant challenge for the UK's creative businesses, and a proportion of managers working in the sector appear to lack the appropriate management and entrepreneurial skills to grow these businesses.

- How should creative firms organize as they grow larger?
- How is creative integrity maintained as the organization grows larger?
- What are the barriers to growth?
- What are the skills required for self-managing creative professionals?
- How may public policy institutions assist in expanding entrepreneurs' networks?

- How may public policy institutions assist in stimulating innovation in the creative industries?
- Are the existing schemes appropriate for the creative industries, for example R&D tax credits?
- How may universities assist in stimulating innovation in the creative industries?
- How may public procurement stimulate the creative industries?

This is an example of academics proposing areas of interest for further research. When considering your research project, it can be very helpful to see what academics are researching in your area of interest. This focus can be further honed down to a practical example of a large industry-wide research programme attracting international financial backing. Your research project could feasibly be framed on any one aspect of this particular project.

APPENDICES

APPENDIX 1
WORKING WITH YOUR SUPERVISOR

Once you have identified what topic or issue you would like to examine, you need to gain the agreement of a supervisor. Your supervisor will act as a guide to the process and will help you reflect on your learning. Your university may have an extensive list of supervisors, so your supervisor may not be someone you have met before. Alternatively, you may be appointed a supervisor because your university does not have a range of expertise in your chosen research area. However, if you know a member of academic staff who has taught on your course, you may wish to make informal contact with them to discuss an idea. The next stage is to formally submit your project proposal to your supervisor.

Your supervisor's role is to provide guidance and feedback on your aims, objectives, methodology, learning and writing of your project. It is important that you feel an empathy with your supervisor and their subject specialism, and that you will be able to work with them. You should have several meetings with your supervisor, either in person or by email. Your supervisor will allocate at least eight hours of their time to your project, so you need to establish the boundaries of this working relationship and make sure you get the most from this support.

You need to manage the interactions with your supervisor. First, discuss with your supervisor what form your communications will take. If possible, meet regularly with them. If you are located remotely from your supervisor, this is unlikely to be possible very often, if at all. In this case, try to arrange to telephone your supervisor from time to time – a few minutes' discussion about difficulties you are struggling with is very valuable. Use email to keep in touch. If they know what stage you are at with your research and whether

you are experiencing problems, they will know how to assist you. If you don't keep in contact with them, they will be unaware of what you are doing and by the time you seek their advice it may be too late to help you in a constructive way.

SUPERVISION AGREEMENT

Some institutes will ask you to write a supervision agreement, but if not, a formal submission can be helpful if both you and your supervisor agree the following (in written form):

- an agreed (broad) timetable of events
- agreement for the submission of work for review prior to meetings or other interactions
- a formal structure and agreed number of meetings or other contact points (to act as a minimum requirement)
- agreement on the nature of supervision
- agreement on the speed and frequency of feedback from your supervisor

CONTACT

The number of meetings and contact points will depend on your project and individual needs. However, it is unlikely that the processes can be concluded with less than six meetings/interactions (totalling not less than five hours). Often, more may be needed. These meetings/interactions could occur at the following points:

- set-up of the project
- secondary data collection or review

- supporting the research process
- guide to analysis
- review of outcomes and writing

A particularly important aspect of managing your contact with your supervisor concerns the final stage. You should agree a timetable for submission, reading and revision of a complete draft of your dissertation. Supervisors may have other commitments so it is important that they know when to expect it; otherwise they may not be able to meet your deadline. Don't be afraid to ask for feedback. The way you manage your working relationship with your supervisor is almost as important as the way you manage your research. It can and should be a valuable and rewarding part of your learning process.

APPENDIX 2
TIME MANAGEMENT

Postgraduate research projects are a relatively unstructured experience and may be a different experience from the taught part of your programme. You will find that you have a great deal of freedom and flexibility in terms of what you do and when you choose to do it. This can be good or bad depending on how effectively you manage your time.

PREPARATION FOR YOUR RESEARCH PROPOSAL

By completing a project proposal you ensure that you know your goals, objectives and deadlines, and you will gain a more realistic picture of your project timeline. Good time management begins with an appreciation of the 'bigger picture'. If you don't know where you are going, then you will never get there. It is important to establish a deadline for accomplishing your goal, even if it is artificial. You will probably find you work more effectively if you need to meet deadlines. It is important to take time at the beginning to plan how you are going to achieve your goal. The individual, bite-size tasks you will need to accomplish in order to achieve your goal are your objectives. You will need to figure out how much time is needed in order to accomplish each objective. Think about whether or not each objective must be accomplished sequentially or whether any can be tackled independently. This will give you flexibility.

If you use a project outline, you will find it much easier to complete your project on time. Use a day planner to track appointments, telephone conversations, email and any written correspondence related to your research project. Day planners can be extremely powerful tools when used reflectively to help you to prioritize. Establish a regular work schedule that you will be able to sustain. Begin by identifying all your regular activities including time spent commuting, jobs, clubs and sports. Block out time for your research each week and keep to it.

Prioritize

If you aren't used to long-term or short-term planning, you might want to begin by keeping 'to do' lists for each day. Prioritize tasks for the day and work through them in the order of their priority. At the end of the day, evaluate your progress and prepare a new list for the next day. Know yourself and your limitations in terms of time and ability and don't take on more than you can realistically accomplish.

Communicate

Communicate regularly with your supervisor. If you find yourself unable to move forward on any task related to your project, meet with your adviser as soon as possible to discuss possible options and/or solutions. Don't fall into the mindset of thinking that you can only meet with your supervisor when you have obtained positive results from your project. You will make stronger and more consistent progress if you discuss difficulties as well as accomplishments.

Focus

Learn how to stay focused and on task. Until you are confident in your ability, put all your effort into doing one thing at a time. Learn how to say 'no' to requests from your supervisor, friends and family that will divert needed energies from the task at hand. Make sure you completely understand what you are doing before you try to do anything. If you don't understand, ask. If you still don't understand, ask again or ask someone else. It may not seem like this is a time-saving tool but it really is. If you understand what you are doing when you set about to do it you are more likely to do it right the first time.

APPENDIX 3
WRITTEN COMMUNICATION

One of the most important parts of your research project is being able to communicate what you have achieved effectively. Although you may have conducted a very interesting, competent and relevant piece of research, it can be ineffective if you cannot communicate concisely what you have done. This section details seven steps which if followed will result in a reader-friendly major project.

DECIDE WHAT INFORMATION SHOULD BE INCLUDED AND WHAT SHOULD BE LEFT OUT

Try to ensure that the report is focused and that the reader can follow your argument. It can be all too easy to wander off and discuss elements of the project that are important to you but may not be relevant to the reader and can easily detract from their understanding of your work.

REMEMBER WHO THE AUDIENCE IS AND WRITE TO THEM

Different audiences want different things. If this project is for assessment purposes, it should be written for the assessor. If your research project is a piece of action research, you may also want to give a copy to the organization or group of people you have worked with.

You may have to rewrite or refocus parts of the research report specifically for them rather than trying to pack too much into one report to the detriment of the focus on your main audience.

ORGANIZE THE MATERIAL TO MAKE IT EASY TO FOLLOW

This means not only summarizing the key points but also introducing and concluding each section and reiterating what you have already discussed and what you will discuss in the next section.

MAKE SURE YOU EXPLAIN WHO, WHEN, WHAT, WHY AND WHERE

This sets the scene. Explaining who the research is for and who is included in the research, when and where it took place, what the objectives are and why you are doing the research, enables the reader to understand the importance and relevance of your work.

KEEP IT SIMPLE

If the work is written in simple language and logically laid out it will be easier to understand. There is no need to over complicate anything; it will only detract from your work.

BE SPECIFIC

The research report should explain your discussion and your argument, but you will inevitably have a lot more information than the reader will need. Although it is tempting to put everything in that you have discovered or done, try to be specific.

REVISE AND PROOFREAD

A research report will normally need to be revised and rewritten. This is unfortunate, but true, so allocate the time to do this. It can be helpful to ask someone to read it for you and see if they can follow your discussion.

APPENDIX 4
GUIDELINES FOR NON-DISCRIMINATORY LANGUAGE

Academic and professional writing and design visuals should not contain explicit or implicit discriminatory messages. Therefore, you need to be aware of language structures that convey discriminatory ideas and avoid these in your writing. Guides on non-discriminatory language specific to your university or geographical area are normally available to you online. What is acceptable or unacceptable tends to vary depending on where you are in the world. The aim of this section is to provide you with some basic guidelines, as well as to spur you on to seek more specific details before you submit your research project.

NON-DISCRIMINATORY LANGUAGE AND DISCRIMINATORY LANGUAGE

Non-discriminatory language is language which does not discriminate against individuals or groups on the basis of their sex, ethnicity, disability and age. Language is discriminatory when it stereotypes people, treats people unfairly, denigrates or insults people, excludes people or makes them invisible, or focuses on one characteristic to the exclusion of others that are more relevant.

RECOGNIZING DISCRIMINATORY MESSAGES

The following examples show how language can be discriminatory.

Example 1: Language that stereotypes people: 'Anna Leoni, the attractive wife of eminent artist Peter Franks, is the new head of the Dinden Art School.'

Why is this discriminatory? Women are frequently described in terms of their appearance or defined by their relationship to men. Men are rarely described or defined in these ways.

Example 2: Language that treats people unequally: 'Four product design graduates, including one Vietnamese woman, have been offered positions at B-Design Studios.'

Why is this discriminatory? It is not relevant to focus on the background of only one person in this context.

Example 3: Language that denigrates or insults people: 'The men and girls in the engineering faculty team played like a bunch of old women.'

Why is this discriminatory? The language used to refer to the team's performance denigrates both women and older people. Referring to female adults as girls, while male adults are called men, is inappropriate. It suggests that women are not adults.

Example 4: Language that excludes people or makes them invisible: 'In his father's time, the record player was a source of home entertainment.'

Why is this discriminatory? The word 'father's' excludes all the mothers who were entertained by the record player. This form of language makes women invisible to readers or listeners.

Example 5: Language that focuses on one characteristic to the exclusion of others that are more relevant: 'Frank completed his degree, with honours, despite his being blind.'

Why is this discriminatory? Frank's blindness is the characteristic being highlighted, rather than his actual achievement.

APPENDIX 5
SYSTEMS OF REFERENCING

Referencing is a standardized method of acknowledging the sources of information and ideas that you have used in your assignments and submissions. Referencing provides enough information for the reader to find the original source you have quoted or used. There are dozens of different styles of referencing, and most universities have a preferred method. This section aims to give you an awareness of the importance of referencing.

WHAT TO REFERENCE

References should be included in your research project wherever you have used the work of others, whether you are quoting a passage directly or using their ideas to build an argument.

REFERENCING FACTS AND INFORMATION

Much of the information you will use in assignments at university is not the work of any particular scholar. There will, however, be many occasions where you will find information for the first time in a certain book or article. Even though this may be new to you, it was not that particular author's exclusive discovery, and so you don't need to cite your source.

WHY USE REFERENCING IN MY RESEARCH?

Referencing is an important part of your writing/visual work at university. It is essential because referencing is the way you

- show respect for and acknowledge the work of others;
- give your work credibility and reliability;
- show that you have read the relevant literature;
- allow your lecturer to validate and read further on a particular point that you have made;
- follow academic writing standards;
- avoid plagiarism (become familiar with the university's regulations).

Failing to provide appropriate references is a form of academic misconduct called plagiarism. Avoiding plagiarism is the responsibility of every student, and there are penalties. Also, in your future professional life, you will find that plagiarism can negatively affect your reputation as well as that of your colleagues and your employer, and may even prompt legal action from the copyright owner of any work that is not acknowledged.

WHAT DO I NEED TO REFERENCE?

A reference is required when you

- quote another person word for word (direct quotation). It doesn't matter whether it is a phrase, sentence or paragraph; you will need to provide a reference from which it was taken;
- paraphrase or summarize. Ideas or data obtained from another writer must be referenced even if you have changed the wording and/or content;
- use statistics (e.g. population);
- use tables, figures, diagrams and appendices. The source of these must be acknowledged unless they are entirely from your own research work;
- use controversial facts, opinions or a date which might be challenged. However, information of a general nature such as facts which are common knowledge, for example the years of World War I, do not need to be referenced.

In other words, you will need to reference any ideas or data you have used which are not your own. Please note that it is just as important to cite electronic sources as it is to reference print materials since they are both covered by copyright law.

WHAT INFORMATION WILL I NEED?

As you gather information for your research project, you will need to record the details of your sources so that you can cite them in the text of your work and also list the full bibliographic details in your list of references at the end. Both the Harvard AGPS and APA referencing styles are author-date styles so the in-text citations will consist mainly of the authors' surnames and the year (and page numbers if appropriate). The list of references gives the full bibliographical details and also additional information such as date of access, database name and URL for electronic sources. Guides from all these systems are downloadable from the internet or available from your university.

REFERENCING STYLES

Referencing styles may include

- Harvard AGPS
- APA
- Oxford style
- MLA style

REFERENCING AND PLAGIARISM

All academic work builds on the ideas and discoveries of previous scholars. This intellectual input must be acknowledged in every instance with a clear and accurate reference showing readers exactly where the quote, idea or fact can be found. It is not enough to include the source in a bibliography at the end of your research project. Failure to reference your work properly, even through carelessness, is to pass the work of others off as your own. This is plagiarism, which is a serious offence in all education institutes and is dealt with severely. It is worth taking the time to understand how to reference your work. Check your institute's requirements for referencing before submitting your research project.

THE LIST OF REFERENCES

There is a distinction between 'references' and 'bibliography'. References are those sources actually referred to in the text. If, for instance, you reference '(Jones 1980)' in the text of your research, you must provide a full bibliographic reference within your footnotes or list of references at the end of your article or chapter. Short of blatant plagiarism, there are few more serious academic sins than the floating reference! If there is also a bibliography, then it lists those sources which were consulted and found relevant, but are not actually referred to by name in the text. If you use a combined bibliography and list of references (not ideal), make sure this is clear to the reader. A single list of references should be given at the end of the project, not one per chapter. The list must be ordered by name, then year. For this reason the year is usually placed immediately after the name, as it makes ordering simpler (although putting the year last is also logical and conforms more closely to library cataloguing systems). Multiple authors, however many there are, must not be reduced to 'et al.' in the list of references, even though they were in the body of the text.

ENDNOTE

EndNote is bibliographic management software that helps manage references and produce bibliographies in a variety of referencing styles. The main functions of EndNote are as follows:

- Database manager – stores, manages and searches for your references. The information is only entered once and can be imported electronically from a database or entered manually.
- Bibliography maker – builds lists of references cited in a paper and at the click of a button will create the bibliography in a number of different styles.
- Data importer – enables the importing of references from other databases into an EndNote library.

BIBLIOGRAPHY

Amabile, T. M. (1983). *The Social Psychology of Creativity*. New York: Springer-Verlag.

Audi, R. (ed.) (1999). *Cambridge Dictionary of Philosophy*. Cambridge: Cambridge University Press

Bakhshi, H. and Windsor, G. (2015). *The Creative Economy and the Future of Employment*. London: Nesta.

Barron, F. (1963). *Creativity Person and Creative Process*. New York: Holt, Reinhart & Winston.

Berger, P. and Luckmann, T. (1967). *The Social Construction of Reality*. London: Allen Lane. Google Scholar.

Bhaskar, R. (1989). Reclaiming Reality, 2nd edn. Brighton: Harvester.

Boden, M. (1994). *Dimensions of Creativity*. Cambridge, MA: MIT Press.

Bone, J. and Baeck, P. (2016). *Crowdfunding Good Causes*. Online https://www.nesta.org.uk/publications/crowdfunding-good-causes

Borgatti, S. P. and Molina, J. L. (2003). Ethical and Strategic Issues in Organizational Social Network Analysis. *The Journal of Applied Behavioral Science*, 39 (3): 337–49.

Brown, R. B. (2006). *Doing Your Dissertation in Business and Management: The Reality of Researching and Writing*. Sage Study Skills Series. London: SAGE.

Brown, T. (2008). Design Thinking. *Harvard Business Review*, 86 (6): 84.

Burgoyne, J. (1989). Creating the Managerial Portfolio: Building on Competency Approaches to Management Development. *Management Education and Development*, 20 (1): 56–61.

Buzan, T. (1982). *Use your head*. Rajpal & Sons.

Callahan, C. M. (1991). The Assessment of Creativity, in N. Colangelo and G. A. David (eds), *Handbook of Gifted Education*, pp. 219–235. Boston: Allyn and Baco.

Cavandish, R. (1982). *Women on the Line*. London: Routledge and Kegan Paul.

Collis, J. and Hussey, R. (2003). *Business Research: A Practical Guide for Undergraduate and Postgraduate Students*. Basingstoke: Palgrave Macmillan.

Cottrell, S. (2011). *Critical Thinking Skills: Developing Effective Analysis and Argument*. Palgrave Macmillan.

Cousins, S. (2005). Contemporary Australia. 2. National Identity. Monash University National Centre for Australian studies course, developed with Open Learning Australia. National Centre for Australian Studies.

Creative & Cultural Skills (2008). The Creative and Cultural Industries: Impact and Footprint, (www.ccskills.org.uk).

Creative Economy Report (2008). *The Challenge of Assessing the Creative Economy Towards Informed Policy-Making*. Available online http://unctad.org/en/pages/PublicationArchive.aspx?publicationid=945

Csikszentmihalyi, M. (1988). Society, Culture and Person: A Systems View of Creativity, in Sternberg, R. J. (ed.), *The Nature of Creativity*. New York: Cambridge University Press.

Csikszentmihalyi, M. (1996). *Creativity*. New York: Harper Collins.

Davis, M. and Baldwin, J. (2006). *More than a Name: An Introduction to Branding*. Vol. 11. Lausanne: AVA publishing.

DCMS (2001), https://www.gov.uk/government/publications/creative-industries-mapping-documents-2001

DeLarge, C. A. (2004). Storytelling as a Critical Success Factor in Design Processes and Outcome. *Design Management Review*, 15 (3): 76–81.

Design Council (2008). Retrieved 12 December 2009 (www.designcouncil.org.uk).

Easterby-Smith, M., Thorpe, R. and Lowe, A. (1990). *Management Research: An Introduction*. London: Sage.

Easterby-Smith, M., Thorpe, R. and Holman, D. (1996). Using Repertory Grids in Management. *Journal of European Industrial Training*, 20 (3): 3–30.

Eden, C., Jones, S. and Sims, D. (1983). *Messing about in Problems: An Informal Structured Approach to their Identification and Management*, Vol. 1. Oxford: Pergamon.

English, G. (2006). Leveraging Personalities for Business Advantage: Exploring How Age and Character Impact Upon Leadership Development. *Strategic HR Review*, 5 (5). Emerald Group Publishing Ltd. (cited 12 September 2008).

Eysenck, H. J. (1993). Creativity and Personality: A Theoretical Perspective. *Psychological Inquiry*, 4: 147–78.

Finke, R. A., Ward, T. B. and Smith, S. M. (1992). *Creative Cognition: Theory, Research and Applications*, Cambridge, MA: MIT Press.

Florida, R. (2000). *The Rise of the Creative Class*, p. 201. New York: Basics Books.

Florida, R. (2004). *The Rise of the Creative Class: And How It's Transforming Work, Leisure, Community and Everyday Life* (Paperback). New York: Basic Books

Forlizzi, J. and Lebbon, C. (2002). From Formalism to Social Significance in Communication Design. *Design Issues*, 18 (4): 3–13.

Fulton Suri, J. (2008). Informing our Intuition: Design Research for Radical Innovation. *Rotman Magazine*, 52–7.

Geertz, C. (1964). Ideology as a Cultural System. *Ideology and Discontent*, vol. 5, p. 55. New York: Free Press.

Gill, J. and Johnson, P. (2002). *Research Methods for Managers*. London: Sage Publications.

Girard, A. and Gentil, G. (1983). *Cultural Development: Experiences and Policies*. Paris: United Nations Educational.

Glaser, B. G., Strauss, A. L. and Beer, S. (1968). *The Discovery of Grounded Theory*. na,.

Grinyer, A. (2002). The Anonymity of Research Participants: Assumptions, Ethics and Practicalities. *Social Research Update*, Issue 36.

Grunert, Klaus G. and Grunert, S. C. (1995). Measuring Subjective Meaning Structures by the Laddering Method: Theoretical Considerations and Methodological Problems. *International Journal of Research in Marketing*, 12 (3): 209–25.

Hart, C. (1998). *Doing a Literature Review*. London: Sage.

Henry, J. and Martin, J. (1987). *Practical Creative Thinking*. London: Meta.

Higgs, P., Cunningham, S. and Bakhshi, H. (2008). *Beyond the Creative Industries: Mapping the Creative Economy in the United Kingdom*. London: NESTA.

Hirano, T. (2006). Design and Culture: Developing a Nation's Brand with Design Management. *Design Management Review* (cited: 15 September 2008).

Howkins, J. (2001). *The Creative Economy*. New York: Allen Lane.

Janis, Irving L. (1972). Victims of Groupthink: A Psychological Study of Foreign-policy Decisions and Fiascoes. psycnet. apa.org.

Jarzabkowski, P., Balogun, J., and Seidl, D. (2007). Strategizing: The Challenges of a Practice Perspective. *Human Relations*, 60 (1): 5–27.

Johnson, G., Melin, L., and Whittington, R. (2003). Micro Strategy and Strategizing: Towards an Activity-Based View. *Journal of Management Studies*, 40 (1): 3–22.

Johnson, G. (2007). *Strategy as Practice: Research Directions and Resources*. Cambridge University Press.

Johnson, G., Scholes, K. and Whittington, R. (2008). *Exploring Corporate Strategy*, 8th edn. Pearson Education.

Kelly, G. (1955). *The Psychology of Personal Constructs*, 2 vols. New York: Norton.

Kemmis, S. and McTaggart, R. (eds) (1988). *The Action Research Planner*, 3rd edn. Geelong, VIC: Deakin University Press.

Khatena, J. (1992). Myth: Creativity Is too Difficult to Measure! *Gifted Child Quarterly*, 26 (1): 21–23.

Kris, E. (1952). *Psychoanalytic Explorations in Art*. New York: International Universities Press.

Martin, R. L. (2009). *The Design of Business: Why Design Thinking is the Next Competitive Advantage*. Boston, MA: Harvard Business Press.

Maslow, A. (1968). *Toward a Psychology of Being*. New York: Van Nostrand.

Miles, I. and Green, L. (2008). *Hidden Innovation in the Creative Industries*. London: NESTA

Perkins, D. N. (1981). *The Mind's Best Work*. Cambridge, MA: Harvard University Press.

Prosser, J. and Loxley, A. (2008). *Introducing Visual Methods*. Discussion paper (unpublished).

Remenyi, D. and Williams, B. (1998). *Doing Research in Business and Management: An Introduction to Process and Method*. Thousand Oaks: Sage Publications.

Reynolds, T. J. and Gutman, J. (1988). Laddering Theory, Method, Analysis, and Interpretation. *Journal of Advertising Research*, 28 (1): 11–31.

Routledge Encyclopedia of Philosophy; retrieved 12 December 2009, ‹www.routledge.com›

Sapsed, J. Mateos-Garcia, J. Adams and Neel, A. R. (2008). A Scoping Study of Contemporary and Future Challenges in the UK creative industries. http://eprints.brighton. ac.uk/5643/1/A_Scoping_Study_of_Contemporary_and_ Future_Challenges_in_the_UK_Creative_Industries.pdf

Saunders, Mark N. K. (2011). *Research Methods for Business Students*, 5 edn. Pearson Education India.

Simonton, D. K. (1997). Creative Productivity: A Predictive and Explanatory Model of Career Trajectories and Landmarks. *Psychological Review*, 104 (1): 66–89.

Smith, C. (1998). *Creative Britain*. London: Faber and Faber.

Somekh, B. (1995). 'The Contribution of Action Research to Development in Social Endeavours: A Position Paper on Action Research Methodology', *British Educational Research Journal*, 21 (3): 339–55.

UK Creative Industries Task Force (1997). cited in Marcus, C. (2005) Foresight Working Document series: Future of Creative Industries: Implications for Research Policy. EUR 21471.

UK Trade and Investment (2004). Cited in Creative Industries Investment Opportunities in the UK, https://www.gov.uk/ government/publications/creative-industries-in-the-uk-investment-opportunities/creative-industries-in-the-uk-investment-opportunities (accessed 20 July 2016).

UNDP, U. (2013). Creative Economy Report 2013 Special Edition. *Widening Local Development Pathways*. New York and Paris: United Nations Development Program/United Nations Educational, Scientific and Cultural Organization. *Recuperado a partir de* http://www. unesco. org/new/en/ culture/themes/creativity/creative-economy-report-2013-special-edition

Wallas, G. (1926). *The Art of Thought*. New York: Harcourt, Brace & Company.

Wittgenstein, L.(2001). *Philosophical Investigations: The German Text, with a Revised English Translation*, translated by G. E. M. Anscombe. Malden, MA: Blackwell Publishing.

Yin, R. K. (1989). *Case Study Research: Design and Methods*. London: Sage.

SUGGESTED FURTHER READING REFERENCES

Andrews, A. and Bevelo, M. (2004). 'Understanding Digital Futures'. *Design Management Review*, 15: 50–7.

Belk, R. W. (1988). Possessions and the Extended Self. *Journal of Consumer Research*, 15 (2) (September): 139–69.

Blumer, H. (1969). *Symbolic Interactionism*. Englewood Cliffs, NJ: Prentice-Hall.

Creative Commons (2009). Retrieved 18 May 2009, from Projects – Creative Commons: http://creativecommons.org.

Department for Business, Enterprise and Regulatory Reform (2008). *Creative Britain – New Talents for the New Economy*. London: Crown Copyright.

Department for Culture, Media and Sport (2007). *Creative Industries Economic Estimates Statistical Bulletin*. London: Crown Copyright.

Department for Culture, Media and Sport (2009). *Digital Britain – Final Report*. London: The Stationery Office.

Department for Trade and Industry (2005). *Economics Paper No.12 – Creativity, Design and Business Performance*. London: Crown Copyright.

Feucht, F. N. (1989). It's Symbolic. *American Demographics*, 11 (11) (November): 30–33.

Gowers, A. (2006). *Gowers Review of Intellectual Property*. London: HM Treasury.

Heller, M. (2006). *Linguistic Minorities and Modernity: A Sociolinguistic Ethnography*. A&C Black.

Henderson, P. W. and Cotes, J. A. (1998). Guidelines for Selecting or Modifying Logos. *Journal of Marketing*, 62 (2) (April): 14–30.

Leed-Hurwitz, W. (1993). *Semiotics and Communication: Signs, Codes and Cultures*. Hillsdale, NJ: Lawrence Erlbaum Associates.

McCloud, S. (1994). *Understanding Comics: The Invisible Art*. New York: Harper Perennial.

McKenna, H. (2006). *Nursing Theories and Models*. London: Routledge.

McVeigh, B. J. (2000). *Wearing Ideology: State, Schooling and Self-Presentation in Japan*. New York: Berg.

Mollerup, P. (1997). *Marks of Excellence: The History and Taxonomy of Trademarks*. London: Phaidon.

Rollins, N. (2009). 'OPEN Digital Experience Design: A Strategic, Trends-Based Approach'. *Design Management Review*, 20 (1): 31–8.

Schrubbe-Potts, E. (2000). *Designing Brands: Market Success Through Graphic Distinction*. Gloucester, MA: Rockport Publishers.

Uher, J. (1991). On Zig Zag Designs; Three Levels of Meaning. *Current Anthropology*, 32 (4): 437–9.

INDEX

self-reflexivity 49
semantic differential scale 134–5
semiotics 70–1, 164–5
  connotative properties 165
  denotative properties 164–5
  meanings 164
  physical properties 164–5
semi-structured interviews 138
senior managers 73
sensational periodicals 119
sensitivity analysis 167
service blueprint 65
Sharma, Pradeep 108–12
  approaches to creativity 108
  creativity tests 109
  purpose of creativity 111
  studying creativity 108
  systemic viewpoint 110
  understanding creativity 111
signed consent forms 100
signposting 182
slices of data 150
Smith, S. M. 109
social constructionism 48–50
social context stories 145
social research 57–8
stakeholder map 65
stakeholders 40–1
statistical approach 95, 175–6
storytelling 145
  problems 147
  sides of story 146
  types and forms 147–8
Strategy as Practice 72
Strauss, Anselm 51
structural-hermeneutical symbol
    analysis 144
structured interviews 138
structured observation 136
subconscious mental process 109
subjectivism 42, 47, 104
substantive learning objective 37
substantive news periodicals 119

supervisor 195–6
  contact 195–6
  interactions with 195
  role 195
  supervision agreement 195
Suri, Jane Fulton 73
surveys 127
symbolic interactionism 50–1, 105
symbols and artefacts. *See* semiotics
systematic research 7

T
tacit knowledge 39
techniques, qualitative analysis 169–71
  analytical memos 170
  archiving 171
  bits and pieces 171
  capturing conversation 171
  context 169–70
  fluency 170
  iteration 170
  participants voice 171
  prefiguring field 170
  processing texts 171
  reflexivity 170
  rigour 170
  triangulation 170
telephone interview 140
tertiary data 106
test hypotheses 131
testing theory 44–5
test phase 63
theoretical memos 152
theoretical sampling 149–50
theory and practice 39–41
  diagnosis of issues/initiatives 40
  negotiating with colleagues/
    stakeholders 40–1
  tacit knowledge 39
theory-in-use 39
Throsby, David 14
time-based research 127
time management 197

Torrance Tests of Creative
    Thinking 109
trade journals 127
transferability 169
tree diagram 124

U
undisguised observation 136
United Nations Conference on Trade and
    Development (UNCTAD) 1
United Nations Educational, Scientific
    and Cultural Organization
    (UNESCO) 12, 14
University of Strathclyde 70
University of Vienna 157
unstructured interviews 71, 138
unstructured observation 136
unwritten documentary sources 127
US Patent Office 36

V
value chains 12
Vienna Institute for Urban
    Sustainability 157
visible symbols 164
visual communications 101
visual information decoding 158
visual research 141–2
  definition 141
  issues of collaboration 142
  issues of representation 141–2

W
Wallas, Graham 109
Ward, T. B. 109
warm-up 31
written communication 198–9
written consent 88
written documentary sources 127
www.designcouncil.org 17

Y
Yin, R. K. 150